Rethinking *The Fifth Discipline*

'It is in the nature of systemic thinking to yield many different views of the same thing and the same view of many different things. This book offers such a point of view of systemic thinking, which is both important and very rewarding for one to take into account.'
Russell L. Ackoff
Chairman, INTERACT, The Institute for Interactive Management, USA

'Robert Flood describes complex systemic theory and practice in a clear, comprehensible manner, thereby bringing a better understanding of the world and ourselves to his readers. If you are interested in learning and growing, if you wish to manage better, then read this insightful and thought-provoking book.'
Professor Brenda Gourley
Vice Chancellor and Principal, University of Natal, South Africa

'In the present global market, systemic thinking has risen to a position of prominence never before attained. Globalisation, networking, and coalition building, are examples of systemic behaviour that stress the need to view and deal with issues holistically, rather than in isolation. Robert Flood for years has been at the forefront of such studies. This book has to be a must for all apprentices of systemic thinking.'
Ghassan Al Sulaiman
Jeddah Chamber of Commerce and Industry and President of IKEA, Saudi Arabia

The Fifth Discipline is one of the very few approaches to management that has attained a position in the international hall of fame. Robert Louis Flood's book explains and critiques the ideas in straightforward terms.

Rethinking The Fifth Discipline makes significant and fundamental improvements to the core discipline of systemic thinking. It establishes crucial developments in this area in the context of the learning organisation, including creativity and organisational transformation. It is therefore a very important text for strategic planners, organisational change agents and consultants as well as students studying and researching management, business and administration.

Key features of this work include:

- a review and critique of *The Fifth Discipline* and systemic thinking
- an introduction to the gurus of systemic thinking – Senge, Bertalanffy, Beer, Ackoff, Checkland and Churchman
- a redefinition of 'management and organisation' through systemic thinking
- a guide to choosing, implementing and evaluating improvement strategies
- practical animations

Robert Louis Flood is a renowned and authoritative expert in the field of management. He has implemented systemic management in a wide range of organisations in many continents and lectured by invitation in twenty-five countries, including Japan and the USA. Professor Flood has featured on a number of radio and TV programmes. His book *Beyond TQM* (Wiley) was nominated for the 1993 MCA Management Book of the Year.

Rethinking *The Fifth Discipline*

Learning within the unknowable

Robert Louis Flood

London and New York

First published 1999 by Routledge
11 New Fetter Lane, London EC4P 4EE

Reprinted 1999

Simultaneously published in the USA and Canada
by Routledge
29 West 35th Street, New York, NY 10001

Routledge is an imprint of the Taylor & Francis Group

Typeset in Sabon by
J&L Composition Ltd, Filey, North Yorkshire
Printed and bound in Great Britain by
TJ International Ltd, Padstow, Cornwall

British Library Cataloguing in Publication Data
A catalogue record for this book is available
from the British Library

Library of Congress Cataloging in Publication Data
Rethinking The Fifth Discipline: learning within the unknowable/
Robert Louis Flood.
p. cm.
Includes bibliographical references and index.
1. Management – Philosophy. I. Title.
HD31.F568 1999
658–dc21 98–51385
CIP

ISBN 0–415–18529–7 (hbk)
ISBN 0–415–18530–0 (pbk)

Dedication

Of the many lessons I learnt on Christmas Eve 1997, one lives on with me – actually do what you think, do not just think what to do.

In loving memory of my mother – Marjorie Flood née Peacock.

Contents

Illustrations

Figures

Tables

Biography

Professor Robert Louis Flood (Bob) was born in London in February 1955. He is an internationally recognised authority on applied systemic thinking. This was marked in 1997 by the award of Doctor of Science (Econ.) for a sustained and authoritative contribution to the field of management. His previous academic achievements include Doctor of Philosophy (1985) in Systems Science and Bachelor of Science (first class, 1983) in Systems and Management. Bob is also a Chartered Engineer and Fellow of the Institute of Measurement and Control. He has written nine books including *Beyond TQM* (Wiley) which was nominated for the 1993 MCA Best Management Book of the Year. He is founding and current editor of the well-respected journal, *Systemic Practice and Action Research*. Bob has worked nine years full time, including in the film business, the health service, and in an opinion poll agency; plus thirteen years in the university sector. His continued commitment to applied systemic thinking is evidenced in a consultancy and training portfolio, which includes organisations in Australia, the Arabian Gulf, South East Asia, South Africa, and the United Kingdom. He now operates full time as a consultant and is Visiting Professor at Lincoln University Campus (UK) and at Monash University (Australia). Bob has lectured by invitation in twenty-five countries worldwide, including Japan and the USA, and has featured on his travels in a number of radio and television programmes.

Acknowledgements

Dan Cook offered several suggestions that profoundly influenced the way the argument of this book came together.

This book also benefits from two collaborative ventures. I wish to acknowledge Mike Jackson and Norma Romm, with whom I have shared much learning and enjoyment. The detail of our work together is much of the source of whatever new order of thinking emerges herein.

I am grateful to North Yorkshire Police in the UK for the opportunity to work with them in the 1990s and to publish the findings. In particular, I am indebted to Steve Green whose vision opened the gates to the action research that was undertaken in York Division, that provides the main practical animation in this book. May I also thank Keith Cullen, Malcolm Foster, Helen Smith and Roger Smith.

I would like to thank the publishers, Routledge, in particular Stuart Hay, for the understanding manner in which they accepted the late submission of this manuscript following the loss of my mother. I acknowledge International Thomson Publishing for permission to base Chapters 3, 4, 5 and 7, on articles of mine first published in 1998 in *IEBM Handbook Of Management Thinking*, edited by Malcolm Warner (respectively, pages 718–723, 57–65, 1–7, and 122–127). I acknowledge John Wiley and Sons for permission to include Figures 4.1, 6.1, 6.2 and 6.3. Figure 4.1 is a version of Stafford Beer's viable system model that appears in a number of his Wiley books. Figures 6.1 to 6.3 are versions of Peter Checkland and co-workers' diagrams found in one or more of their Wiley books.

I am particularly indebted to friends (Andrew, Dave, Eddie, Geoff, Mal and Tony) at Beverley RUFC for the Sunday sanity sessions; as well as our 1997/1998 Colts Squad who were winners in the final of the Yorkshire Colts Cup (including my son Ross).

Norma Romm held out her hand of friendship to me over the duration of the preparation of this book, which happened to be a most difficult period of my life.

As ever, Mandy and Ross calm me in the maelstroms and revive me from the doldrums.

Robert Louis Flood
October, 1998
Dunnington, East Yorkshire, UK
robertflood@compuserve.com

1 Introduction

Effective and meaningful operation of any organisational set up nowadays is a tough occupation. For commercial enterprises competition has become a global phenomenon. For Governmental agencies the belt has tightened with an increase in public accountability and fiscal control. For non-profit making organisations purpose and identity often have become increasingly elusive. For all organisational set-ups the information matrix within which they operate has taken on a mind-blowing sophistication. Furthermore, consumers have become acutely aware of their rights. And wide-ranging social issues such as gender, race and disability, are found on many organisational agendas. All of these things and many more have contributed to an organisational upheaval that has changed what counts as relevant management, from organisational management to the operations that it ultimately supports.

As Brenda Gourley states on the back cover, the world has become far more complex and far less certain. Traditional management strategies that seemed sufficient as recently as a generation ago are found wanting today. To survive and/or to improve in the current era requires up-to-date knowledge of contemporary management strategies as well as skills and competencies needed to work with them. Failure to perform in this way will have a detrimental impact on organisational viability. Commercial organisations might as well hand over business to their competitors. Governmental agencies might well grind to a halt. Non-profit making organisations might quietly disappear. It is in the interest of all organisational set ups and indeed us as individuals, to seek guidance from contemporary management strategies in the struggle for effective and meaningful practice. One potentially important strategy is the application of systemic thinking.

Systemic thinking hit the headlines in the 1990s with Peter Senge's book about learning organisations called *The Fifth Discipline*. The learning organisation is said by Peter Drucker to be the organisational concept of the future. A learning organisation in fact is one that continually expands its capacity to create its own future. Senge argues that five disciplines underpin learning organisations. The fifth discipline is systemic thinking that provides substance to the other four disciplines and hence to the learning organisation as a whole. Systemic thinking helps us sense as well as appreciate our connection to a wider whole. We can only meaningfully understand ourselves by contemplating the whole of which we are an integral part. Systemic thinking is the discipline which makes visible that our actions are interrelated to other people's actions in patterns of behaviour and are not merely isolated events.

Senge, however, stuck close to a narrow, albeit important, strand of systemic thinking called system dynamics. There exist many more accounts about the systemic character of the natural and social worlds – e.g. complexity theory, open systems theory, organisational cybernetics, interactive planning, soft systems approach, and critical systemic thinking. Each one yields different and potentially valuable insights. Together, they offer a diversity and strength vital to our ability to cope within an exceedingly complex world.

Of particular additional interest to this book is complexity theory that, like Senge's work, also came to the fore in the 1990s. It promises exciting new possibilities for the way that the natural and social worlds might be understood. Complexity theory begins, as does Senge's work, by acknowledging the interrelated nature of things as well as emergence, where the whole is experienced as greater than the sum of its parts. However, it recognises a special form of emergence called spontaneous self-organisation. What exactly gives rise to spontaneous self-organisation is difficult if not impossible to know, at least by the human mind.

Complexity theory appreciates the world as a whole, comprising many, many interrelationships expressed in endless occurrences of spontaneous self-organisation. The great extent and dynamic nature of the interrelationships and spontaneous self-organisation means that it is only possible for us to get to grips with some things and only those that are local to us in space and time. Local in space and time refers respectively to 'things that we are immediately involved in' (it is not a geographic concept) and 'not very far into the future'. In straightforward terms, we have a restricted understanding about what is going on around us, and a limited capability to know what will happen next.

Systemic thinking thus takes issue with grand narratives of strategic planners who think globally and believe that with intention they can create a better future. In their reports they innocently indulge in fictional script writing. There is no more chance of their long-term plans coming true than a *Star Trek* movie – it could happen for all we know, but it seems most unlikely. A refreshing and far more in touch conceptualisation of 'management and organisation' based on systemic thinking is desperately needed.

Both Senge's *The Fifth Discipline* and complexity theory suggest if not fully explain a hidden order, or simplicity, in the seemingly impenetrable complexity of the world. Tools of systemic thinking facilitate learning about this order. However, it is not realistic to believe that we can learn about all the things that might affect us, or what is going to happen as things unfold. We will always be faced with uncertainty.

If *The Fifth Discipline* and complexity theory have their say about uncertainty, then the way we think about and approach 'management and organisation' will change. We will operate in conscious recognition of the following three paradoxes:

- We will not struggle to manage over things – we will manage within the unmanageable.
- We will not battle to organise the totality – we will organise within the unorganisable.
- We will not simply know things – but we will know of the unknowable.

Now the title of this book comes clear. It is about rethinking *The Fifth Discipline* – i.e. getting to grips with systemic thinking – and, with systemic thinking, learning within the unknowable. Hence we have, *Rethinking The Fifth Discipline: Learning Within The Unknowable.*

This book is organised into two parts. Part I offers a state of the art account of *The Fifth Discipline.* Peter Senge's work on learning organisations is reviewed and made sense of by its comparison to the concepts and approaches of five other key systemic thinkers – Bertalanffy's open systems theory, Beer's organisational cybernetics, Ackoff's interactive planning, Checkland's soft systems approach, and Churchman's critical systemic thinking. What emerges from this review is a new order of thought. The emerging whole opens up a way to Part II and to complexity theory. Part II is presented in three sections – concepts, approach, and a detailed practical animation. A summary of chapters follows.

Part I

2 *Senge's* 'The Fifth Discipline'

The book *The Fifth Discipline* is Peter Senge's account of the *learning organisation.* For Senge, five disciplines are necessary to bring about a learning organisation – *personal mastery, mental models, shared vision, team learning,* and *systems thinking* (referred to as systemic thinking in this book). Systemic thinking is the discipline that makes as one all five disciplines. Each discipline is introduced in this chapter with the emphasis placed on systemic thinking, the central theme of the current book. The resulting overview establishes Senge's framework of thought. Each of the next five chapters introduces the work of one additional key systemic thinker and makes comparisons with Senge's learning organisation.

3 *Bertalanffy's open systems theory*

Ludwig von Bertalanffy was a biologist whose organismic conception of biology otherwise known as *open systems theory* came to pervade many disciplines, including 'management and organisation', the impact being vastly more than the sum of its parts. He was the first person on the European continent to develop open systems theory in biology as a working hypothesis for research. It is central to his publications from the mid-1920s. Open systems theory profoundly influenced the way organisations are conceived and consequently managed. It helped to shape management and organisation theory in the 1950s and 1960s. It pervades management practice today. Von Bertalanffy was also the prime mover of general system theory that subsequently emerged in his work in the late 1930s. *General system theory* aims to reveal through the open systems concept the interdisciplinary nature of systemic thinking. Von Bertalanffy from the 1950s until his death in 1972 applied open systems theory and general system theory to a wide range of social studies, the result becoming known as his *systems view of people.*

4 *Beer's organisational cybernetics*

Stafford Beer is essentially a cybernetician working in the field of operational research and management sciences (ORMS). Beer argues that techniques of ORMS have high utility only when employed in the light of a scientific description of the whole situation. Whole situation descriptions come through models built with *cybernetic logic*. These models must be homomorphic or isomorphic (i.e. they draw direct correspondence to reality) not metaphorical or analogical. The models are formulated using tools of rigorous science – mathematics, statistics and logic. Beer's most famous homomorphism, the *viable system model* (VSM), draws correspondence between 'management and organisation', and human brain structure and function. The VSM stipulates rules whereby an organisation (biological or social) is 'survival worthy' – it is regulated, learns, adapts and evolves. Beer invented *team syntegrity* to complement the VSM when applied in organisational contexts, adding his statement of participatory democracy.

5 *Ackoff's interactive planning*

The work of Russell L. Ackoff has made and continues to make a significant impact upon many fields in 'management and organisation'. He largely co-defined with C. West Churchman *operations research* in its early years (the 1950s). By the 1970s, however, he concluded that operations researchers had failed to change with the times. An operational and tactical mode dominated their work, whilst corporate managers had progressed into a strategic mode. Ackoff, who admits he is market led, responded in accordance with his observations. He moved out of operations research and began a new phase of work that addressed purposeful systems of corporations and systems of interacting problems ('the mess') that characterise them. By the 1980s, Ackoff had consolidated his ideas in a participatory approach to planning, labelled interactive planning. *Interactive planning* encourages people to conceive unconstrained idealised designs and to invent ways of realising them. In the 1980s and particularly in the 1990s, Ackoff's concern for participation surfaced in another guise, in a structural notion for a circular organisation. The *circular organisation* is in fact an expression of a democratic hierarchy.

6 Checkland's soft systems approach

Peter B. Checkland is an action researcher who focused attention on systemic thinking. Commitment to action research began during his initial fifteen years' career at ICI Fibres. He consulted literature on management sciences as he assumed increasingly senior positions with management responsibility. He found that the literature failed to resonate with his experiences and needs as a manager. Subsequently, Checkland chose to research into this dilemma and took up a Professorship at Lancaster University in the United Kingdom. He launched an action research programme and developed through this a soft systems approach. Three strands might represent the main output of his programme – an *interpretive-based systemic theory*, an original brand of *action research*, and principles for action that he labelled *soft systems methodology* (SSM).

7 Churchman's critical systemic thinking

C. West Churchman is a philosopher with an intense *moral commitment* to employ systemic thinking for the betterment of humanity. Along with Ackoff, he largely co-defined *operations research* in its early years (the 1950s). For Churchman, operations research was always a systemic activity. Employing mixed teams coupled to an interest in parts of the organisation and how they might interact, is an early expression of this. Churchman might also be considered the main founder of the critical systemic approach. After operations research he developed a caravan of critical systemic concepts and concerns. These include an *anatomy of system teleology* and, of particular significance, ways of *exploring and bounding action areas*. He argued that improvement, say in terms of efficiency and/or effectiveness, always raises *questions of an ethical nature*. He also stressed the importance of *securing improvement*. More broadly, he developed a vision of *systemic wisdom* – thought combined with a concern for ethics; and *hope* – a spiritual belief in an ethical future. Churchman's work can be criticised as esoteric, yet he still impressed on the minds of many researchers the recurrent systemic question of whether they can justify their choices and actions.

8 Senge's 'The Fifth Discipline' *revisited*

In this chapter, Senge's *The Fifth Discipline* is revisited in the light of comparisons made with the works of Bertalanffy, Beer, Ackoff, Checkland

and Churchman. A critique is put together that points to important insights uncovered by these five systemic thinkers which Senge does not fully take into account. Bringing together their insights with Senge's insights results in a whole with much more potential than its parts in isolation. The emerging whole opens up a way to complexity theory and to Part II of the book.

Part II

Concepts

9 Towards systemic thinking

In this chapter the scene is set for a thorough reworking of systemic thinking. To start the ball rolling the conventional wisdom of reductionism and the counter-view, systemic thinking, are introduced and juxtaposed. Reductionism breaks things into parts and attempts to deal with each part in isolation. It has made and continues to make a significant contribution to traditional science and technology. The experiment of reductionism in organisational and societal settings, however, has not been plain sailing. It has struggled primarily because it misunderstands the nature of human beings (yet it remains a dominant wisdom). Social settings are different and exhibit spiritual and systemic qualities. Spiritualism appreciates the wholeness of human being. Systemic thinking builds holistic pictures of social settings. It suggests systemic ways of coping with them that challenge the very idea of problems, solutions, and normal organisational life.

10 The demise of problems, solutions and normal organisational life

Complexity theory is introduced in this chapter. The suggestion made through complexity theory is that problems, as such, do not exist. There are no problems clearly identifiable 'out there' that can be solved on the way to re-establishing normal organisational life. The notion of 'problem and solution' inadequately characterises the complexity of organisational and societal settings. Rather, such settings are more usefully understood in terms of wholes, that is, people, purposes and interacting issues that bring them together in emerging conflict and/or co-operation. Some issues arise from conflict and turn out to be insoluble. Insoluble issues are dilemmas. In place of problems, solutions and the maintenance of normal organisational life, therefore, it is more helpful to think in terms of interacting issues and dilemmas that emerge and are coped with over time. Systemic thinking gets to grips with such complexity through a form of reasoning called boundary judgements.

11 Getting to grips with complexity

In this chapter complexity theory is employed to illustrate that systemic thinking involves, in the first instance, drawing tentative boundaries around stakeholders, focusing primarily on clients, and raising issues and dilemmas relating to those clients. The bounded space is usefully conceived of as an action area. Put succinctly, the extended questions for dialogue are, 'Who is embraced by the action area and thus benefits? Who is outside of it and does not benefit? What are the possible consequences of this? And how do we feel about that?' Boundary judgements thus raise questions of an ethical nature, as well as an interest in efficiency and effectiveness. Boundaries are always subject to further debate and are thus *temporary*. Boundaries result from choice of client. For each choice there always exists other options with different clients. Boundary judgements therefore are also *partial*. The temporary and partial nature of boundary judgements reminds us, following choices we have to make, that we remain somewhere between mystery and mastery. Yet, there remains scope for deepening systemic appreciation of any bounded action area.

12 Deepening systemic appreciation

Once boundaries are drawn creating an action area, albeit temporarily, there is value in deepening systemic appreciation, albeit partially, through further dialogue. Deepening systemic appreciation is likened to opening four windows on the action area. The four windows are – systems of processes, of structure, of meaning, and of knowledge-power. Each window offers a different view on issues and dilemmas. Bringing together and debating these views through prismatic thought helps us to build up systemic interpretations of the manifold and interrelated issues and dilemmas. Each systemic picture suggests possible creative courses of action and transformation from which choices for improvement can be made. The following five chapters introduce the four windows and prismatic thought, but at all times it must be borne in mind that the context of discussion is that given by complexity theory.

13 Window 1: systems of processes

One angle on improvement as a feature of systemic appreciation is to approach issues and dilemmas in terms of efficiency and reliability of systems of processes – i.e. process design. Efficiency means to work without any unnecessary waste in time or resources. Reliability means dependable and accurate performance. Processes are explained in this chapter along with possible action to take when encountering inefficiency and unreliability. A spectrum of action is identified, from radical change to continuous incremental improvement. The well-known approaches, business process reengineering and kaizen, are positioned respectively on this spectrum. The next window recognises that any system of processes flows within and is supported by a system of structure.

14 Window 2: systems of structure

Another perspective on improvement is to approach issues and dilemmas in terms of effectiveness of systems of structure – i.e. structural design. Effectiveness means to achieve chosen tasks. Structure is explained in this chapter along with possible actions to take when encountering ineffectiveness. A spectrum is identified, from rule bound to rule free structures. A range of structures is positioned on this spectrum, including tall and flat, circular, organic, and less formal ones. However, working with a purpose such as effectiveness or, indeed, efficiency and reliability, assumes some form of agreement has been struck that accommodates people's systems of meaning.

15 Window 3: systems of meaning

A third 'take' on improvement is to enhance the quality of agreement and understanding between people and hence the potential of decisions that are taken. Agreement and understanding is considered in this chapter in terms of systems of meaning people ascribe to issues and dilemmas. A number of approaches are introduced that facilitate dialogue about systems of meaning. A spectrum of possible outcomes of dialogue relating to these approaches is identified, from consensus through accommodation to tolerance. However, outcomes, such as agreements, may not be meaningful to some people when their ability to participate in dialogue is severely restricted by knowledge-power relationships that directly affect them.

16 Window 4: systems of knowledge-power

Additionally, a fourth angle on improvement looks for knowledge-power relationships that influence the shape of designs and the outcome of supposed dialogue. Examples include those relating to race, class, sexuality, culture, age, disability, the expert, and management hierarchy. A spectrum of ways in which patterns of entrenched behaviour might be transformed and made fairer is suggested. At one end of the spectrum is emancipation of the privileged from their ideologies and power structures. At the other end is unshackling of the underprivileged from impoverished conditions that result from dominant ideologies and power structures. Perspectives that are formed by looking through each of the four windows just introduced are subsequently transformed through a process of prismatic thought.

17 Prismatic thought

Perspectives generated by opening in turn all four windows on the action area gain in insight through a holistic, creative interpretation and transformation. Plausible systemic explanations of issues and dilemmas can be developed as well as optional courses of action. This may be likened to prismatic thought. A prism refracts light creating many bursts of colour. Prismatic thought similarly creates many coloured stories of events that inform choice of action. On completion, this chapter rounds off discussion about deepening systemic appreciation of issues and dilemmas, as well as possible ways of dealing with them. However, it begs the question of how to make choices between those possibilities and how to implement and evaluate changes in line with ideas about improvement? This challenge is addressed in the approach introduced in the next section

Approach

18 Organisational learning and transformation

An approach to organisational learning and transformation is developed in this chapter. It draws on scenario building, but incorporates boundary judgements and subsequently deepening systemic appreciation. The idea of scenario building is to facilitate learning a way into the future, not to establish medium- or long-term plans. Three types of learning scenario are created. The first scenario learns in the context of the future we might be heading towards. The current boundary judgement is interpreted and a systemic appreciation is developed that explores the sorts of events that are happening and why they might be occurring. The second scenario learns about ideal futures. Possible alternative boundaries are suggested and ideal systemic properties are worked out for each one. The third scenario learns about possible ways of closing the gap between what appears to be the situation and preferred ideal futures – i.e. ways to move towards ideal systemic properties and/or to shift the boundaries. Projects to close the gap are chosen, formulated and implemented. All three learning scenarios are continually revisited. (This process is applied, in the appendix of the chapter, to Senge's idea of personal mastery.) Systemic evaluation of projects is a learning imperative that follows implementation.

19 Systemic evaluation

Systemic practice is not complete without systemic evaluation that indicates progress towards chosen and specified improvement. Systemic evaluation traverses issues and dilemmas of systems of processes, of structure, of meaning, and of knowledge-power. It indicates performance of projects in these terms. It provides information for reflection on, and where necessary reworking of, projects under way. Choosing, implementing and evaluating projects, through the approach outlined in this section, seeks to achieve a balance between instrumental action (based on method) and experiential action (built from experience).

20 Instrumental and experiential action

The approach outlined in the previous two chapters can be interpreted as recommending either instrumental action or experiential action. In this chapter it is argued that neither interpretation is adequate in its own right. A balanced approach is preferable, that draws people's experience into instrumental action adding meaning to possible forms of action, and lays instrumental thinking over people's experience offering them possible direction. This notion seeks to balance the mystery of our experience, with a certain mastery of the moment coming from instrumental thinking. The concepts and approach introduced in this section of the book set up the reader for an instructive engagement with the substantial practical animation that follows.

Practical animation

21 Local Area Policing (LAP) in York, UK

This chapter offers an extensive practical illustration that animates the concepts and approach introduced in the last two sections. Most insights generated by the practical animation have relevance to all sorts of organisational learning and transformation. Lessons learnt therefore might be transferable to other organisational contexts. Choosing, implementing and evaluating Local Area Policing in York as an improvement strategy makes up the bulk of the practical animation. In addition, I comment on my role as researcher. The practical animation then becomes a case study with which the reader is encouraged to participate. A case study guide is given that facilitates reflection on the concepts and approach of the book in the context of the practical animation. Trainers and educators may also employ the case study as an experiential exercise that helps their learners to engage in learning within the unknowable.

22 Reflections and key insights of systemic thinking

The closing chapter initially crystallises my thoughts and feelings around the time I drew this project to a close. It then rounds off the book with a summary of key insights of systemic thinking that result from *Rethinking The Fifth Discipline*. These key insights remind us that effective and meaningful 'management and organisation' and, indeed, all other aspects of living, will be greatly enhanced by *Learning within the unknowable*.

Part I

Knowing oneself following a system of thought, will simply create a result, i.e., oneself, produced by that system of thought – not knowing oneself.

2 Senge's *The Fifth Discipline*

The learning man

Peter Senge follows in the tradition of the learning organisation, which came to the fore in the 1970s, for example, through the research of Chris Argyris and Donald Schön, and the practice in Royal Dutch/Shell of Arie de Geus. It is Senge, however, who leveraged the concepts and methods of the learning organisation into popular currency through his now widely known book *The Fifth Discipline*. The learning organisation as articulated in *The Fifth Discipline* ranks amongst just a few approaches to 'management and organisation' that have acquired a position in the international hall of fame. Central to the popularisation is the fifth discipline itself, systemic thinking, that has otherwise struggled on the margins of the social and educational mainstream. An introduction to Senge's learning organisation is presented in this chapter. Each of the five disciplines is reviewed with emphasis placed on systemic thinking, the central theme of the current book.

Systemic thinking, system dynamics

Systemic thinking explores things as wholes and is highly relevant, Senge insists, because the world exhibits qualities of wholeness. These qualities relate to every aspect of our lives – at work and at home. Events appear to be distinct in space and time, but they are all interconnected. Events, then, can be understood only by contemplating the whole. Life events can be made sense of in a meaningful way only in the knowledge that our actions contribute to patterns of interrelated actions.

The world is whole and the whole is complex. It is increasingly complex with more and more information, intense interdependency, and relentless change. Senge sorts two types of complexity from this – detail complexity and dynamic complexity. *Detail complexity* arises where there are many variables, which are difficult, if not impossible, to hold in the mind at once and appreciate as a whole. *Dynamic complexity* arises where effects over time of interrelatedness are subtle and the results of actions are not obvious; or where short term and long term effects are significantly different; or where effects locally are different from effects on a wider scale. A model of detail complexity can be likened to a snapshot photograph that allows detail to be studied in freeze frame. A model of dynamic complexity can be likened to an animation that allows patterns of behaviour to be studied over time. Dynamic complexity is the main concern of Senge's systemic thinking.

The trouble is, Senge argues, that we are taught from an early age to make complexity apparently more manageable by breaking wholes into parts. This makes understanding wholes pretty much impossible since we can no longer appreciate results of actions because the whole is stripped of an essential quality – interrelatedness. Similarly, if we think of ourselves as a disconnected part, we lose sense of our connection to a wider whole and inadvertently alienate and disempower ourselves. We are disempowered because we cannot grasp why events happen in our lives in the way that they do.

Accentuating the difficulty, people then attempt to reassemble the fragments resulting from breaking wholes into parts in the belief that it is within our power to recreate the whole. Senge appeals to systemic sense on this score through the writings of David Bohm, who likens such recreation to reassembling fragments of a mirror with which, of course, a true reflection never again can be seen. I also appreciate D.T. Suzuki's way of picturing this matter in *The Gospel According To Zen*. He notes that we murder wholes by dissecting them into parts, yet expect to put the parts back together to recreate the original living whole.

The tools of Senge's systemic thinking derive from an approach called system dynamics (linked in its name to dynamic complexity). The tools attempt to put to rest the illusion that the world is made up of separate parts. They also attempt to dismiss the simplification that the world is linear, with beginnings and ends. The tools help to picture the world as interconnected through ongoing cyclical patterns. In fact, Senge observes, apparently there are a number of types of pattern that recur. These he calls systems archetypes.

Systems archetypes, the message goes, reveal a kind of simplicity underlying the dynamic complexity of, say, management action. Dynamic complexity may be understood in terms of the relatively small number of systems archetypes as they are shown to explain each original situation. One systems archetype, or several interconnected systems archetypes, may capture observable patterns of behaviour and offer an explanation to the puzzle, why a complex of events occurs. Extending one's knowledge of systems archetypes expands one's ability to get to grips with management issues and, consequently, particularises opportunities that exist for improvement.

Working with systems archetypes helps to locate these opportunities, that Senge calls points of leverage. Bringing about informed change at points of leverage facilitates a disproportionate and desired impact to be achieved on important aspects of the whole – whole in space and time. Leverage is thus achieved when action is taken that leads to significant and enduring improve-

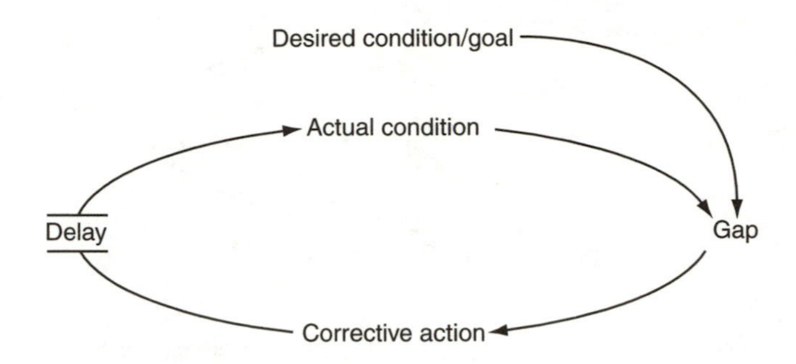

Figure 2.1 Corrective action with delay

ment. Working on leverage points realises focused action that is normally less than obvious to most people operating solely from intuition.

Senge reckons that about a dozen systems archetypes have been distinguished. These make up some kind of generic set. Kim's *Systems Archetypes* reviews the lot. Senge covers nine in *The Fifth Discipline* and, with colleagues, in *The Fifth Discipline Fieldbook*. The core nine are introduced below both as a story and a diagram. (Senge's name for them is given in brackets where different from that employed below.)

Corrective action with delay (balancing process with delay)

An actual condition and a desired condition/goal differ. That is, there is a gap between how things are and the way we want them to be. Corrective action is taken to close the gap. However, the impact of the corrective action is delayed. That is, the results of the corrective action are not observed right away. The gap does not appear to be closing and so further corrective action is considered necessary. The impact of the initial corrective action then closes the gap as desired. Later, the second corrective action has an impact leading to a gap in the other direction. Further corrective action in ignorance of the delay leads to a repeat performance and an oscillation in the actual condition. (See Figure 2.1.)

Eroding goals

This is similar to the previous systems archetype 'corrective action with delay'. However, rather than take further corrective action when the impact of the initial corrective action is delayed, a strategy is adopted to close the gap by adjusting the desired condition/goal. This action perpetuates with continual erosion of the desired condition/goal. (See Figure 2.2.)

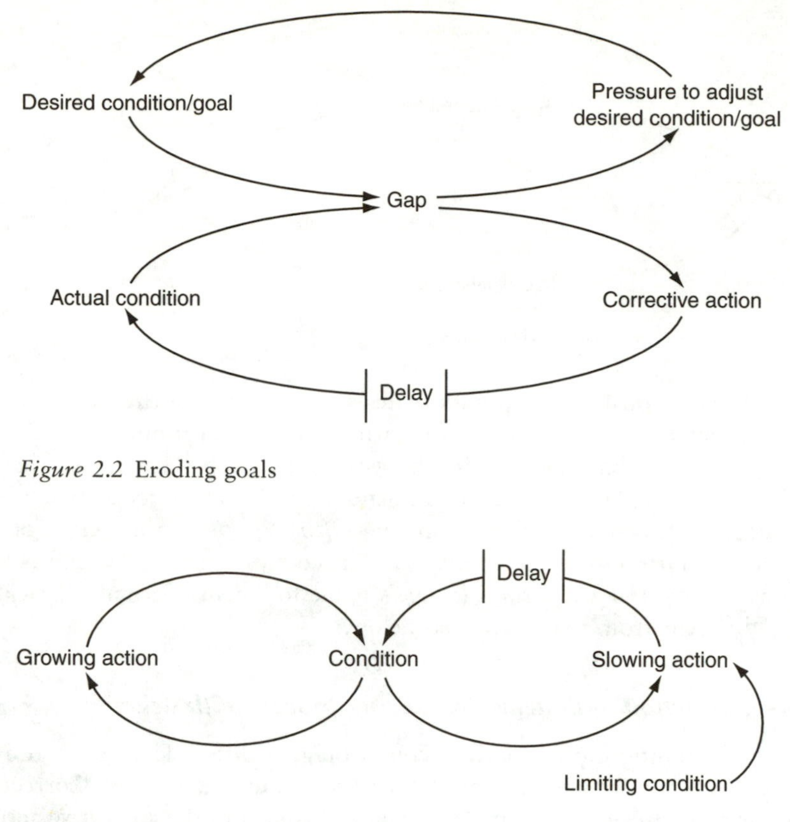

Figure 2.2 Eroding goals

Figure 2.3 Limits to growth

Limits to growth

A condition feeds on itself through a growing action to produce a period of accelerating growth. Growth approaches a limiting condition and consequently experiences a slowing action. Growth eventually comes to a halt. However, if delay occurs in the slowing action, then the growth action may overshoot the limiting condition and will later be forced to contract to or even dive below the limiting condition. (See Figure 2.3.)

Tragedy of the commons

This is a story that shows how rational, isolated decision-making may sum to irrational decision-making for the whole. There is a common resource and two individuals/groups drawing on it (there may be many more). Each one maximises their gain, increases activity and thus demand on the resources. Initially, the common resource sustains growth, but in due course

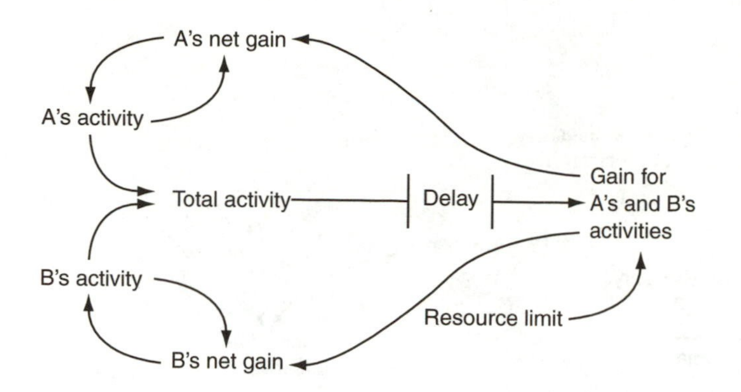

Figure 2.4 Tragedy of the commons

a resource limit is inevitably encountered. This impacts negatively on the gains for A's and B's activities and depletes resources. It becomes a cycle with the tragic consequence that resources as well as A's and B's activities wither away, that is, unless A and B are able to make decisions about the whole that are mutually beneficial and sustainable. (See Figure 2.4.)

Growth and under-investment

An organisation's demand and supply increases, say, for a product or service, leading to a growing action. This improves performance, for example, in terms of number of sales. Existing capacity for the product or service is met and so performance in this respect reaches its limit. However, the performance standard for the sales of the product or service is raised and a perceived need to invest surfaces. Investment experiences delay in realisation. Meanwhile, demand continues to rise, but performance in terms of ability to deliver what is promised severely falls, leading to a reversal and slump in demand. The performance standard of sales (and indeed quality) is then lowered to justify the slump and the perceived need to invest drops away, limiting demand that can be met. Investment should have gone ahead in capacity and future investments made that stay ahead of demand. (See Figure 2.5.)

Treating symptoms, not fundamental causes (shifting the burden)

A problem condition arises. A strategy is worked out to treat fundamental causes and is implemented, but experiences delay. The symptoms of the problem condition, however, can be and indeed are treated, with an immediate result. An increasing reliance on addressing symptoms leads to the side effect that fundamental causes are treated less and less until,

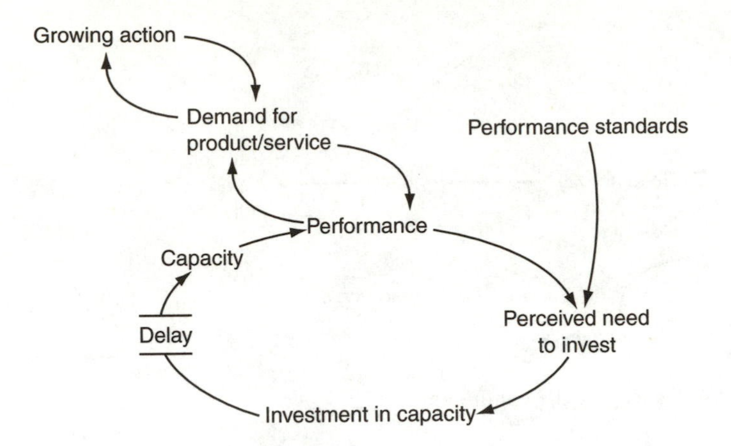

Figure 2.5 Growth and under-investment

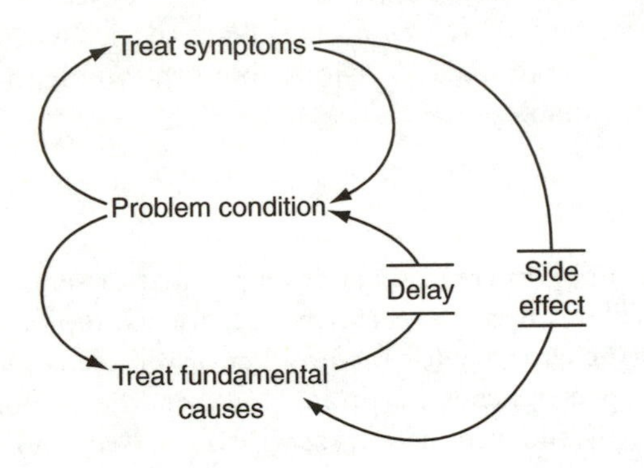

Figure 2.6 Treating symptoms, not fundamental causes

eventually the strategy to deal with the fundamental causes becomes disabled. (See Figure 2.6.)

Corrective actions that fail (fixes that fail)

A problem condition is encountered and a corrective action is worked out that is considered to be a solution. However, this corrective action leads to unexpected and unseen consequences that feed back into the problem condition. Since these consequences are also unseen, the reaction is to administer more of the same corrective action, but this leads to more of the same consequences. (See Figure 2.7.)

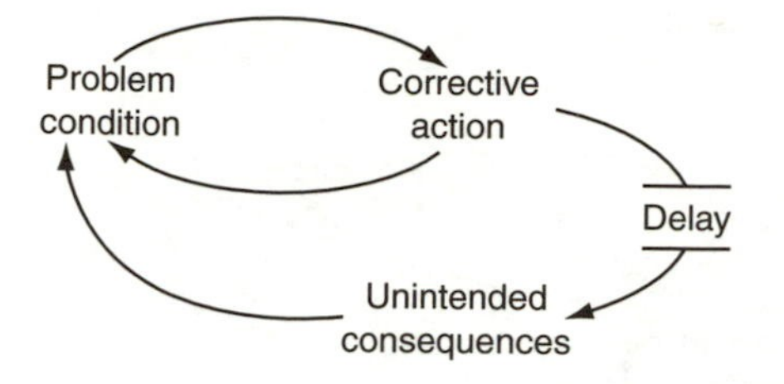

Figure 2.7 Corrective actions that fail

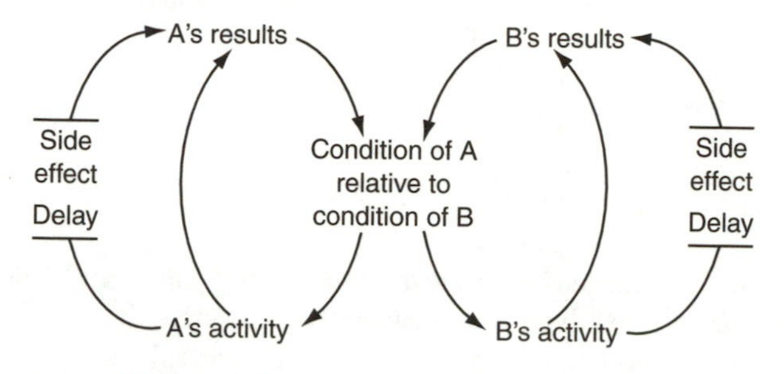

Figure 2.8 Escalation

Escalation

A and B are in a competitive relationship. If A or B achieve an improvement in their condition, then the other one responds, leading to an improvement in their own condition. This cycle repeats itself in an escalating fashion. However, escalation may slow or even stop due to lack of sustainability of the dynamic, or due to delay in impact of side effects. (See Figure 2.8.)

Success to the successful

A resource allocation procedure distributes limited resources according to a given criterion of success. At a certain allocation point, A is considered more successful than B and so A is allocated a larger share of the resources than B. This increases A's chances of success and diminishes B's chances of success, when measured against the criterion of success for the next round of resource allocation. (See Figure 2.9.)

As seen, systems archetypes are employed to describe, predict and explain patterns of behaviour. The nine systems archetypes covered above illustrate how this is done qualitatively, for example, with qualitative simulation that predicts and/or explains certain forms of behaviour. Qualitative simulation is aided by translating a story into a diagram, called an influence diagram, where points of leverage are easier to locate. The nine figures presented

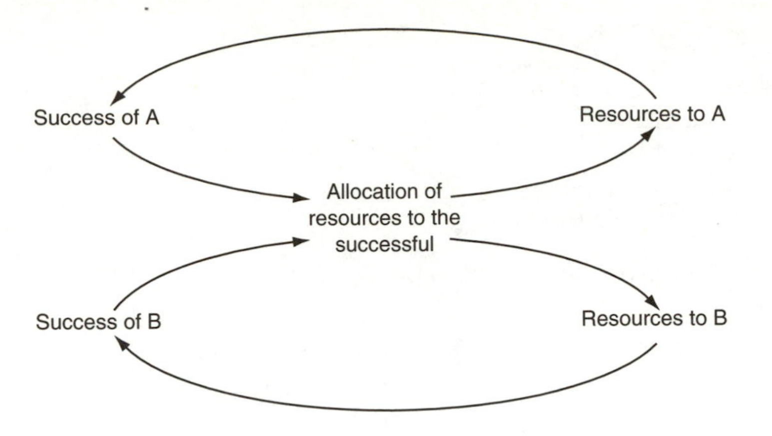

Figure 2.9 Success to the successful

above are all examples of influence diagrams. In special cases influence diagrams may be translated into dynamic mathematical models that predict quantitatively certain forms of behaviour. A valid mathematical model may be employed to test out a range of possible strategies for improvement. Mathematical descriptions are most relevant when modelling natural processes, such as physical and biological ones, where laws of behaviour are established. *The Fifth Discipline Fieldbook* warns, however, that system dynamics can all too easily be reduced to process-based thinking alone, whilst the broader argument of systems archetypes and underlying structure of behaviour goes unheeded. We now turn to Senge's four other disciplines.

Personal mastery

Personal mastery means developing one's own proficiency. It does not mean achieving dominance over people or things. Personal mastery is likened to a journey with no ultimate destination. In other words, it is a lifelong discipline. The journey consists of processes whereby a person continually clarifies and deepens personal vision, focuses energy on it, develops patience in seeking it, and in this way apparently increasingly views reality objectively. It thus leads people to do positive things towards achieving personal vision.

Personal vision is a calling of intrinsic desires, not a purpose to pursue. It is about focusing energies on what you do want, rather than on what you do not want. As a result, people hold a sacred view of work because work now is valued for itself, rather than posing a chore to be done as a means to some other end. Senge argues that people who achieve high levels of personal mastery therefore tend to be committed and exude initiative, have a broader and deeper sense of responsibility in their work and, of key importance, learn faster.

Personal mastery is not something you can force people to do. It is a potential organisational strategy, the importance of which needs to be explained to people. People can engage in discussion and dialogue about the possible implications of their personal vision. They are able to shape how their strategy might be implemented. It must be made clear in discussion and dialogue that personal mastery is not about developing people as a means towards organisational ends; rather, along with the four other disciplines, it seeks what Senge calls a covenant between people and organisation.

There are two sources of tension and conflict that most likely will become part of the journey – creative and emotional tension, and structural conflict.

Inevitably a gap will exist between personal vision and current reality. This is a source of tension that contains both positive and negative elements. *Creative tension* is positive and arises from a commitment to change. A person experiences energy and enthusiasm. This moves current reality towards personal vision. It needs feeding. *Emotional tension* is negative and arises from a lack of belief that change is possible. This can lead to feelings and emotions associated with anxiety. It pulls back personal vision towards current reality. It requires dampening. An important task is to sort out these two types of tension and then manage them accordingly. This prepares the way for concerted action to bring reality more in line with personal vision. Senge also emphasises the importance of being honest with oneself about the gap, so both a clear vision *and* an accurate, insightful view of current reality are given equal importance. Being honest about the gap avoids fooling oneself and consequent misdirection of concerted action.

Structural conflict may arise when there is disbelief in one's own ability to fulfil intrinsic desires. Such disbelief may rest on assumptions of powerlessness or unworthiness. Whichever, a lack of belief in oneself threatens to erode personal vision. Therefore, a need exists to attack negative beliefs, reducing structural conflict whilst preserving personal vision. Again, Senge emphasises a commitment to the truth. Only by these means is it possible to uncover ways with which we deceive ourselves, such as with negative beliefs, and then challenge why we have them. People with a high level of personal mastery excel in this regard.

In *The Fifth Discipline Fieldbook* a number of methods are introduced in support of the discipline of personal mastery. The fieldbook can be consulted for details. One of the methods is called 'drawing forth personal vision'. The purpose is to help people define their personal vision. A suitable atmosphere for reflection is essential. The process begins by 'creating a result'. This is a form of idealistic thinking, seeking out a result in life that is deeply desired. Three questions are asked. What does it look like? What does it feel like? What words would you use to describe it? The process continues by reflecting on answers to those three questions. For example, were there reasons that made it hard to conceive an ideal position? How would it feel to achieve the ideal? What is the complete picture relating to the ideal? Other methods introduced by Senge and colleagues pursue different aims. These include real time reflection and seeking innovations in structure that encourage personal mastery.

Systemic thinking is the discipline that integrates all five disciplines into a combined theory for the learning organisation. With personal mastery, for example, it helps to clarify the dynamic nature of structures in our lives. Systemic thinking illustrates the interrelated nature of creative tension and emotional tension, and how we can better achieve our intrinsic desires by amplifying creative tension and attenuating emotional tension. Systemic thinking points to the link between negative feelings we might have about ourselves and the way that this may impact on erosion of our goals.

More broadly, systemic thinking enables us to appreciate our connectedness to the world, to see more and more of the interdependencies between our actions, our reality, and how our intrinsic desires fit in with this. A systemic view allows us to learn about structures in the world in which we live our lives and to avoid a blinkered reaction to experiences, resulting in blame and guilt. It is systemic structures that explain events, not the actions of individuals. Systemic recognition of the way things work is an important step towards commitment to the whole.

Mental models

Mental models are conceptual structures in the mind that drive cognitive processes of understanding. They influence people's actions because they mould people's appreciation of what they see. People therefore observe selectively. Mental models most often invisibly define our relationship with each other and with the world in which we find ourselves.

The issue with mental models, Senge says, is not whether they are right or wrong, but whether they discharge routines in a person's life without them knowing it. In this case mental models undermine systemic thinking by limiting the vision of what can be seen and done. They hold back learning by restricting possible ways of conceptualising things. It is the argument of *The Fifth Discipline*, of course, that limited vision restrains learning and leads to inertia for individuals and for organisations.

An example of a limiting mental model that Senge chooses to spotlight is hierarchy in management. This in his opinion is a firmly entrenched mental model that people subscribe to, mainly unwittingly, which dominates management practice. The kind of routines hierarchy discharges include game playing and decision-making based on bureaucratic politics. Senge would prefer a mental model with values and principles more congruent with human nature as he sees it. Here he emphasises openness and merit.

The discipline of mental models aims to train people to appreciate that mental models do indeed occupy their minds and shape their actions. People need to discover mental models currently at work that shape their patterns of reasoning. They must learn to manage them. This will involve developing skills of inquiry, for example, bringing assumptions of mental models to the surface and testing advocacy with inquiry. In the learning organisation, people become able to test many mental models – our own and other possible ones – in each situation as it arises, ensuring that each one and a range of them are well considered. In the learning organisation such skills will be institutionalised through organisational practices that most likely will involve a facilitative organisational structure.

Methods for reflection and inquiry are considered central to the discipline of mental models. Senge is keen here on the work of Chris Argyris and Donald Schön called action science. Action science is concerned with spontaneous, tacit theories-in-use that enter into discussion and dialogue. These include actions such as unilateral control, unilateral self-protection and defensiveness, smoothing over and covering up. Such actions are employed whenever feelings of embarrassment or threat come into play. People are often unaware of these so called intrapsychic forces and the consequences that they lead to in discussion and dialogue.

One method that addresses intrapsychic forces is called 'the left-hand column'. The purpose is to become aware of the tacit assumptions that shape conversation and often prevent us from achieving things we set out to do. A table with two columns is drawn up for the exercise. The idea is to place in the right-hand column things said in a situation experienced as difficult. After reflection, other things are recorded in the left-hand column that were thought and felt but not said. Further reflection on the table some time later may help to clarify issues such as why things in the left-hand column were not said, what comments were made that contributed to the difficulty, and what prevented a different form of action from happening. In short, the question is, what/which mental model(s) was/were in force?

Systemic thinking helps further by testing if mental models are systemically flawed in the sense that they neglect critical feedback or delay, or miss points of high leverage. It helps to expose assumptions mental models are making about the dynamic nature of reality and to evaluate the validity of the assumptions. The aim is to better understand and indeed to improve our mental models of the world, not to draw elaborate systemic diagrams of the world.

Shared vision

Personal vision amounts to the pictures an individual carries around in their head and heart. A personal vision is about intrinsic desires. Shared vision, on the other hand, amounts to pictures people throughout the organisation carry. It is a vision to which many people are committed since it comes out of and is thus created from each person's personal vision. Shared vision refers to shared operating values, a common sense of purpose, indeed, a basic level of mutuality. It extends insights and principles from personal mastery into a world of collective aspiration and shared commitment.

Shared vision provides a focus and energy for learning. Here, Senge means generative learning rather than adaptive learning; that is, expanding an organisation's capacity to create its own future, rather than be created by events of the moment.

Senge says that it is not possible to have a learning organisation without shared vision. Shared vision fosters risk taking and experimentation. It generates leaders with a sense of vision who wish to communicate this in such a way that other people are inspired to share it and incorporate such ideas in their personal vision – the art of visionary leadership. Shared vision in Senge's view may be generated from the top in this way, but may in other cases bubble upwards (note here the structural assumption of hierarchy). Whichever way, a truly shared vision takes time to emerge and to shape how things are done.

The core idea on which methods for shared vision are constructed is intensive dialogue between people involved and those affected by the dialogue. The process is developmental. This is the antithesis of visioning exclusively from the top of a management hierarchy. *The Fifth Discipline Fieldbook* suggests how to move visioning from the top of the management hierarchy to widespread intensive dialogue – from 'telling' to 'co-creating'. Telling is where those at the top believe that they know what the vision should be and the organisation is going to have to follow it. People do what they are told either because they think that those at the top know best, or simply believe that they have no other choice. There is little generative learning. Co-creating, on the other hand, is a widespread and collaborative process where a shared vision is built in a mood of generative learning.

Systemic thinking explains the spread of shared vision in generative learning as a reinforcing process. Communication of ideas gathers pace and the vision becomes increasingly clear, leading to rising enthusiasm. As with any process of growth, system dynamics encourages us to look for limiting factors in the dynamic. Potentially there are several of these.

One possible limiting factor comes into play as more people get involved. Although a certain amount of shared vision is achieved, the more people who are involved, the greater the potential for a diversity of views to break out. This dissipates focus and may generate conflict. Equally, as with personal vision, it is possible that people may see a gap between shared vision and how things actually are, which gives rise to negative feelings and erosion of the goals of shared vision. Furthermore, it is possible for people to forget their connection to one another and that they are part of a whole, which lets slip the approach from one of joint inquiry to one of individuals in conflict.

Team learning

The aim of team learning is to achieve alignment in people's thoughts and energies. Growing a common direction creates resonance so that the whole team achieves more than the sum of team members, if each one were to work on her or his own. If, however, people are not aligned, then qualities valued in the learning organisation, such as empowerment, may actually increase conflict, yielding a whole team that achieves less than the sum that its members can, if they were to work in isolation.

Successful team learning may happen if team members master a balance of practices of discussion and dialogue. Senge defines *discussion* as communication where different views are presented and defended in a search for a best view to support a decision that must be made. *Dialogue* is communication of a fundamentally different nature, where people suspend their views and enter into deep listening, in the sense that the listener visits and explores mental models of other team members. The listener in this way attempts to see through the eyes of other team members.

Discussion and dialogue are necessary counterparts in a quest for consensus. However, there may be forces at work that prevent productive discussion and dialogue. Again, Senge makes reference to the research of Argyris and Schön called action science. Action science attempts to identify the defensive routines people employ in discussion and dialogue that break down those processes. For example, even when one team member knows that another one has made a mistake, they might prefer not to comment honestly about this because it can cause embarrassment or offence. Senge sees the challenge as transforming all forms of defensiveness into inquiry, indeed, reflective inquiry. This is the discipline of team learning.

Team learning in Senge's outlook is best pursued through methods of dialogue. Senge makes reference to David Bohm's book *On Dialogue* in which he writes about a stream of meaning flowing within us and between us. In this way people make a genuine attempt to appreciate matters of concern through the eyes of people who raise the concerns. People learn from this by expanding their understanding of circumstances that prevail. The basic components of a dialogue session as set out in *The Fifth Discipline Fieldbook* are as follows. Invite people and give them a chance to participate. Enter into generative learning where close attention is paid by all to what is said. Create time and silence where people have the chance to reflect on their own and other people's thoughts. And suspend assumptions to avoid the possible imposition of ideas on other people.

The perspective and tools of systemic thinking feature strongly in team learning. In particular, the tools of systemic thinking bear relevance to many forms of team learning. Take management teams as an example. The primary task of all management teams is dealing with complexity. Management teams deal with a variety of complex situations. Attention may be directed towards possible structures that support the learning organisation. Management teams inquire into the future through strategic visioning and policy analysis. The trouble is that conventional analysis tends to employ language that seeks to analyse such situations as somewhat static, relatively simple situations. Systemic thinking offers a language through systems archetypes that helps people get to grips with dynamic complexity. It helps to bring together people's mental models in a shared systemic language, generating team learning and understanding, and a shared sense of purpose.

Openness and localness

Senge emphasises openness and localness in his idea of a learning organisation. There are two types of openness in Senge's view – participative and reflective. *Participative* is the most common. It is the freedom to speak one's mind and to state one's views. It encourages wide involvement in decision-making. However, Senge argues, this mode of contribution leads to very little learning. A more potent generative learning comes from *reflective* openness. This entails challenging one's own thinking. It necessitates surfacing assumptions that shape our views and then subjecting the assumptions to open criticism. Senge speculates a little about positive synergy between participative and reflective openness.

Senge goes out of his way to reinforce ideas of openness as a challenge to power and politics in organisations. He expresses sorrow at the many examples of power and politics today. There is both formal and informal power which couple with game playing, and an acceptance that such games represent convention. This 'given' is challenged by learning organisations in a search for openness. What motivates people is questioned. The idea that power, wealth and self-interest are sole motivators is challenged. Senge's learning organisation assumes over and above self-interest that a person wants to be a part of something larger. A person desires to build something important with other people. The learning organisation in this sense is about co-operative relationships between people.

As well as enjoying co-operative relationships, Senge reckons, people also want to take responsibility for their actions, which is where localness comes in. People learn most rapidly when they have a genuine sense of responsibility. A genuine sense of responsibility results from empowerment of people at a local level, where people experience things that matter most to them. Responsibility invites initiative, gets people going, and encourages them to share and to come up with new ideas. Systemic thinking and localness are partners in learning that work together by focusing on matters of proximate relevance whilst preventing myopic thinking.

Commentary

Systemic thinking is the discipline that brings together all five of Senge's disciplines in pursuit of a combined body of theory and a mode of practice for the learning organisation. For example, systemic thinking in personal mastery helps us continually to see our connectedness to the world, and more and more of the interdependencies between our actions and our reality. Systemic thinking in mental models exposes assumptions and tests if these are systemically flawed, for instance, by identifying feedback not previously accounted for. Systemic thinking in shared vision clarifies how vision radiates through collaborative feedback processes and fades through conflictual feedback processes. Systemic thinking in team learning identifies positive and negative synergy in discussion and dialogue where, respectively, the whole becomes greater than or less than the sum of its parts.

Pockets of committed people across the globe have studied and practised systemic thinking. They have kept alive aspirations of systemic thinking since its entrance in the 1930s and 1940s into western thought. Apart from a number of forays that gave hope, but did little more than raise dust, systemic thinking has remained pretty much in the outback. Systemic thinking endured mainly as a vision of marginalised groups struggling to penetrate the educational and social mainstream. The rise and sustained impact of Senge's work in the 1990s suggests a possible revolution of thinking in the making, one that promises to enter and to redefine the educational and social mainstream. It is in my view a revolution long overdue. It offers a platform for change that I wish to build upon and innovate in this book, in the spirit of transformational learning that Senge endorses.

Reading *The Fifth Discipline* stimulated in me new insights into the potential of systemic thinking for transforming personal and organisational living. Many of the insights resonate with experiences from my life when I felt disempowered, but might not have done with *The Fifth Discipline* in mind. I might have been empowered, for example, by appreciating the counteracting forces of creative tension and emotional tension, or systemic flaws in mental models shaping my actions. Perhaps these experiences offer a clue to the question why *The Fifth Discipline* has gained such wide currency at this time. Is it not at least in part because *The Fifth Discipline* and its concepts and tools of the learning organisation promise to empower people? Does it not help us to understand and to put meaning back into our lives that modern society has taken out?

The Fifth Discipline is a counter-product of present-day living. It challenges mainstream thinking. It does this most poignantly by locating mystery in our lives that is inevitable because we cannot know everything. This is a humbling thought. Expecting to know everything in due course, as we are taught by mainstream thinking, manifests in our misery as we consistently fail to command absolute knowledge and control, let alone transform every aspect of our lives. *The Fifth Discipline* to an extent recognises this. For these reasons, further developments in the theory and practice of Senge's learning organisation warrant considered attention.

Senge and his co-producers' *The Fifth Discipline Fieldbook* is one such development. It makes substantial additions to the concepts, tools and techniques of the learning organisation. In particular, it expands on ways of approaching personal mastery, mental models, shared vision and team learning. However, there is little elaboration of or challenge to the mental model that is Senge's view of systemic thinking. In fact, Senge's original view is strongly reinforced in a series of vignettes that occupy a common vantage point. This vantage point sees systemic thinking through the lens of system dynamics, which is just one of many systemic approaches that might be taken into account. Senge's two books make little reference to a wider extant body of complementary systemic approaches. True, Senge recognises that the origins of system dynamics lie in subject domains traversing the physical and social sciences (see J.W. Forrester's work). System dynamics emerged from and embraces certain concepts of engineering and management, and the tools and techniques of cybernetics and servomechanism engineering theory. However, other path-breaking offshoots of systemic thinking are passed over with barely a reference to them. For example, in *The Fifth Discipline* the only such recognition is in a footnote on page 401 noting Checkland's soft systems approach. In *The Fifth Discipline Fieldbook* there is only a brief reference on page 185 to Ackoff's interactive planning. There is mention only in passing on page 89 to Ackoff's interactive planning as well as Bertalanffy's open systems theory, amongst names of some other researchers and research topics, that includes complexity theory.

System dynamics does bring forward important insights offered by systemic thinking. Yet, in sticking so close to system dynamics, Senge fails to recognise and take into account other important insights systemic thinkers have to offer. In my view he underplays the potential role of systemic thinking in his learning organisation. Russell Ackoff says on the sleeve of this book that, 'It is in the nature of systemic thinking to yield many different views of the same thing and the same view of many different things.' Senge with system dynamics manages only to generate the same view of many different things. With tongue in cheek, then, I note a touch of irony in *The Fifth Discipline* and its sister fieldbook stressing only a part of the whole of 'systemic thinking'.

A need exists for a thorough review of Senge's mental model of systemic thinking. That is the role of Part I of this book. To facilitate such a review, the next five chapters each presents the ideas of a most influential systemic thinker, drawing out comparisons with Senge's work where appropriate. Part I of the book concludes in Chapter 8 with 'Senge's *The Fifth Discipline* revisited', where the findings of comparisons are consolidated and worked into an extensive critique of Senge's view of systemic thinking. The emerging whole opens up a way to complexity theory and to the crucial enriching insights that it offers, which are set out in Part II of the book. So, let us begin this exercise by exploring the historical roots of systemic thinking in this century, as they arise in Bertalanffy's open systems theory.

3 Bertalanffy's open systems theory

The seminal man

Ludwig von Bertalanffy's seminal contribution to science usefully can be broken down into three interrelated categories. First, came biology and open systems theory (from the mid-1920s). General system theory and the unity of science followed (from the late 1930s). Application of these theories, for example, to symbolism, psychology and education, came next (from the mid-1950s). These three categories reflect progression in his research. Concepts from each category influenced theory and practice in 'management and organisation' to different degrees – the impact of open systems theory is profound; that of general system theory transforming; whilst work on symbolism, psychology and education, bear on those subject areas. Each category is presented below in an allocated space commensurate with its importance to the argument of this book.

Open systems theory

Ludwig von Bertalanffy's research challenged the relevance of nineteenth-century physics to the appreciation of living things. Physics offered many insights into the physical world by employing reductionism. Reductionism breaks things into parts and studies forces acting on them, seeking to establish laws and principles of their behaviour. It does this by treating parts as closed systems, that is, separate independent units of analysis.

In the late nineteenth century research into living things encountered limitations to reductionism. A counter-position in biology took on a coherent form by the mid-1920s. Several scientists began to think in a new way. Paul Weiss, Walter B. Cannon (credited with homeostasis) and, in particular, Ludwig von Bertalanffy, came to the fore. Von Bertalanffy demonstrated that concepts of physics were helpless in appreciating dynamics of organisms. Existence of an organism cannot be understood solely in terms of behaviour of some fundamental parts. A whole organism demonstrably behaves in a way that is more than the sum of its parts. It exhibits synergy. Furthermore, much of an organism's existence is characterised by increasing or at least maintaining order, which is negentropic. Biology therefore required new concepts to explain phenomena like synergy and negentropy.

In this regard, von Bertalanffy developed a theory of open systems in biology (otherwise known as organismic biology). Open systems theory employs functional and relational criteria rather than reductionist analysis of fundamental parts. An organism co-exists in relation to an environment. Its functions and structure diversify or are maintained by a continuous flow of energy and information between organism and environment. An organism is a complex thing comprising many interrelated parts, resulting in a whole with an overall integrity. Key concepts here include *self-organisation* by way of progressive differentiation, *equifinality* as the independence of final state from initial conditions, and *teleology* as the dependence of behaviour on some future purpose 'known in advance'.

As time passed, both closed systems theory and then open systems theory swept across and bid for ownership of emerging disciplines, like management, as discussed below.

Relevance to 'management and organisation'

One example of reductionism at work is the experiment of closed systems thinking in organisational settings. Senge, along with others who followed Bertalanffy's lead, objected to closed systems thinking employed in this way. It assumes behaviour of organisations is based on fundamental principles and laws just like physics. Operations are routine, repetitive, and perform predetermined tasks. There is a strict hierarchy of control, exact obedience by standardised parts (including people), and much emphasis is placed on efficiency and effectiveness. Analysis employing tools like work-study methods is seen to prevail. Senior managers are governors, whilst middle managers and supervisors are engineers keeping the machine well oiled (by commanding people) so that it can relentlessly achieve the purpose for which it was assembled. Workers operate and supervisors maintain the machine, keeping it in good working order.

The closed system experiment remains active today with many organisations adopting some, if not all, of the ideas it nominates. It has rendered some success, helping to perform routine tasks and to achieve repetitive production of a single product. This is something that Senge fails adequately to acknowledge in dismissing the idea out of hand. It assists in the accomplishment of set purpose, especially in stable environments that barely need to be taken into account, at least in the short term. However, efficiency and effectiveness is in part and at times undermined because people experience drudgery. They become demotivated by tasks that they are expected mindlessly to perform. Furthermore, organisational activities are increasingly impacted on by turbulence in operational and administrative environments. They are simply unable to respond swiftly enough. Open systems theory promised to address these concerns.

Open systems theory applied to 'management and organisation' portrays concepts of physics as helpless in appreciating dynamics of organisations. Rather, open systems theory observes organisations as complex systems made up of parts most usefully studied as a whole. An organisation is open to its environment. Action is taken to hold an organisation in a steady state. The primary aim is to ensure survival, by transforming inputs and by adapting to changes when they occur. Since parts comprise people, management is concerned about the nature of people at work. Parts, or subsystems, have lists of needs that must be met. Individual motivation requires attention. For example, jobs can be enriched leading to greater satisfaction and productivity. The whole organisational structure may facilitate participation. Leadership can encourage democracy and autonomy.

Open systems theory has attracted its fair share of criticism. It suggests structure and function in bounded organisations and that they are physical entities just like organisms. This encourages people to seek out and to identify systems in the world. Writers such as C. West Churchman and Peter Checkland (see later chapters), in various ways, argue that human systems are different. Human systems, they say, are better understood in terms of systems of meaning (ideas, concepts, values, etc.) people ascribe to the world, rather like Senge's mental models. To appreciate human systems therefore requires learning and understanding about systems of meaning and conflict that arises between them. Organisational boundaries diminish in importance or at least are redefined in this way. Ideas such as open systems theory, then, are useful only in so far as they stimulate learning and understanding as one possible model for analysis. This is precisely Gareth Morgan's approach in *Images Of Organisation*, employing an open systems metaphor as one possible image of organisational dynamics.

The impact of von Bertalanffy's open systems theory on 'management and organisation' is profound. It helped shape 'management and organisation' in the 1950s and 1960s. It is the conception point of systems archetypes recognised in the 1970s that Senge attaches so much importance to. It pervades management practice today. Planning and decision-making nowadays is often couched in terms such as differentiation, environment, functions, growth, interrelatedness and teleology. Beyond these influences, open systems theory turned out to be the forerunner of general system theory.

General system theory

Von Bertalanffy generalised the open systems concept for other fields of study. This led him to the idea of general system theory and a new vision of the unity of science. General system theory aims to formulate and derive principles applicable to systems in general. Von Bertalanffy developed general system theory throughout the 1940s and into the 1950s.

In 1954 he and three other distinguished scholars with similar ideas spent time together as Fellows of the Centre for Advanced Study in the Behavioural Sciences in Palo Alto, California. Von Bertalanffy along with Kenneth Boulding (economist), Ralph Gerard (physiologist) and Anatol Rapoport (mathematical biologist) became founding fathers of the systems movement. The systems movement, Kenneth Boulding recollects, began in conversations of four Fellows around a luncheon table.

Von Bertalanffy subsequently was prime mover in organising the systems movement. He was central in establishing the Society for the Advancement of General Systems Theory. It was initiated as a group of the American Association for the Advancement of Science at its Berkeley meeting in 1954. The society launched both a yearbook in 1956 and an annual conference (both still going today). The society was founded with four aims.

- To investigate the isomorphy of concepts, laws, and models from various fields, and to help in useful transfers from one field to another.
- To encourage development of adequate theoretical models in fields which lack them.
- To minimise the duplication of theoretical effort in different fields.
- To promote the unity of science through improving communication among specialists.

The first three of these aims live on in a different guise in Senge's systemic thinking. In particular, we see systems archetypes employed in many different fields, helping in the development of theoretical models. This arguably helps to minimise duplication of theoretical effort.

Von Bertalanffy's main worry was increasing specialisation, leading to a breakdown in science as an integrated realm. He saw specialists encapsulated in their own private universe, finding it difficult to get messages from one cocoon to another. He wished to prevent closed, isolated research. He foresaw a system of laws and generalised theories to unify all sciences.

Robert Rosen (1979) described von Bertalanffy's general system idea with forceful simplicity. If two systems S and S′ are physically different but nevertheless behave similarly, then there is a sense in which we can learn about S through S′. Learning, von Bertalanffy insisted, is through isomorphy or homology, not vague analogy.

[For the record, Alexander Bogdanov (1873–1928, see 'Further reading'), a Russian thinker, developed 'tektology' that is likened to general system theory. It was published in Russian in the years 1912–1928. Soviet authorities suppressed tektology. In the 1980s tektology became available in English.]

Systems view of people

Consolidated in the book *A Systems View Of Man* (edited by La Violette, 1981), von Bertalanffy's reasoning on symbolism, psychology and education, illustrate applications of his systemic theories. Besides certain biological differences, von Bertalanffy states, what distinguishes human beings from other creatures is the creation and use of symbols. Symbols are freely built, representative of some content, and transmitted by tradition. They are conscious representations of thought and values. Von Bertalanffy's systemic thinking sees systems of symbols, or symbolic universes. Through this conception, he suggests, language, science, art and other cultural forms, achieve existence transcending the personalities and lifetimes of their creators.

In the domain of psychology, von Bertalanffy wrote of people as intrinsically active psychophysical organisms that possess autonomous behaviour. This challenged the reactive, mechanistic stimulus-response model. He emphasised many organismic principles from open systems theory.

In the domain of education, von Bertalanffy saw stifling of creativity in North American pedagogical practices that taught within confines of disciplines. He recommended an interdisciplinary approach. Interdisciplinarity is a big topic in the 1990s, particularly in tertiary education. It is supported, for example, with many universities encouraging synergy from research groups to counter the trend of decline in resources. Ironically, interdisciplinary studies are not well supported by external research grant awarding bodies or newfangled research assessment exercises that determine the distribution of elements of resource. Lessons may be learnt here from J.W. Forrester, Senge's early mentor, who has contributed with system dynamics, an interdisciplinary education for children that is widely taken up in the USA.

A systemic discipline emerges

In 1957 the Society for the Advancement of General Systems Theory changed its name to the Society for General Systems Research. Under this umbrella organisation, systemic thinking burgeoned into many offshoots – including system dynamics and seminal work on complexity theory. Offshoots then sprouted yet more specialist offshoots. Many national systems societies formed, either to promote a specialism or to align offshoots to gain coherence amongst like-minded people.

In 1980 the International Federation for Systems Research was incorporated, fittingly in Austria, von Bertalanffy's home country. The aim was to stimulate all activities associated with the scientific study of systems and to co-ordinate such activities at an international level. It launched the journal *Systems Research* (now incorporating *Behavioural Science*). The independent *International Journal of General Systems* was launched in 1974. In 1988, the international journal *Systems Practice* (renamed *Systemic Practice and Action Research* in 1998) was launched in which many new possibilities for systemic thinking have emerged. Specialist journals mushroomed – including *System Dynamics Review* and recently, dealing with complexity theory, *Complexity In Human Systems* and *Emergence*. Sensing this growing plurality and 'competition', in 1988 the Society for General Systems Research changed its name to the International Society for the Systems Sciences. And in the 1990s Senge's *The Fifth Discipline* and an ever maturing complexity theory came on to the scene. Evidently, systemic thinking has become diverse and through this diversity offers many insights worthy of exploration, as we will discover in subsequent chapters.

4 Beer's organisational cybernetics

The recurring man

Stafford Beer is an exceptional person. In a most distinguished of careers, he made and continues to make a sustained and authoritative contribution to operational research and the management sciences (ORMS). He pursued a highly successful career in industry and commerce and as an international consultant whilst, *at the same time*, he produced a stream of influential books. Broadening the scope of ORMS, he defined and practises organisational cybernetics of decision and control. Cybernetics is generally defined as the art and science of communication and control. Beer subsequently invented the viable system model for effective organisation and the complementary team syntegrity, adding to the viable system model a statement of participatory democracy.

Beyond ORMS, however, Beer's artistic character flourishes, that is an essential element of his life and works. He has a lifetime interest in the classical languages Latin, Greek and Sanskrit. He practises and teaches yoga. He has published poetry and a few exhibitions of his paintings have been held. In particular, his *Requiem Meditation*, consisting of nine interactive oil paintings, was installed in the apse of the Metropolitan Cathedral of Christ the King in Liverpool (1992 and 1993). He has broadcast frequently on radio and television. Stafford Beer, then, might be considered a man of cybernetic genius and, within this mould, a recurring and indeed wide-ranging capacity to create and invent. His work is reviewed below under the headings – cybernetics, viable system model, and team syntegrity.

Cybernetics

Stafford Beer essentially is a cybernetician working in the field of ORMS. His leading three books offer an appreciation of these subjects – *Cybernetics and Management* (1959), *Decision and Control* (1966) and *Management Science* (1968).

ORMS in Beer's argument needs to be cybernetic to be effective. The techniques of ORMS are of high utility only when employed in the light of a scientific description of the whole situation. This means managing the whole, not just the parts. Managing the whole involves drawing together potential organisational developments, in part generated by ORMS techniques, to form new higher order plans. Techniques that Beer recommends include but go beyond system dynamics, the core of Senge's systemic thinking.

A cybernetic mode of operation involves interdisciplinary teams, since it is not possible to say in advance of any cybernetic intervention which branch of science is needed. ORMS, however, is not a science in itself. Rather, it is doing science in a management sphere. An ORMS activist does not have to be concerned with laws governing natural phenomena, but must however operate across scientific disciplines, being sufficiently knowledgeable and mentally agile to identify a relevant interdisciplinary model. There are laws of an interdisciplinary nature, Beer argues, that support the quest for knowledge and agility. Cybernetics is the science of interdisciplinary laws and offers a systemic matrix through which ORMS is done and higher order plans are accomplished. The way in which Beer achieves this, however, yields a quite different yet complementary result to Senge's systems archetypes.

Science for Beer is both rational and rigorous. It is the precise formulation of method that yields something clear and definite, testable and repeatable. Science aspires to free will through rigorous choice (a point made in *Decision and Control*, then amplified in *Designing Freedom*). In *Decision and Control*, Beer argues that, ordinarily, belief is fixed. He refers to three habits of fixing drawn from Charles Peirce's work – tenacity through the process of conditioning, authority when people believe they are an indivisible part of a system, and apriority in which conclusions arise from an underlying language. Scientific fixing at least emancipates us from such uncritical patterns of 'choice making'.

In scientific mood, an ORMS team begins by defining the scope of the problem. The problem, to use Beer's expression, does not necessarily reside where the symptoms are found. Therefore, a team approach is crucial and must encompass the whole problem situation. This requires consultation across departmental barriers. Cybernetic ORMS does not reward departmental minded people. A problem is tentatively defined, facts on this are collected and collated, and suitable courses of action are examined. Options are then evaluated in terms of probabilities, costs, risks and potential benefits. The precise problem, as Beer sees it, is pinpointed. From here on, Beer envisages committee debates whereby informed, rational and rigorous decisions are made. This is in contrast to the dialogical practice that characterises Senge's disciplines, shared vision and team learning.

Clearly, Beer's notion of ORMS, and subsequent decision-making, is that it must balance the whole. He observed in *Decision and Control* that ORMS techniques tend to maximise only one variable with one purpose in mind. This might conflict with other purposes. The way ORMS jobs seem to escape this flaw is by unwittingly limiting the scope of inquiry. The old ORMS methodology cannot face up to extreme complexity. Beer thus declared the need for a new methodology for ORMS, one with a cybernetic orientation.

Cybernetics operates without regard to the specialised viewpoint of any one branch of science, offering the systemic capability Beer sought. Cybernetics, of which system dynamics is one realisation, became popularised in the mid- to late 1940s through the work of Warren McCulloch and Norbert Weiner. They described a new science of cybernetics, observing that many disciplines were saying essentially the same thing with regard to control, information, measurement and logic. Cybernetics recognised an underlying unity between control mechanisms in different sciences. Cybernetics is thus considered to be the general theory of control and hence is often called the science of communication and control.

In particular, in *Cybernetics and Management*, Beer explains the concepts of cybernetics. He concludes that there are three main properties of a cybernetic system. They are exceedingly complex, probabilistic, and self-regulatory. They are also purposive, meaning that from a particular viewpoint the system is organised to achieve some end. Cybernetic systems are characterised by feedback and control that guide the purposive system. Many systems that are exceedingly complex cannot be specifically defined. Behaviour is studied by discovering the logical and statistical relationships that hold between information that goes in and instructions that come out – the system is treated as a black box.

Beer traces cybernetics to information theory and the work of Claude Shannon. Effective operation of a system depends on an ability to store, transmit and modify information. Information kills variety, which is Beer's term for complexity, and the reduction of variety is one of the main techniques of regulation. This is not a process of simplifying the system, but making it more predictable.

The main tool of the cybernetician, Beer asserts, is 'the model'. Beer's models are logical cybernetic descriptions of a system. The change of state of a system can be represented as a transformation of the logic. Dynamic systems are thus described by a model together with a set of rules for making it change state. ORMS work is undertaken with the logic of a model in mind. The initial task, Beer observes, is coming up with a logical cybernetic description. It is from hereon that Beer's cybernetics notably diverges from Senge's systemic thinking, being far more scientific in mood.

Models by definition are about comparison. For Beer, the formal scientific process begins with comparison between conceptual models. There are two conceptual models; one of the managerial situation about how the 'system really works', and one that resembles the first selected from the scientific situation by ORMS practitioners about how the 'situation really works'. Practitioners then question to what extent does the behaviour of the one model throw light on the behaviour of the other? In what ways do the theories currently maintained by scientists in the one area transplant into the other? Are the actual techniques of research and computation appropriate? Moreover, do conclusions that hold for the one model hold for the other? Ultimately, the researcher is asking under what methodology can correspondence be regarded as rigorously validated?

Beer recognises various ways in which comparison can be made. Metaphor offers a poetic identity relation. The research scientist wishing to be more exact may test the ideas through analogy. Yet this tends to destroy the identity relation that, 'the metaphor poetically enshrines'. In any case, analogy by definition is open to dispute. The research scientist, Beer stresses, needs to formulate models precisely, using tools of rigorous science – mathematics, statistics and logic. The aim is to produce two deeper level homomorphic models (that may well be isomorphic). An example used by Beer is modelling 'learning rats' and transposing this into a model for 'a learning industrial plant'. Another example is Beer's sketch for a cybernetic factory. He constructs a machine capable of adapting to its environment in the guise of an intelligence amplifier modelled on the homeostat (a word derived from homeostasis). The result is an industrial concern looked at through cybernetic eyes as imitating functions of a living organism. The question then asked is, what kind of organic control system can be proposed to pursue environmental adaptation?

Beer's most famous homomorphism, the viable system model, discussed below, draws correspondence between 'management and organisation', and human brain structure and function. In his model, Beer offers a clear view of how a participatory structure might be conceived, an offering that Senge notably fails to make. The managerial situation is modelled, drawing on the science of neurophysiology, set out in *Brain of the Firm*, as a brain-directed organism operating in an environment. To prove his point that there are laws of an interdisciplinary nature, Beer also constructs the viable system model in *Heart of the Enterprise* from cybernetic first principles. Appreciating Beer's views on ORMS and cybernetics, in particular those on science and modelling, is an essential prerequisite to getting to grips with the viable system model.

Viable system model

A full exposition of the viable system model (VSM) is found in the trilogy: *Brain of the Firm* (1972), *Heart of the Enterprise* (1979), and *Diagnosing the System for Organisations* (1985).

The VSM is a model that in Beer's argument encapsulates effective organisation. It is a model of any viable system, biological or social. The VSM stipulates rules whereby an organisation is, 'survival-worthy' – it is regulated, learns, adapts and evolves. It is an organisation constructed around five main management functions – operations, co-ordination, control, intelligence and policy (see Figure 4.1). Beer respectively labels these systems one to five. The key to their organisation is a set of laws of interconnection in the form of a complex of information and control loops.

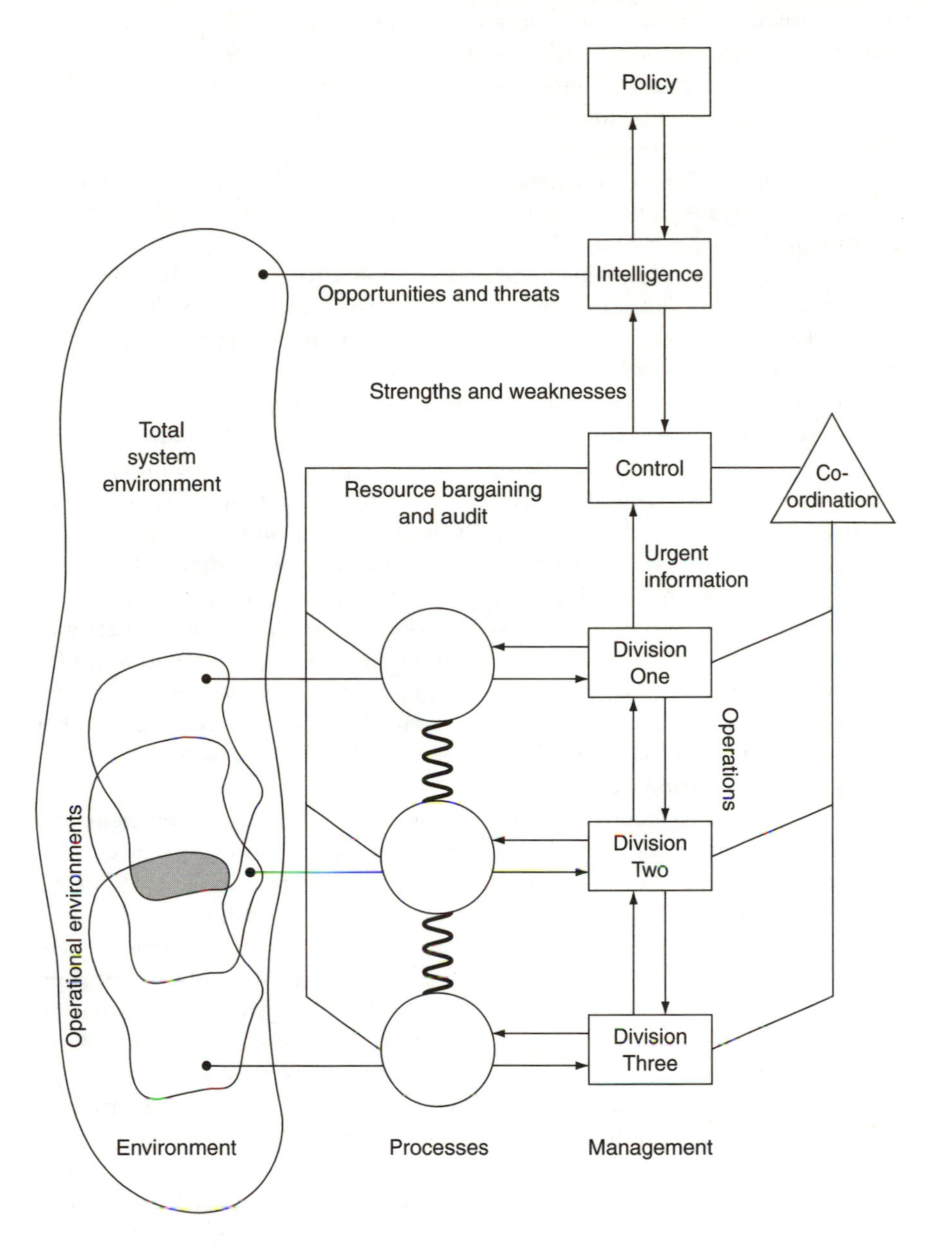

Figure 4.1 Viable system model

The VSM employs, amongst other things: amplifiers to increase impact of activities where needed; attenuators as activities to absorb variety; and transducers to translate information into a usable form as it passes, for example, between functions. The VSM employs an interdisciplinary law, that all distinct organisations contain themselves, which Beer calls recursion (described later). Another critical principle is that each contained organisation, and each of the five functions which it comprises, must be allowed as much autonomy as possible whilst maintaining the integrity of the whole. For 'management and organisation', it sets out details of how enterprises might work in contrast to organisational charts that Beer rejects as merely devices for apportioning blame (pitching in cybernetic logic against hierarchical logic).

The model as depicted in Figure 4.1 is shown to separate out the main operations of an organisation organised as divisions. It specifies the relationship between these divisions and the remaining four management functions that serve them – co-ordination, control, intelligence and policy. Operations (system one) performs the primary activities of the organisation, that is, it works to achieve what the organisation is set up to do. System dynamics might be employed to model the operations as processes and to investigate their efficiency and reliability. Operations comprise a number of divisions each with operational managers. Each division is considered to be a viable system in its own right. Viability here means that each division holds a guarantee of continuity, that it too is survival worthy. Each division is allowed as much autonomy as possible whilst maintaining the integrity of the whole. A division is connected to an operational environment, amplifying its own impact on the environment and attenuating variety entering from the environment. The divisions are serviced through four management service functions which are coupled by transducers, and which attenuate variety as information flows 'upwards'.

Co-ordination (system two) aims to ensure that there is an efficient and stable use of resources achieved in a harmonious fashion. It receives vital information about short-term problems faced in operations. It dampens uncontrolled oscillations between divisions. It also, or even primarily, manages conflict that might arise between divisional managers. Control (system three) acts as a control function that maintains relatively stable equilibrium between the interdependent divisions. Control deals with vital information about problems in operations that short-term co-ordination is not able to cope with. Control manages resource bargaining. Control also audits the divisions in a regular and routine manner. Audit may include operational, quality and financial audits, such as budget reviews. Control action is taken when audits show up operational problems that have not or cannot be dealt with through co-ordination. Additionally, control interprets policy decisions and ensures that they are effectively implemented throughout operations.

The intelligence or developmental function (system four) captures information about the total environment. This comprises internal and external environments. Intelligence is gathered about *strengths* and *weaknesses* of internal processes. A model of the external environment is provided that identifies *opportunities* and *threats*. This SWOT information is brought together in an operations room, which is an environment for decision-making. Vital intelligence information is disseminated throughout the organisation to those who will benefit from it. Intelligence rapidly transmits urgent information to policy (system five), alerting policy makers to serious problems in operations, co-ordination and control. Policy deals with strategic decisions and issues of management style, as well as urgent information. It receives all relevant information from intelligence about strengths, weaknesses, opportunities and threats, and, on the basis of this SWOT information, reviews and modifies policy. It arbitrates between antagonistic internal and external demands. It represents the essential qualities of the whole just described.

Recursion, mentioned earlier, means that the whole can be found in the parts. That is, whole viable systems can be found as divisions of a viable system (the divisions that make up operations, which is system one in Beer's terminology, see Figure 4.2). A viable system is itself a part of a larger viable system. Recursion offers a novel way in which a shared vision and related policies can penetrate an organisational activity. Shared vision or identity is determined by the policy function using a participatory method (see 'Team syntegrity' below). At higher resolution recursive levels, the shared vision is interpreted within the identity of the whole and is subsequently implemented.

Using a recursive design aims to avoid the negative effects of coercive structures. Recursion implements through management function, whereas traditional hierarchy implements by management authority. Recursion for example promotes autonomy. The parts have as much independence as is possible given the constraints that exist when co-ordinating and controlling to maintain a whole. The viable system organisation allows for participation to be fulfilled in terms of functions. For example, channels for resource bargaining exist between operations and control. *Vertical loading* is encouraged. This means loading down responsibility to the 'lowest level' at which it can be managed. *Task formation* is encouraged to produce whole jobs and to reverse mechanical, reductionist tendencies. People consequently take responsibility over their work. They can determine the needs of their customers and work out for themselves how this best can be achieved. A customer is any person or group who we provide with a product, service or information. *Job grouping* is encouraged to bring together efforts that are naturally related. This would gather sets of jobs, for example, by geographical location, client type, or some other logical grouping.

The central concern with the VSM expressed in the literature is that it underplays the purposeful role of individuals. For example, who in the VSM is responsible for determining the purpose of the organisation? Does the VSM emphasise control at the expense of individual freedom? Does a quest for harmony and stability tend to assimilate rather than integrate people? Do the five management functions constitute an imposition on people? Do they mask undercurrents of resistance, difference and tension that operate informally? Do these concerns undermine the VSM as a systemic structure able to support Senge's five disciplines? What might be Beer's response?

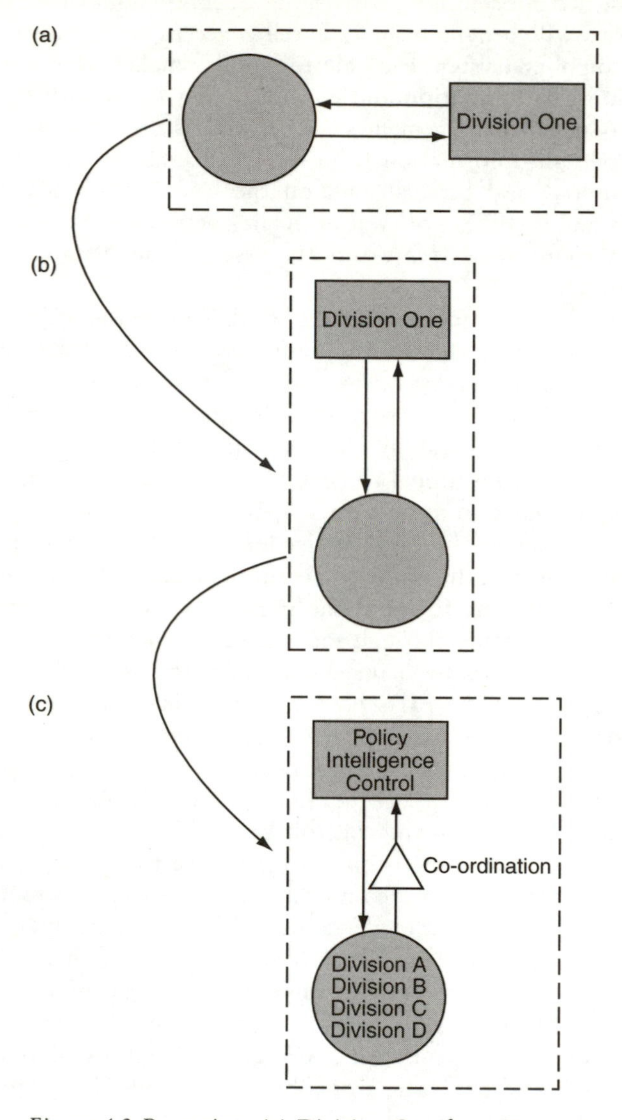

Figure 4.2 Recursion: (a) Division One from Figure 4.1; (b) transposition of Figure 4.2 (a); (c) Figure 4.2 (b) as a simplified viable system model

Beer was aware as early as *Decision and Control* (1966) that special problems exist in maintaining a clear and distinct idea of what cybernetics is about, free from emotive and other misleading connotations of words and language (revisiting Peirce's apriority). He is gravely concerned that the analogue of the systems language has unavoidable connotations which he would rather be without; for example, the absurdity, as Beer puts it, that cybernetics pictures people as deterministic and predictable thinking machines. Although Beer rarely comments on criticisms other than in passing, a careful reading of his consistent argument strongly suggests he handles criticism of his work in this way. Furthermore, in recent times, Beer developed team syntegrity that might be considered his ultimate statement of participatory democracy.

Team syntegrity

Team syntegrity presented in *Beyond Dispute* (1994) complements the VSM. The VSM offers cybernetic principles of organisation. Team syntegrity adds to this Beer's notion of people's participation in organisational activities. The invention seeks to organise normative, directional and strategic planning, and other creative processes. It addresses the question of effective group work. In particular, it suggests how to form work processes in which each group member can make maximum use of her or his capacity, as well as benefit from synergistic effects of group dynamics.

The underlying model is a regular icosahedron. It has 20 sides with 30 edges, each edge representing a person. A team syntegrity 'infoset' thus consists of 30 people with a common commitment and interest in an area they wish to investigate, perhaps for setting policy. A protocol creates an internal network. The role of the protocol is to maintain productivity and creativity. There are three parts to the protocol – problem jostle, topic auction and outcome resolve.

Problem jostle encourages the infoset to generate an agenda for their meeting. Five sessions each of four hours are put aside. The infoset then agrees on 12 agenda topics. At the same time, the infoset works towards and develops a self-organising system.

Topic auction is where each of the 30 members of the infoset is given two discussion topics out of the 12 that result from the problem jostle. The aim is for people as far as possible to receive topics of her or his highest preference. Teams form around discussion topics in a group of five. Each member also acts as a 'critic' in two other teams. Therefore, each member has four roles yielding overall 120 roles in a team syntegrity activity.

Outcome resolve is where the infoset work with their topics, and develop and refine them, resulting in final statements of importance. This is undertaken through at least three iterations of debate. That is, each group of five members and five critics meets at least three times. Meetings are structured as follows. Group members discuss the topic for about 30 minutes. Critics listen. Then in about 10 minutes critics offer comments and proposals. A draft is made of the statement of importance.

As group members and critics participate in other group meetings, they gain information, ideas and impressions. Debate flows around and around the conscious network. It, 'reverberates and hums'. The sphere created becomes a group consciousness with no hierarchy. Beer argues that a group organised in this way is an ultimate statement of participatory democracy, since each role is indistinguishable from any other one.

Cybernetics makes its mark

Cybernetics as understood today is an interdisciplinary activity. The cybernetic notion of communication and control is found in all forms of human thought – from biology to 'management and organisation' and international relations – and in all forms of human action – from engineering to strategic planning and international economics. We have seen so far in Part I that cybernetics underlies three systemic approaches – Bertalanffy's open systems theory, Beer's organisational cybernetics, as well as Senge's systems archetypes. Together, Bertalanffy, Beer and Senge offer many useful insights and contribute to a potentially powerful tool kit to support cybernetic thinking in 'management and organisation'. Cybernetics has made its mark. However, cybernetics is far from the whole story of systemic thinking. Systemic thinking goes beyond principles and archetypes of communication and control in developing a rich understanding of human circumstances. The next three chapters, covering Ackoff's interactive planning, Checkland's soft systems approach, and Churchman's critical systemic thinking, increasingly explore systemic thinking in terms of the interpretive nature of human beings.

5 Ackoff's interactive planning

The planning man

The work of Russell L. Ackoff has had and continues to have a significant impact upon many fields in 'management and organisation'. Wherever he has had his say, Ackoff is without compromise in promoting messages of participation, creativity, problem dissolving, improving the future, and seeking to *plan or be planned for*. In this, he has generated a whole too massive to cover here. Nevertheless, there are perhaps four main contributions that stand out and provide a representative account – fables and foibles, operations research, interactive planning, and circular organisation. The first of these points to a wry streak in Ackoff that pervades his work, sometimes explicitly, yet at other times quite subtly.

Fables and foibles

In creating his own future, reviewed below, Ackoff led himself into many experiences. He has consolidated these, often with most welcome humour, in several publications of fables and foibles. An account of Ackoff's work would not be complete without at least brief reference to this side of the man's intellectual character.

Ackoff's writings on 'management and organisation' are insightful and practical. They are also irreverent and witty. *Ackoff's Fables* (1991) epitomises these last qualities. His fables are very short stories with very sharp points, about personal experiences that are essentially true. According to Ackoff's mentor, the late Tom Cowan, they are stories that may not be completely true, but ought to be. The following sharp points give a flavour of Ackoff's fables and, indeed, foibles.

- The best system designer is one who knows how to beat any system that others design.
- The best response to an arbitrary requirement is one that is itself as arbitrary as the requirement.

- Intelligence and creativity are producers, not products, of education, but they are often its victims.

More fables and foibles are located in Ackoff's column in the first ten volumes of the journal *Systems Practice*. We now turn to the 'more serious' side to Ackoff's work.

Operations research

Operations research in the 1950s and 1960s promised to satisfy Ackoff's appetite for doing real, practical work, which his time in philosophy departments did not offer. He moved on to co-define with Churchman operations research in its early years (the 1950s). *Introduction to Operations Research* (1957, with Churchman and Arnoff) was the first international textbook in the field. In the 1960s he co-produced *A Manager's Guide to Operations Research* (1963, with Rivett), and *Fundamentals of Operations Research* (1968, with Sasieni). In this trilogy, he heads a comprehensive account of operations research. He emphasises, as does Beer, the importance of a mixed team approach. An organisation is diverse and requires at least equal diversity in operations research teams. The mixed team approach in the 1960s distinguished North American operations research from operational research in the UK, and points to a systemic interest in managing the whole.

In the 1960s, Ackoff states, operations researchers learnt that their techniques are best suited to certain types of problem. They are suited to machines and machine-like behaviour. Operations research problems tended to be operational and tactical in nature, rather than strategic and normative. Operations research became defined by operational and tactical problems. At the same time, Ackoff reckons problems of corporations were changing. After World War II, demand rose rapidly and production responded. This posed problems suited to the technology of operations research. By the early 1960s, western industry had built more production capacity than required to meet demand. Corporate leaders switched attention to handling competition for demand and creation of new demand. They exhibited purposeful behaviour. Most operations researchers, however, stuck with their techniques and interest in operational and tactical problems. A gap developed between corporate managers' needs and operations researchers' provision. Operations research thus became relegated to lower levels of management.

Further changes, in Ackoff's view, led to a widening gap. There were limits to growth obtainable by manipulating marketing variables. Corporations increasingly turned to internal development of new products and services. This required strategic planning in Ackoff's judgement, not operational and tactical problem solving. It required dealing with complex systems of interacting problems that Ackoff labels, 'messes'. It was the failure of operations research to change with the times that moved it down the hierarchy and even out of organisational enterprises. At the same time, Ackoff observes, instructors increasingly taught and learnt from textbooks, not from practice. Furthermore, Ackoff concludes that by the 1980s professional operations research journals were almost completely devoid of discussion about real, practical issues. Isolation of operations research from the real world was now virtually complete. (Since the 1980s, however, a soft operational research movement, based mainly in the UK, has attempted to redirect the field of study and address the wider issues Ackoff has located.)

Ackoff, who admits he is market led, responded in accordance with his observations. He moved out of operations research. He began a new phase of work that addressed purposeful systems of corporations and the messes that characterise them. Ackoff's work came together in an approach called interactive planning.

Interactive planning

At every stage of a diverse career, Ackoff has maintained a commitment 'to improve the future'. He does not claim to be a scholar in this regard, although his research record defies this denial. Instead, Ackoff says, he works out his own thoughts rather than thoughts of others. Interactive planning is one result of this. Interactive planning asks what can be done *now* to create the future, not what will be the future independently of what we do now? The main aim is to assist participants of an organisation to design a desirable future and to invent ways of bringing it about. This reflects Ackoff's firm belief in the maxim, *plan or be planned for*.

Interactive planning builds on the premise that obstruction to change sits mainly in the minds of participants, rather than separately 'out there' in the problem context. Obstructions are often nothing more than assumptions made by participants. They are mental models that are lodged in place. Ackoff dismisses approaches that attempt to surface and sweep away assumptions of mental models, because the task is not practically feasible. There are probably thousands of assumptions. In any case, how will we know when all assumptions have been surfaced and dealt with critically? Rather, Ackoff advocates formulating an idealised design and creative ways of seeking to achieve it. Participants can assume that existing fixtures of the problem context became destroyed last night; so what ideal future will participants choose today now they are freed up in this way? In a process of closing the gap between their ideal future and the future they are already in if no changes are made, participants find that obstacles, 'dissolve' – that is, they disappear out of participants' minds. In Senge's terms, mental models are challenged and transformed.

Interactive planning is a methodology that leverages the preceding ideas into the world of practice. It is a form of scenario building that offers in tangible form helpful guidelines about realising intrinsic desires and shared vision, guidelines that remain somewhat intangible in Senge's work. Interactive planning is set out in *Creating the Corporate Future* (1981). An instrumental version is given by Ackoff and co-workers in *A Guide to Controlling Your Corporation's Future* (1984). The methodology has five stages.

- Formulate the mess.
- Ends planning.
- Means planning.
- Resource planning.
- Design of implementation and control.

The original contribution of interactive planning is located in the first three stages that are elaborated on below.

Formulate the mess. As noted, Ackoff's notion of mess, is a complex system of interacting problems. Formulating the mess aims to help people get to grips with an organisational mess and thus work out the future that they are already in if nothing is done about things. This involves synthesising the following three types of study, yielding a reference scenario vital to means planning.

- *Systems analysis* – formulate a detailed picture of the organisation as it is today in terms of its processes, structure, culture and relationship with its environment.
- *Obstruction analysis* – surface existing obstructions to corporate development.
- *Preparation of reference projections* – animate the output of systems analysis and obstruction analysis to generate plausible projections about future performance.

Ends planning. This is where idealised design is located. Idealised design encourages participants to design the organisational enterprise that they would have today, if they were free to choose any design they so desired. Idealised design is qualified as follows.

- The design must be *technologically feasible*, not science fiction.
- The design must be *sustainable*, which means that it must demonstrate qualities of a learning organisation.

Three strategic steps are followed.

- *Select a mission* – formulate a general-purpose statement that generates commitment and direction.
- *Specify desired properties of the design* – based on the ideal mission, formulate a picture of the ideal properties of the design in terms of processes, structure, culture, and the design's relationship with its environment.

- *Idealised design* – move from idealised properties to a detailed idealised design.

Ackoff recommends passing through these steps twice, once constrained by the environment and once unconstrained by it. If significant differences arise, then an additional task must be performed to influence the environment.

Means planning. The reference scenario and idealised design are compared, and strategies for closing the gap are generated. This needs to be a highly creative process. Means planning can be likened to Joseph Juran's project-based approach to clearing up quality failure cost, except with Ackoff projects are aimed at improvement in some wider sense. Strategies become clearly defined projects in terms of, for example, purposes, resource requirements, ownership, time scale, and measures of performance. In this way, means planning moves into *resource planning* and *design of implementation and control.*

Interactive planning promises many benefits to learning organisations. Participation generates motivation and commitment, thus unlocking much potential creativity. It aims to achieve consensus among participants, thus increasing chances of smooth implementation. It reminds us that it is participants' own mind traps (i.e. their mental models) that prevent them from achieving their ideal future.

Criticisms have been levelled at interactive planning. Its consensus worldview assumes all participants are willing to engage in open and free debate. What if there are political undercurrents at work? People may wittingly or unwittingly act in this way. There is no indication in interactive planning of how to recognise and manage contexts of this sort.

Ackoff responds to this criticism as just another obstruction that dissolves if participants are creative enough in finding ways around resistance, for example, from powerful stakeholders. A counter-argument is that Ackoff can only claim that he has not in his experiences come across irresolvable conflict simply because the scope of his projects does not challenge his client's fundamental interests. Ackoff then points to a picture on his office wall, of a violent management–union clash, and a letter from the union some time later thanking him for dissolving the conflict. The debate continues.

Circular organisation

Ackoff's concern for participation surfaces in another guise, in a structural notion for a circular organisation. Participatory structure is a significant point where Senge falls short and Ackoff may step in, although we might also consider Beer's viable system model sketched out in the last chapter. The circular organisation is in fact a democratic hierarchy. It is a form of organisation that is meant to cater for a more active contribution of people in co-defining their involvement in the organisation. It opens the way for organisational members to operate Ackoff's interactive planning, amongst other things. *Creating the Corporate Future* (1981) provides a first account of the circular organisation, whilst *The Democratic Organisation* (1994) is the main reference text. Each account is written in Ackoff's typical precise fashion, replicated in the summary below.

There are three principles put forward by Ackoff that exemplify his notion of participation through structure.

- The absence of an ultimate authority.
- The ability of each member to participate directly or through representation in all decisions that affect her or him directly.
- The ability of members, individually or collectively, to make and implement decisions that affect no one other than the decision-maker(s).

The main structural characteristic of a circular organisation is the board (see Figure 5.1). A board is a body of people from a local area in the organisation. Each person in a position of authority is automatically a member of a board that they chair. Each board, except the ones at the top and the bottom of the hierarchy, has a minimum membership – the manager whose board it is, that manager's immediate subordinates, and that manager's immediate superior. Any board may, as seen fit, add members from within or beyond the organisation, as long as it improves representation of the principal stakeholders. The number of representatives should not exceed the number of subordinates, thus maintaining a majority with the latter.

Boards at the lowest level of the hierarchical organisation should include all their subordinates. If the number is too large for them all to serve on one board, then they should be divided into semi-autonomous work groups. Each group selects a leader who reports to the lowest level manager. The leader has a board comprising themselves, the lowest level manager, and all members of the group.

There are six responsibilities of each board.

- To plan for the unit whose board it is.
- To make policy for the unit whose board it is.
- To co-ordinate plans and policies for the immediate lower level.
- To integrate plans and policies with those immediately below it and those at higher levels.
- To improve the quality of work life of the subordinates of the board.
- To enhance and evaluate performance of the manager whose board it is.

The circular arrangement overcomes some of the concerns levelled at traditional hierarchy, such as bureaucracy. It enhances people's chances of participating and making a rapid as well as meaningful contribution. This is quite consistent with the aim of Senge's learning organisation and could be

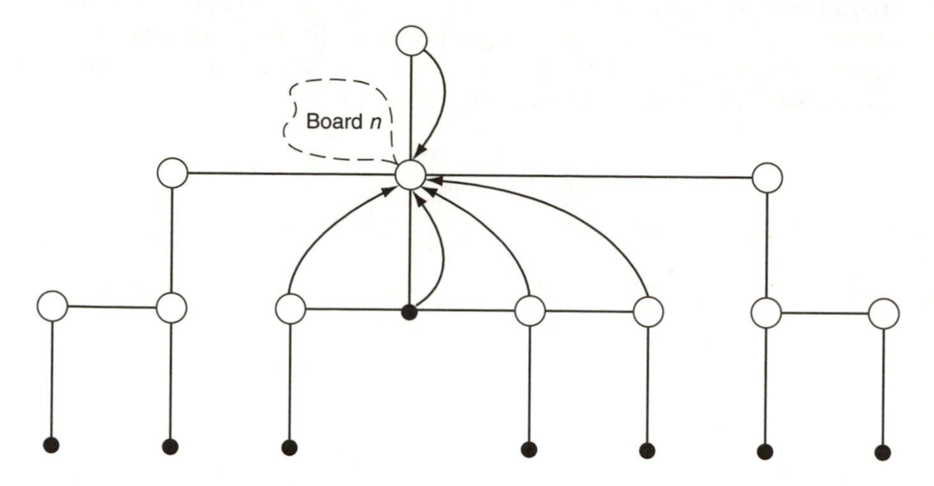

Figure 5.1 Circular organisation (indicating one board at one level)

employed as an innovation in infrastructure that *The Fifth Discipline* alludes to. It breaks with strict vertical thinking, thus introducing more responsibility throughout the organisation. It does this by spreading participation, whereas bureaucracy spreads responsibility only in terms of an individual's competency. The circular organisation increases flexibility to respond to changing circumstances, although much still depends on the nature and extent of governing rules.

Of the numerous options to organisational design, circular organisation may have an advantage since it complements traditional hierarchy, which dominates today's organisations. It does not ask for radical overhaul as required with Beer's viable system model, with the danger of organisational trauma. On the other hand, it could be seen as a rather conservative response to worries about traditional hierarchy. It also fails to unravel different management functions and how they might be organised, for example, as achieved by Stafford Beer. Finally, the circular organisation sticks with the idea that organisations are clearly defined and bounded entities, a concept that has been severely criticised in recent literature on organisational analysis.

A soft turn

Russell Ackoff has a career stretching six decades. His contribution has a strong practical orientation that increasingly focuses on people as interpretive beings. This indicates a soft turn in systemic thinking. By a soft turn, I mean a leaning towards working with people's cognitive processes in a purposeful way. Such an aptitude extends to Ackoff's accomplishments not covered herein, for example, in applied social science and management information systems. In each area the messages are broadly the same – encourage participation, be creative, let problems dissolve, and consequently improve the future. And if there is one resounding message Ackoff wishes to give to managers, it is, perhaps, *plan or be planned for.*

6 Checkland's soft systems approach

The man of passion and structure

Peter B. Checkland spent fifteen years at ICI Fibres before taking up a Professorship at Lancaster University in the United Kingdom, where he remained for the rest of his working life. During his career at ICI, Checkland was appointed to positions increasingly with management responsibility. This new role encouraged him to consult the literature of the management sciences. What he found was disappointing. It failed to resonate with his experiences and requirements as a manager. Frustration triggered off for Checkland an interest in management sciences as a research domain, with an emphasis on systemic thinking. Thus Checkland launched a new career at Lancaster University where he very quickly assumed the leading role in a project that developed and clarified a soft systems approach.

The findings of Checkland's research project are consolidated in three books – *Systems Thinking, Systems Practice* (1981), *Soft Systems Methodology in Action* (1990, with Scholes) and *Information, Systems, and Information Systems* (1998, with Holwell). Running through and maturing in this trilogy are three important strands that may be considered key features of his soft systems programme. These are: the realisation of a unique brand of *action research*, and, from this, the crystallisation of an *interpretive-based systemic theory*, as well as the establishment of principles for action in ill-structured problem contexts that he labelled *soft systems methodology* (SSM, by far his best known contribution). The current chapter comprises a review of each of the three strands of Checkland's soft systems approach.

Perhaps we should note, first off, as did Mike Jackson in the *IEBM Handbook of Management Thinking*, that Checkland is a person with a love of English literature, jazz and rock climbing. Both jazz and rock climbing involve passion and structure. These two qualities are key ingredients that readers of his books soon encounter, and which we will discover in Checkland's soft systems approach as it unfolds below.

Action research

Action research has its roots in Kurt Lewin's work in the 1940s. Since then it has branched out into many different strands (see the special issue of *Systems Practice* listed under 'Further reading'). Consequently, action research is difficult to summarise in a paragraph or two, although the following account might point to some of its more important insights.

Action is undertaken. Reflection on action yields insights that may support a deeper appreciation of what is going on. Insights are fed into and improve current actions, and may be transferred to some other domain where another reflection–action cycle gets under way. The process continues, improving understanding of what we know about action contexts and how we might act within them. In this process, practitioners and researchers cannot be separated out of the situation as external observers of it. They are co-interpreters and co-creators of the systems of meaning constructed in the process of action research. Practitioners and researchers participate in action and research about action. The divide between practitioner and researcher is thus closed down. The two roles become one. All involved are co-workers, co-researchers, and co-authors of reports and research output.

Checkland and Holwell (on page 22 of their book) summarise action research through Argyris *et al.*'s terms as follows.

- Action research is a collaborative process between researchers and people in the situation.
- It is a process of critical inquiry.
- It places a focus on social practice.
- It is a deliberate process of reflective learning.

Checkland and Holwell find that this summary and hence action research as such, 'has one serious deficiency'. It has omitted, 'the need for a declared-in-advance intellectual framework of ideas. A framework is needed that defines and expresses what constitutes knowledge about the situation. This helps to draw a distinction between research and novel writing'. It makes the research recoverable, which means that the process is supposedly recoverable by anyone interested in subjecting the work to critical scrutiny. Such a criticism might well be levelled at Senge's somewhat anecdotal writings.

Checkland (1985) therefore recommends that we think along the following lines. There are some linked ideas in a framework, a way of applying these ideas, and an application area. After employing a methodology there is reflection on what learning has been achieved, learning about all three elements – framework, methodology, and action area. (See Figure 6.1.) This, Checkland argues, is a very general model of the organised use of rational thought and is an essential form of reasoning for action research.

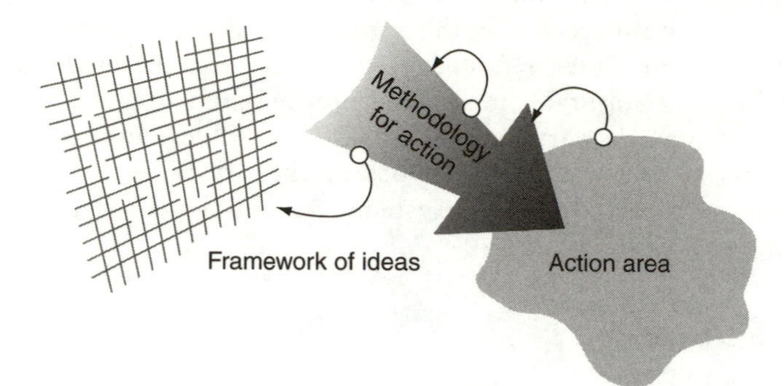

Figure 6.1 Action research

Checkland applied such action research principles to a programme of research for the management sciences and in particular systemic thinking. The programme generated a framework of ideas that might be known as an interpretive-based systemic theory. It also led to principles for action in ill-structured problem contexts known as soft systems methodology. These findings are covered respectively in the next two sections.

Interpretive-based systemic theory

Checkland's interpretive-based systemic theory is concerned with situations defined through action concepts. It might be described in the following way. Understanding does not simply arise from observation or theory. The human being has intentions that lie behind each action. For example, slapping somebody on the back might be interpreted as a friendly or hostile action. Observation or theory does not provide sufficient learning and understanding to appreciate what is happening in such circumstances. It is necessary to progress beyond observation and theory to realise an 'authentic' explanation about what is going on in the minds of the people.

A specific action concept can only be transparent in the deeper context of a certain set of social rules. It is in these terms that an actor can be said to be doing some particular thing. Social rules lead to a social practice. Lying behind social practice is constitutive meaning. Constitutive meaning 'puts in' meaning to the social practice, since it is the fundamental assumption that underlies what is done and what makes it meaningful. Insisting on such an appreciation promises to deepen intellectual rigour in the literature on, and the practice of, the learning organisation.

To understand the whole therefore requires an appreciation of constitutive meaning, social practices and actions taken. Interpretive thinking is systemic in outlook because it helps all involved to 'see' people's lives as a whole by uncovering what is meaningful to them in terms of social rules and practices, and underlying constitutive meaning. To achieve an interpretive-based systemic understanding, it is necessary both to study the cultural aspects of any situation as well as the interpretations and perceptions that individual people form within the cultural context. Interpretive-based systemic theory thus strongly recommends participation of all stakeholders in a kind of multi-agency approach. As we will see below, the principles for action recommended by Checkland in soft systems methodology reflect quite clearly such interpretive thinking.

Soft systems methodology

Checkland's action research programme led him to appreciate the goal seeking character of mechanistic and biological based systemic thinking, in terms of framework, methodology and action area (refer back to Figure 6.1). Systems engineers for example consider that the world comprises many systems. Systems engineers designed methods to identify a system, name the system's objectives, and identify resources that are necessary to achieve the system's objectives in an optimal way. This is often referred to as a means–ends approach. Checkland, however, found little relevance in the systems engineer's means–ends thinking for his tasks at ICI, and subsequently in his consultancy work undertaken from Lancaster University. He concluded for a means–ends approach that both means and ends are problematical. It is a matter of interpretation how we appreciate the world systemically, what is considered to be the most desirable ends, and what might be the most suitable means of achieving them. A new angle on framework of thought, methodology and action area, was worked out through action research. The result is congruent with an interpretive-based systemic theory. Emerging from this reconceptualisation were principles for action in ill-structured problem contexts. The principles became known as soft systems methodology (SSM).

SSM is not a method that can be laid out in a set of steps to follow systematically. Checkland was fully aware of this difficulty when he formulated a 'seven stage' diagram to act as a pedagogical tool to put forward SSM principles (see *Systems Thinking, Systems Practice*). Considerable effort was made to explain the diagram as a continuous process of learning with which action researchers begin anywhere and move in any direction (see Figure 6.2). The figure must be understood as a learning cycle, even when it is explained, as below, within the limitations of linear prose.

Stage 1 suggests that a problem situation might arise that a number of people feel uncomfortable with. They wish to explore the situation with a view to making some improvement. The problem situation is expressed with stage 2, attempting to avoid structuring the problem situation that would close down original thinking and hence learning. Use of systems archetypes here would, in Checkland's view, put in structure to thought before learning had had a chance to unfold in a creative fashion. Rich pictures are advocated

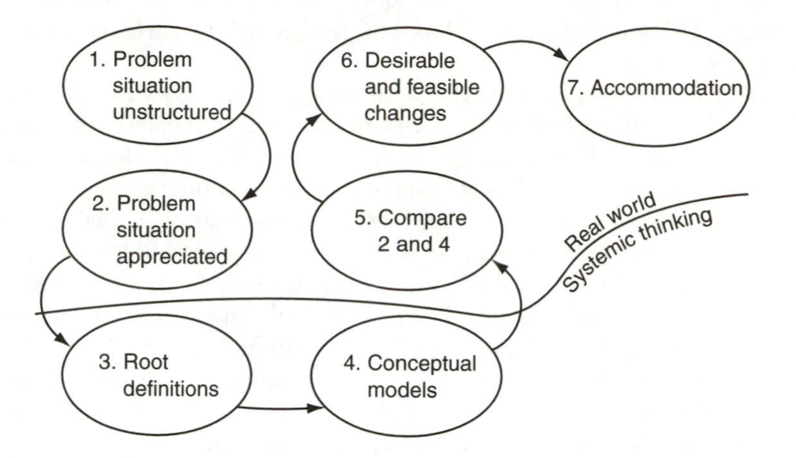

Figure 6.2 Soft systems methodology, mode 1

as one suitable means of expression. They are cartoon type representations that allow people to express their experiences and, as is the case with cartoons, accentuate points that stand out in their minds.

Stage 3 recommends systemic thinking about the real world. The transition to stage 3 is made by naming possible human activity systems that may offer insight into the problem situation, and may generate debate leading to action to improve the problem situation. A human activity system is a systemic model of the activities people need to undertake in order to pursue a particular purpose. Stage 3 develops root definitions of relevant systems. Root definitions are built around the world-view that states the constitutive meaning underpinning the purpose of a human activity system. The transformation process is then conceptualised. Customers, actors and owners, are subsequently named. Environmental constraints are taken into account. Construction of root definitions embraces customers (C), actors (A), transformation processes (T), world-view (W), owners (O), and environmental constraints (E) – that can be remembered with the CATWOE mnemonic.

Stage 4 elaborates on root definitions by drawing up conceptual models. Conceptual models in the first instance are the minimum set of verbs (action concepts) necessary to describe the actions of the human activity system, that was seeded in a relevant system and grown in the root definition. The verbs are ordered systemically, drawing out the loops that describe the interactions of the human activity system. System dynamics might be employed here. Conceptual models, which are the result of systemic thinking about the real world, are taken into the real world in stage 5, where they are compared to the problem situation expressed in stage 2. Debate is generated whereby world-views inherent in conceptual models are thoroughly questioned and their implications understood. The conceptual model is also employed to surface possible change proposals.

With stage 6, the change proposals are thought through in two ways. First, the *desirability* of the human activity system captured in the systems model is raised and discussed. Second, the issue of *feasibility* is explored in the context of the problem situation, attitudes and political interactions, which dominate. Stage 7 seeks to explore possible accommodation between contrasting opinions and interests that surface in the process of SSM. Note here that Checkland seeks accommodation, whereas Senge seeks consensus. Implementation of agreed upon change proposals gives rise to another problem situation and so the process of SSM continues.

Interpretation of these seven stages can all too easily default to the dominant instrumental way of thinking. I have seen Checkland handle this tendency to default in two ways in his seminars. My favourite is a joke he has with the audience. He announces that he is about to screen on the overhead projector a representation that illustrates SSM. All present who are familiar with SSM expect to see the seven-stage figure. Instead, Checkland projects an unused transparency on to the screen. The message is that the methodology of SSM is what you make of it from the principles. The second way deals with the question, 'Where do I start with SSM?' with the answer, 'Just begin'. There is no starting place, nor finishing point to SSM. SSM is, in principle, a continuous process of learning and understanding.

As Checkland's action research programme continued, a maturing appreciation of a framework, methodology and action area became evident. Checkland and Scholes in *Soft Systems Methodology in Action* separated out two modes of SSM in action. Mode 1 is as just described. It is the explicit application of SSM to guide an intervention. However, Checkland and Scholes reasoned that practitioners are immersed in an organisational context on a day-by-day basis, and surely could benefit from SSM principles in this greater portion of their working lives? SSM is not just about intervention; it may also help people to make sense of the rough and tumble of everyday affairs. If internalised, SSM affords the opportunity for action researchers to reflect on their experiences and to make some sense of them. There is a need for mode 2 SSM.

Mode 2 SSM is a conceptual framework to be incorporated in everyday thinking. The main feature of mode 2 SSM is recognition of two equally important strands of analysis – a logic-based stream of analysis and a stream of cultural analysis. The *logic-based* stream of analysis encourages practitioners to investigate the situation they are in, to look for new opportunities, and to seek ways to achieve accommodation between people, thus closing the gap that exists between them. The stream of *cultural analysis* is an intertwined inquiry into the intervention itself. It is both a 'social systems' analysis and a 'political systems' analysis. Three things are focused on. First, is the intervention itself, exploring the role of the client, problem

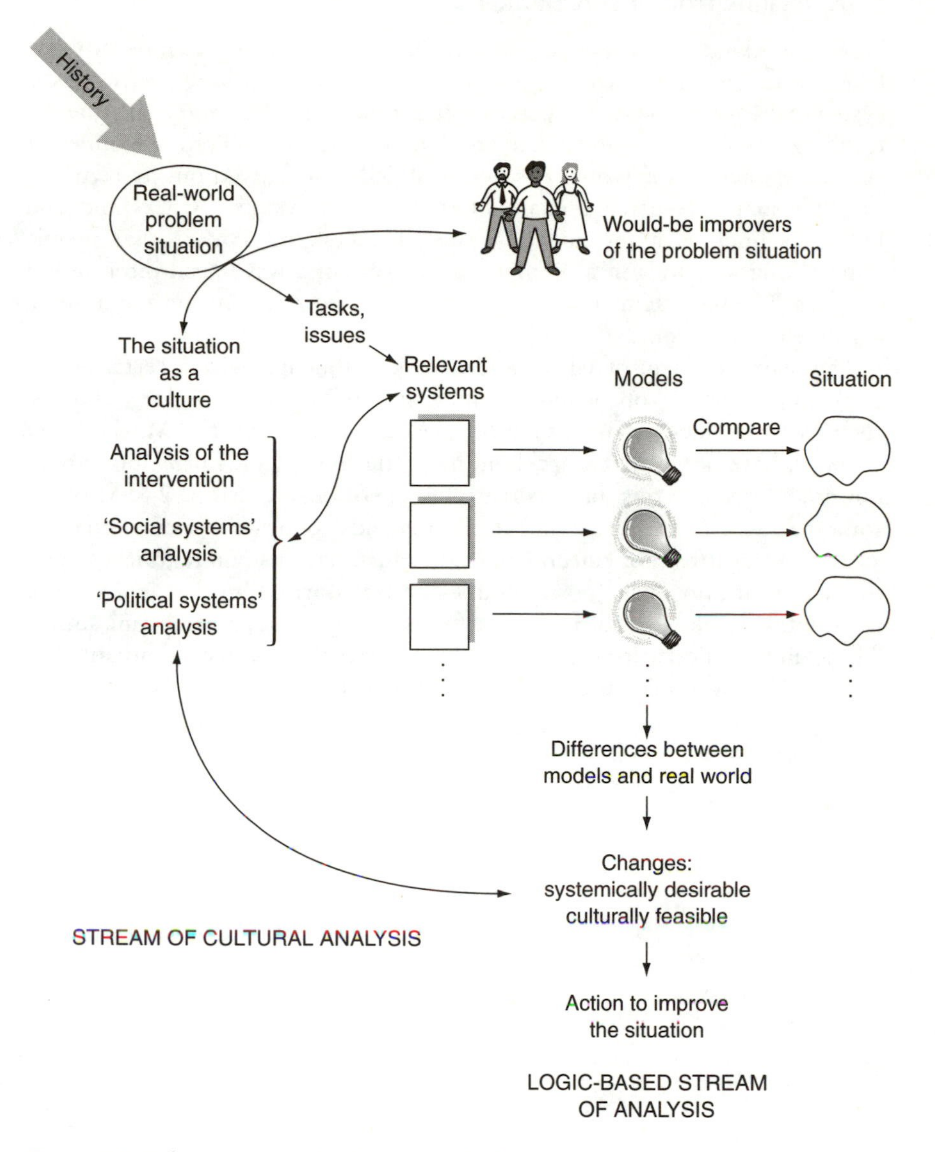

Figure 6.3 Soft systems methodology, mode 2

owners, and problem solvers. Second, 'social systems' analysis looks at roles, norms, and values as they influence behaviour. Third, 'political systems' analysis investigates political interaction, coalitions and the use of power as it makes an influence on decision-making. (See Figure 6.3.)

Hard lessons from a soft thinker

Peter Checkland in his research project founded at Lancaster University has brought to the fore, with masterful clarity, what an interpretive-based systemic theory and systemic practice might look like. His brand of systemic thinking has had most impact in the UK, but has influenced a number of researchers across the globe. Furthermore, SSM has carved out its own line of study in the research domain of information systems. Checkland and Holwell's book is a testament to this. The link to SSM is that people undertaking activities in a human activity system always need information support. The paradigm shift from goal seeking to relationship maintaining is offered in this context.

The main criticism of Checkland's work is that it neglects certain difficulties in achieving open and meaningful debate. In particular, scholars, such as Mike Jackson in his *Systems Methodology for the Management Sciences*, have noted that Checkland has little to say in his principles about power and the way this distorts the outcome of debate. Mode 2 SSM offers some response to this criticism. It recommends 'political systems' analysis as part of the stream of cultural analysis. However, this barely touches upon the notion of knowledge-power and social transformation that is discussed later in this book. The idea of social transformation seems to be missing in Checkland's concern for feasible changes, given the history, dominant attitudes, and power structures of a problem situation.

7 Churchman's critical systemic thinking

The moral man

Whilst Ludwig von Bertalanffy is generally accepted as the main founder of the modern systems movement, C. West Churchman might be considered co-definer with Russell Ackoff of operations research, and the main founder of a critical systemic approach. This chapter looks in detail at those two seminal contributions, with greater emphasis placed on systemic thinking where Churchman's most important insights are located. To set the scene, however, we must look first at Churchman's moral commitment.

It is simply not possible to appreciate C. West Churchman's contribution without grasping, indeed *feeling*, the intensity of his moral commitment. A deep ethical concern is rooted in an early Quaker education. Since then, Churchman has spent his life dedicated to humanity. His commitment begins and ends with humanity in scientific research. He insists that scientists must take responsibility for the social consequences of their work. Science, as well as philosophy, should be employed to study serious dilemmas like hunger, poverty and war. This is why Churchman became fed up with life in philosophy departments where people, in his words, 'asked silly questions'. It is why he lost patience in his editorship of *Management Science* with the large number of submissions containing mainly mathematical content that were never applied. Churchman, inspired by his mentor Edgar A. Singer, called for increasing human purposefulness and participation in systems design in a never ending cycle that entertains attack from its worst enemies. (Singer's influence is evident in each of Churchman's main publications.) Churchman is thus relentless in his quest for critically reflective and moral practice. He does this by raising questions. There are no answers, he states, just more questions. For example, ask Churchman if a value free science is possible and he will question if a value free science is moral. Ethical alertness, then, is a key feature of Churchman's form of critical systemic thinking. Senge's notion of learning organisations lacks this quality of ethical alertness, leading to a dramatically different realisation of systemic thinking, as we will see in the next chapter. Let us first turn to Churchman's contribution to operations research.

Operations research

In 1951, Churchman and Ackoff joined the Case Institute of Technology and formed the Operations Research Group under Churchman's directorship. Their purpose was to apply philosophy, through operations research, to industrial and governmental issues. Churchman concluded that to apply philosophy he had to find a home outside of a philosophy department. In that period, the two largely co-defined operations research. *Introduction to Operations Research* (1957, with Ackoff and Arnoff) was the first international textbook in the field. One-third of the book is devoted to philosophical and methodological aspects of an interdisciplinary approach to real world issues. The remainder of the text covers techniques such as linear programming, inventory control, production scheduling, queuing problems and sequencing.

Distinguishing North American operations research from operational research in the UK in the 1960s, Churchman emphasised the importance of mixed teams that bring to bear a range of expertise on diverse problem situations. This is a form of team learning that Senge's work parallels. Teams might comprise people from any or all functions of the organisation, depending on context. A team approach is an early expression of systemic thinking in Churchman's work, in its recognition of the diverse nature of the whole problem situation. It reflects an interest in parts of organisations, how they might interact together and with their environment. Churchman developed his ideas in relation to operations research in *Prediction and Optimal Decision* (1960), focusing on scientific consideration of value judgements in applied science.

Churchman, however, grew increasingly unhappy about developments in operations research in what he called, 'the dreary '60s'. He did not take issue with techniques in themselves as long as they demonstrated practical utility *and* were used in a systemic manner. He employed systemic awareness to show limitations in what is now labelled traditional operations research. The following optimal inventory policy is a classic, well cited example (e.g. see *The Design of Inquiring Systems*, 1971).

It is not feasible, Churchman declares, to design an optimal (efficient and effective) inventory policy without considering all conceivable alternatives to holding an inventory. The best of the forgone opportunities represents an inventory's opportunity cost. He asks, how can we judge whether an inventory policy is sound without knowing the opportunity cost? Beyond any technique there is a need to investigate the larger system of an organisation's opportunities. There is no rational design for improvement without knowledge about the total relevant system. Operations research, then, was always a systemic activity for Churchman.

Critical systemic thinking

The case for Churchman's systemic thinking is made in the last two sections. First, ethical alertness comes from thinking systemically. Second, efficiency and effectiveness come from thinking about the total relevant system. Churchman's systemic thinking is about ethics, efficiency and effectiveness. His systemic thinking is captured in four principles and seven central concepts chosen for review below. The principles are presented first.

- The systems approach begins when first you see the world through the eyes of another.
- The systems approach goes on to discover that every world-view is terribly restricted.
- There are no experts in the systems approach.
- The systems approach is not a bad idea.

The first two principles are emphasised in Senge's discipline of mental models. The four principles are embodied in the following seven central concepts of Churchman's systemic thinking.

Teleology

(As in *The Design of Inquiring Systems*, 1971; and *The Systems Approach and Its Enemies*, 1979.) Churchman, in his anatomy of system teleology, set out nine conditions that must be fulfilled for 'a system' to demonstrate purposefulness. These conditions are as follows.

- A system is teleological.
- A system has a measure of performance.
- There is a client whose interests are served.
- A system has teleological components.
- A system has an environment.
- There is a decision-maker who can produce changes in the measure of performance of a system.
- There is a designer whose design of the system influences the decision-maker, leading to changes in the measure of performance of the system.
- The designer aims to maximise the system's value to the client.
- There is a built-in guarantee that the purpose of the system defined by the measure of performance of the system can be achieved and secured.

Any such appreciation of a system, however, raises questions of system identification that Churchman addresses through 'sweep in'.

Sweep in

(As in *Systems Approach and Its Enemies*, 1979.) For Churchman, systems are not real entities existing 'out there' waiting to be identified. Rather, systems are whole system judgements, that is, judgements made in the knowledge of the totality of relevant conditions. This suggests, following Singer, a sweep in process, that is, sweeping in ever more features of the problem context. Sweep in helps participants to become more aware and increasingly able to appreciate contrasting systems of meaning. It is an attempt to raise understanding, rather than to realise absolute knowledge. Sweep in is a process of critical reflection that helps people think or debate their way out of mind traps (borrowing Geoffrey Vickers' terminology) or mental models (in Senge's language). However, the sweep in process in isolation suggests ever expanding boundaries which is not very helpful if things are to get done. Senge fails to recognise the expanding boundary difficulty in any meaningful way, as we will discuss in the next chapter. Churchman on the other hand was fully aware of the expanding boundary dilemma and recognised a need for unfolding.

Unfolding

(As in *Systems Approach and Its Enemies*, 1979.) The process of unfolding was brought to light in recent times by Werner Ulrich (1988). Unfolding draws upon the nine conditions of Churchman's anatomy of system teleology (whereas Senge employs systems archetypes to make sense of things). The conditions help people to add structure and meaning to their experiences. People may employ them to surface plausible interpretations of events. This aids them to identify possible clients, designers, decision-makers and other affected people. It helps participants to consider measures of performance and who might gain or suffer from a particular design. Unfolding is therefore the critical counterpart to sweep in. Sweep in and unfolding culminate for Churchman in boundary setting.

Boundary setting

(As in *Systems Approach and Its Enemies*, 1979.) Defining an action area from the problem context through sweep in and unfolding, centres on drawing boundaries around possible clients, and consequently surfacing issues and dilemmas relating to those clients for discussion. Boundary setting is an issue of great importance to systemic thinking. Put succinctly, the questions are, 'Who is embraced by the action area and thus benefits? Who is out and does not benefit? What are the possible consequences of this? And, how might we feel about that?' Boundary setting thus raises questions of ethics, efficiency and effectiveness, in a search for improvement and shows them to be inextricably linked. Boundaries are always open to further debate through sweep in and are thus temporary. Boundaries are the result of choice. For each choice located by unfolding, there are always other possible options that will arise by sweeping in. Boundaries are therefore partial. The temporary and partial nature of boundary setting is suggestive of improvements to make, for now, but raises the question of how improvement is to be secured.

Securing

(As in *The Design of Inquiring Systems*, 1971.) According to Churchman, to secure improvement means that over time improvement persists, i.e. improvement must be sustainable. Systems of measurement are central to knowing that improvement has been secured. As Werner Ulrich (1994) notes, this means considering choices for improvement by critically taking into account and tracking long term environmental and developmental implications. The aim is to make choices that deliver ecologically viable in addition to socio-economically and socio-culturally desirable future improvements. So, the sweep in process, for example, must embrace our children's future. Our children, some yet to be born, must be recognised as possible clients of today's decision processes. This leads us to Churchman's two fundamental intrinsic desires – wisdom and hope.

When asked to define what he means by hope, Churchman (1997) replied as follows. 'I used to think, because I'm a logician, that definitions had to be rigorous. It's a paradox. You can explain A by B, but B is not clear enough so you do C, but C is not clear enough because it doesn't define rigour. You can't do that except by D. It's a lot of nonsense. Definitions should be meaningful. And meaning goes deep to the spiritual side of me. It can't be made rigorous at the present time.' Churchman's struggle with a meaningful definition of hope that captures its spiritual quality holds too for his notion of wisdom. So we must be content with our own holistic reflections on his following brief words.

Wisdom

(As in *Thought and Wisdom*, 1982.) Wisdom is thought combined with a concern for ethics.

Hope

(As in 'In search of an ethical science', 1997.) Hope is the spiritual belief in an ethical future.

Suffice to say, the apparent simplicity of Churchman's sentiment of wisdom and hope belies each one's importance and potency. Having the courage to undertake serious engagement with these most fundamental of concepts in fact is having the courage to invite Churchman to become one's moral conscience.

The people's conscience

C. West Churchman has made and continues to make a giant-sized contribution to intellectual thought in operations research, management sciences and systems sciences. This takes second place only to the intensity of feeling about a moral commitment to human betterment that his writing demands. Churchman's work can be criticised as esoteric, yet he still impressed on many people's minds the recurrent question of whether they can justify their choices and actions. Churchman thus earned himself a reputation as the moral conscience of operations research, management sciences, systems sciences and, indeed, all other fields of 'management and organisation' that dare to consult his work. The extent and impact of Churchman's work is marked by his nomination in 1984 for the Nobel Prize Award in the field of social systems.

8 Senge's *The Fifth Discipline* revisited

Taking stock

The main drift of Part I to this point is that Peter Senge's *The Fifth Discipline* has leveraged systemic thinking into the educational and social mainstream. To millions of people he brought insights about our lives and the world in which we find ourselves that are afforded by systemic thinking. However, there is a wider body of literature on systemic thinking not incorporated into Senge's work. In this material is found both plurality of thinking and recondite understanding that invites further attention. The last five chapters review a representative sample of this literature, choosing to concentrate on authors recognised as influential in the field. We are now well prepared to revisit *The Fifth Discipline*.

An empowering quality

Peter Senge has made popular in management thinking the learning organisation and the many valuable insights that come with it. If attended to thoughtfully, these insights can enrich both our personal and working lives. Senge's account of the learning organisation is potentially empowering as the following examples relating to his five disciplines illustrate.

Personal mastery may empower people by helping them to clarify and deepen personal vision and to come to grips with intrinsic desires. *Mental models* may empower people by educating them about the way cognitive processes shape what they see and define their relationship with other people and the world. *Shared vision* may empower people by generating a common sense of purpose on which they focus energy in a meaningful way. *Team learning* may empower people by aligning their thoughts and energies that triggers-off resonance and synergy in learning. *Systemic thinking* may empower people by enabling them to begin to appreciate rather than be confused by the interrelated nature of the world and how this might cast insights into their experiences. It is systemic thinking, Senge argues, that integrates all five disciplines and brings about the empowering potential of the learning organisation.

Senge offers a view of systemic thinking from the vantage point of system dynamics. System dynamics explains people's experiences through systems archetypes and the underlying structure in behaviour that they help to locate, which is one useful insight. However, contributions from other systemic thinkers locate many more central insights that systemic thinking can offer and which people might take into account. Senge misses out on these. He therefore stops short of drawing together a wide-ranging and coherent theory of systemic thinking. Senge's readers are continually referred back to the narrower focus of system dynamics for an account of what systemic thinking has to offer. Consequently, whilst enjoying a certain sense of empowerment from the many valuable insights Senge spotlights, people may still battle with an unnecessary confusion arising from their unconvincing systemic encounters with a profoundly systemic world.

Incorporating insights from other accounts of systemic thinking may enhance the empowering quality of Senge's work. This possibility is explored in the next two sections. First, I extract from the preceding reviews a number of commonalities and similarities sufficient to proclaim our prime movers to be of one movement. Second, I locate from the reviews two central issues for systemic thinking not dealt with by Senge in any meaningful way, which lead to a metamorphosis of the systemic idea and open up a way into Part II of this book.

Commonalities and similarities

Comparing Senge's conceptual framework to Bertalanffy's, Beer's, Ackoff's, Checkland's and Churchman's, reveals a number of commonalities and similarities worthy of note. To begin with, each person is concerned about coping with complexity. Sharing a systemic view leads all six to conceive of complexity as dynamic rather than merely a matter of detail. Each one visualises dynamics in terms of interrelatedness, although the constitution of each visualisation varies.

Because of the complex and interrelated character of things, Beer, Ackoff and Churchman, each in their own way, recommend the deployment of interdisciplinary teams. These teams bring with them diversity in expertise that is necessary, it is argued, to deal with the diversity of any practical situation. Senge, however, offers a much-enhanced appreciation of the team role. Rather than teams merely bringing expertise, they learn and grow as individuals and as a group in the situation. The result is synergistic. Experiential learning releases people from mental models that otherwise shape their view of the world. It sharpens team ability and capacity.

Challenging mental models is expressed in Checkland's action research learning cycle in terms of exploring world-views. Checkland places greater emphasis than Senge on learning by explicit reflection on the framework of thought in use that shapes people's actions and experiences. This offers a certain rigour to the learning process possibly lacking in Senge's account? In contrast, Churchman quite simply states that systemic thinking (i.e. learning) begins when you see through the eyes of another.

Another link is found between Bertalanffy's pioneering research and the systems archetypes that Senge employs. In fact, popularisation of ideas like growth, adaptation and steady state, originated in biological studies including Bertalanffy's open systems theory. Bertalanffy experimented with the open systems concept across many disciplinary areas. He sought the unification of science through a general system theory. Whilst Senge stops short of such grand aspirations, he persists with systems archetypes treating them as templates able to explain dynamic behaviour across disciplines. Beer is more positive than Senge that he has discovered cybernetic principles of viability for the natural and social sciences, with his viable system model.

In Checkland's soft systems approach systems archetypes may be employed to facilitate thinking about the world. So too can the viable system model or any other systemic model. Checkland prefers to employ his own CATWOE model. These and other exemplars perform the role of thought generation, not reality representation. The aim is to get debate going about desirable and feasible improvement strategies. Checkland's approach is doubly systemic in the way he employs systemic models to explore the world in a systemic cycle of learning. Double systemicity is found in Senge's five disciplines too, in particular through team learning in harmony with systems archetypes.

Both Senge and Ackoff share a deep interest in scenario building. Senge refers to the Royal Dutch/Shell approach. For Royal Dutch/Shell, scenario building helps people to learn about the kinds of thing that happen and why they happen, not what will happen. It challenges people's mental models. People become better able to learn and to deal with change. Ackoff, however, sees no point in analysing mental models by questioning assumptions that shape the way things are understood. He goes straight for idealised design. He states that we must come up with an ideal scenario for the future we really want. Then we seek to achieve it. On the way, obstacles to change dissolve. That is, deeply rooted mental models, although not explored, are exposed as cognitive blocks rather than material ones.

These and many more commonalities and similarities link up our six systemic thinkers. They are of the same movement. Each one excels in some ways but less so in others. Collectively they present a formidable intellectual force that promises empowerment of individuals and improvement in the way we know ourselves and live our lives. However, systemic thinking faces two central issues that threaten right from the outset to undermine the entire holistic endeavour that we have been so diligent in getting to know.

Two central issues for systemic thinking

Systemic thinking is about holism, or holistic thinking, which means formulating appreciation in terms of wholes. As we have seen, one common insight that characterises the systems movement appreciates wholes in terms of an interrelated complex. Yet, we are not able to progress far with this idea before encountering the first of two central issues for systemic thinking. Taking 'interrelated complex' as a key concept leads to the following tautology – the discovery made when conceiving of things as interrelated is indeed that everything appears to be interrelated with everything else. So what! And worse is to come. In practice, then, *systemic appreciation is an ever-expanding exercise*. What use is that to anybody? Inevitably, to be pragmatic, systemic appreciation must operate within some limits. The first task of systemic thinking, therefore, must be to bound thought, yielding a viewpoint that is both relevant and on a manageable scale.

In this act of boundary setting we locate a second central issue for systemic thinking, that is, *who is to judge that any one viewpoint is relevant*? Each judgement is based on a rationality that decides where a boundary is to be drawn. This defines who is in and benefits and who is out and does not benefit. Systemic thinking is a process that quite simply cannot avoid ethical judgements of this sort. Systemic thinking therefore must remain ethically alert. Ethical alertness is a key principle of systemic thinking and can be located in C. West Churchman's work. As far as I am aware, Senge in his writings has grappled neither with these two central issues of systemic thinking italicised above, nor the dilemmas of ethical practice that they point to.

So, how does Senge deal with boundary judgements? Senge is not at all clear about this and could be accused of sidestepping the issue. By inference, however, it may be observed that he allows boundary judgements to happen through 'problem identification'. If a problem can be known, then clients and other stakeholders who are interrelated through the problem situation can also be known. And so 'a system is identified' that can be investigated with systems archetypes in search of structural explanations for behaviour and leverage points for change. A crucial question here is, therefore, can 'a problem' be known? Senge is clear on this point.

In *The Fifth Discipline* on page 283 the notion of convergent and divergent problems is introduced. We are told that *convergent problems* do have correct solutions. Intelligent study leads to answers that converge. For example, Senge claims that finding the best site for an oil refinery is a convergent problem. A correct solution can be found once production and final distribution points, volume of demand, and costs of transport are identified. *Divergent problems* on the other hand have no correct solution. The more they are studied the more contradictory answers appear to be. Genuine openness allows people to deal productively with them. Seeking the best way of educating children is an example of a divergent problem referred to by Senge.

The impression set by Senge that so called convergent problems have correct solutions is immediately refutable. For example, finding the best site for an oil refinery is not clear-cut given that certain technical parameters are in place. Only a wave of reductionist thought could come to this conclusion. No problem exists that is purely technical. People are always involved. All sorts of people may be involved or affected and thus want to participate in discussion or dialogue about the siting of an oil refinery – environmentalists, government, farmers, residents, and promoters of tourism, are just a few possible ones. A so-called convergent problem is the phantom of an uncritical choice of boundary and a lack of awareness of the ethical nature of boundary judgements.

The idea of divergent problems also runs into difficulties. It is not so much the idea itself, but the way Senge handles divergent problems. Openness is needed, we are told, for a productive journey to a result – but what exactly is the character of the result? The desired result for Senge is consensus.

Senge introduces his perspective of consensus in *The Fifth Discipline* (on page 248). There are two types of consensus – a focusing down consensus and an opening up consensus. A *focusing down consensus* seeks the common denominator in multiple individual views. It is constructed from the content of our individual views. It is a process of discovering what part of my view is shared both by you and by others. Discussion is considered adequate here. An *opening up consensus* on the other hand seeks a picture larger than any one person's view. Each person must look at things from each other person's viewpoint. Dialogue is necessary here. Presumably, opening up consensus differs from focusing down consensus in the way people's views are expanded before consensus is achieved. In any case, at some point a consensus is achieved, which means a certain form of unanimity.

Unanimity is a switch that dims critical reflective inquiry. This makes opaque the inevitable result that a boundary judgement is made and that some people benefit and others do not, just like in the oil refinery example. The purported 'solution to the problem' is nothing more than 'a problem to other people that demands a solution'. And so it goes on. Here we encounter a vicious circle of problem–solution–problem–solution and so on. This loop may be escaped from with a fundamental shift in thinking, replacing the idea of 'a problem to be solved or at least dealt with by consensus' with one of 'interacting issues and dilemmas to be managed on a continuous basis'.

One possible explanation for Senge's apparent erroneous belief in consensus is a limited appreciation of forces that can break down the discussion and dialogue that precede consensus. This in turn restricts thinking on what is required in critical reflective inquiry to counter such forces. As we have seen, Senge hangs on Argyris and Schön's action science. Action science usefully recognises factors (e.g. intrapsychic forces and defensive routines) in discussion and dialogue, which mask people's true feelings. This makes problematic team learning and shared vision. Senge therefore recommends methods such as a 'left-hand column' to subdue the bias and bring about open and meaningful discussion and, in particular, dialogue. However, action science does not make much of politics and power.

Senge does discuss politics in organisations and appeals for his readers to consider the negative impact that political dynamics have on people's learning and a learning organisation. Senge does not elaborate on his worry. In fact, he stops well short of a central concern in the social sciences – knowledge-power and social transformation. Knowledge-power recognises that what is considered to be valid knowledge may be determined by powerful people. Remember, 'The ruling ideas are forever the ideas of the ruling class', is the way Marx and Engels expressed this point some time ago in *The Communist Manifesto* in their search for transformation to a classless society.

In modern society the knowledge-power concern is broadened to incorporate management hierarchy, gender, race, disability and other issues. In each of these cases, knowledge-power relationships are argued to exist that lead to entrenched patterns of behaviour that bias outcomes from discussion and dialogue. Some people are alienated and disadvantaged. Patterns of behaviour undermine disadvantaged people's capacity to create their own future. It undermines the learning organisation as such. Bias can be removed only through social transformation that alters twisted patterns of behaviour. Transformation requires skills in reflection and inquiry that have so far evaded Senge's account of the learning organisation.

Senge does prescribe treatment for one of these knowledge-power relationships – management hierarchy – as we have already seen. His reductionist prescription is to abandon management hierarchy in favour of some other model, which he only loosely describes in terms of openness and merit. Senge refers to the Royal Dutch/Shell participatory model. He does not mention that all forms of structure have both strengths and weaknesses including those sold as participatory. For example, implementation of a participatory approach is threatening to some people and often leads to casualties. There is no perfect way of getting around this, not even with ideas of the learning organisation. How ethical is that? On the other hand hierarchy has endured a century. Why is that? Does it not hold positive qualities for certain contexts, such as where it is necessary to perform routine tasks to achieve some agreed upon goal? Of course, there are no absolute answers to these types of question, but a systemic approach at least encourages such reflective discourse in the process of choice making.

Ironically, Senge's dismissal of management hierarchy in a search for more participation is a kind of confining act. He is in a sense laying down his law to all people for all situations. From a systemic point of view this is absurd. The idea of systemic thinking, we are reminded, is to develop whole appreciation, in this case a whole appreciation of possible organisational structures. Such an appreciation may be achieved only through wide ranging discourse about the relevance of optional organisational structures *in each local context*, that is, local in space and time. From a systemic point of view, this must include management hierarchy as one option, as well as, for example, Beer's viable system model and Ackoff's circular organisation. People must be allowed to decide for themselves. If not, then we confine them in their thinking and do not open up to them every possible opportunity to learn.

Senge has certainly recognised an importance in localness, as noted earlier, but has not grasped what this fundamentally means for systemic thinking. Localness means that there can be no pre-set judgements concerning, for example, the relevance of any model or method to any situation – such as management hierarchy. It means therefore that systemic thinking in practice is nothing more or less than a directed process of critical reflective inquiry looking into the nature of a situation and the relevance of possible different ways of handling the situation (including systems archetypes). It is a process that guides people to their own appreciation of matters of direct concern and how they might deal with them.

Reflections on Part I

Part I began with an exposition of Peter Senge's *The Fifth Discipline*. The aim was twofold. First, a clear and concise appraisal gave easy access for the reader to all five disciplines. Second, a precise review made possible a critique of Senge's work in terms of the many positive contributions it makes as well as potential areas in which it might be enhanced. The central interest for this book is improving Senge's notion of what he names the fifth discipline, i.e. what I have called systemic thinking.

Senge's view of systemic thinking is limited to system dynamics and the systems archetypes that it has produced. Thinking in these terms can generate a meaningful appreciation of our experiences, at work and in life more generally. However, relying too heavily on system dynamics rather restricts the potential of systemic thinking. The headlines of this story follow.

System dynamics does model emergent phenomenon, but it does not model the emergent process. It does present interdisciplinary principles, but it does not extend them to principles of cybernetic viability. It does suggest the need for a participatory structure, but it does not offer one. It does offer principles for action, but it does not deliver principles for action research. System dynamics does not grapple with systemic appreciation as an ever-expanding exercise. It does not question who is to judge that any one viewpoint is relevant? It does not appreciate systemic thinking as a process of ethical judgements.

What is needed is an appreciation of systemic thinking that meaningfully addresses both the concerns *of* system dynamics and the concerns *with* system dynamics. The two types of concern are aired in Part I of this book. Part II offers my attempt, employing complexity theory, to develop the said appreciation. It does this in three sections – concepts, approach and a practical animation. However, this is not a process of construction, planned and built on Part I. Rather, Part II emerges from Part I as a possible new order of thought, with a particular focus on systemic practice.

Part II

There are some people who establish a brilliance and command over a system of thought. I am not one of them. All I know seems forever to be in a state of change.

Concepts

9 Towards systemic thinking

Introduction

Peter Checkland begins the argument of his book *Systems Thinking, Systems Practice* on page 13 by observing that, 'We find ourselves for a brief span inhabiting a mysterious universe.' Captured here with startling clarity is the essence of human being – we are self-aware, we are aware of the fleeting nature of our current existence, and our existence is not at all a clear matter. We human beings are inquisitive and consequently wonder, what on earth is going on? And, what is the purpose of what is going on? We seek an explanation to these questions. This chapter begins with an explanation offered by western rational thought coming from the Enlightenment.

The Enlightenment

A view came to the fore in Europe in the eighteenth century that belief systems, like supernatural forces and divine manifestation, lack rational analysis, are unreasonable, and seduce and ensnare people. The retort was the Enlightenment that made a major bid to free people from belief systems characterised by dogma and tradition. It represented in some quarters, abandonment of theistic ideas and a plunge into objectivity, captured in the philosopher Nietzche's *The Antichrist* and his statement, 'God is dead.'

Enlightenment thinkers argued that human thought seeking scientific truth would become independent of belief systems. They fought for rational analysis, seeking to identify natural connections between empirical events yielding an objective and true picture of our existence. When applied, scientific thought would enable people to understand completely and thus control the world. It would support the purpose of human progress. Here, progress means betterment of the human condition. The Enlightenment therefore opened up ways for people to rethink their previously handed-down notions of the world and human existence. It signalled the go-ahead for the rise of science with its attendant reductionist mode of thought.

Reductionism

Until the late nineteenth century, science was founded on concepts of physics. Physics promotes reductionism. Reductionism advocates analysis of phenomena. Analysis means resolution into and the study of simple elements. In the groove of reductionism, then, comes rational analytical thinking that involves identification of fundamental parts and study of the behaviour of and forces acting upon each one. For example, atomic theory in traditional physics considered an atom to be the smallest particle of an element that can take part in a chemical reaction. For a while, an atom was declared to be the fundamental particle of matter. Forces acting on atoms in chemical reactions were thus of central concern. According to more recent atomic physics, all matter, and therefore atoms, consists of two kinds of particle – leptons and quarks. With traditional physics, a reductionist mood prevails.

Coupled to reductionism in physics is a closed systems view. The closed systems view assumes phenomena can be explained as completely isolated events. These systems are thought to operate effectively without reference or response to an external world. This view is in large part a consequence of thinking that both 'the system' and 'the environment' are separate, deterministic and predictable. Fundamental principles and laws are assumed to exist that define the behaviour of their parts. An example is Isaac Newton's closed mechanical universe. The behaviour of closed systems is thought to be in accordance with the second law of thermodynamics, which broadly speaking affirms that things move from an ordered to a disordered state. This dynamic is known as entropy. Traditional physics thus sees only closed, isolated, mechanical systems moving ever closer to disorder.

The scientific method is employed to discover principles and laws of behaviour. Parts are isolated and experiments are carried out on them to establish how the one affects the other. This is a process of inquiry that seeks to establish cause and effect relationships. The scientific method then attempts to falsify the principles and laws, which are held as increasingly rigorous the more they withstand attempts to falsify them. This logic of scientific discovery is attributed to Karl Popper and his book *The Logic of Scientific Discovery*. Popper's method is known as critical rational science. To scientists of like persuasion, phenomena that defy explanation of this sort are dismissed as metaphysical, transcending boundaries of science and not worthy of scientific study.

So, as Russell Ackoff says in his book *Redesigning the Future*, with reductionism reality is assumed to be physical and physics therefore is considered to be the basic experiential science. With reductionism, Ackoff concludes, all objects and events, their properties, and our experience and knowledge of them, are made up of ultimate elements, that is, elements that can be reduced no further. Explanations of the whole come from the cumulative properties of the parts. This reductionist conception of nature encourages discipline-based thinking, which makes disciplines in effect distinct and definitive elements of logic. Following such explanations, human being and the perceived nature of the universe falls into line with a reductionist impression.

The reductionist way arguably has demonstrated a relevance to the physical world. That part of the world we know as non-living things to an extent can be learnt about in terms of physical relationships of cause and effect. Knowledge of this sort has made possible new ways of living moulded by technological developments in an era of modernisation. Some of these developments are very impressive. However, technological progress has led to changes in biological and social behaviour that some people experience as oppressive. For example, some people are doomed to a life of drudgery as a result of monotonous work in factories and offices. Oppression of this kind often results from managers' obsession with technology under their control, rather than the technology itself. Technocrats have lost touch with people and this includes their own self. Modern living it turns out has in certain senses led to impoverishment rather than improvement of the human condition.

As a consequence of these misfortunes of modernisation, the current and oft said to be postmodern era has witnessed a decline in belief of purpose as well as a rise of suspicion in divine law and scientific reasoning. People's experiences at the present time are said to make them feel hollow and purposeless. This new sensation may well be a driving force behind waves of enthusiasm in the western world for spiritualism, where anxiety over meaningless life becomes tranquillised. Being out of touch with people and ourselves may in fact mean that we have lost touch with our human spirit. We can go east to discover one systemic account of the human spirit.

Spiritualism

A brief overview of Zen based upon ideas mooted in *The Gospel According To Zen* captures the essence of what we need to know of spiritualism for the purposes of this book. Zen is an oriental philosophy. It is concerned with the spirit of a person. In contrast to the western obsession with the meaning of life, Zen quite simply sees life as living. Thus, Zen might explain the so-called progress of science and technology as a belief with which people escape what otherwise feels like meaningless life, through production and ownership of things, making money, and in a shallow way trying to have fun. Zen similarly might explain religion *that assumes existence of a super-human being* as an ideological reaction to insecurity and aloneness, seeking salvation through a transcendent father. (Religion purely is a spiritual experience with Zen.)

In these ways, Zen suggests, people are alienated from human being. Life is deadened. Rationalism of science is followed to the point of complete irrationalism in the pursuit of a good life. Belief in a super-human being is defended in bloody war in the name of peace and love. In an obsession with purpose and things, people become out of touch with existence and wholeness.

Zen's holistic philosophy pictures each person as a flash of consciousness in existence that is of existence. What a person is, is what everything else is. Thus, a person looking out at the world is in fact the world looking at itself. The world is therefore nothing more or less than a projection of one's self. To understand the world we must understand one's self.

An understanding of one's self comes through experience of the essence of things, labelled *satori*. Each person has the capacity to be awakened or enlightened through *satori*. *Satori* is a sort of inner perception – a perception of wholeness, not of an individual object. *Satori* cannot be analysed and logically explained because that involves reduction, which of course denatures the wholeness of *satori*.

A narrative about a Zen Master and a young Confucian illustrates the message of *satori*. A young Confucian studied with a Zen Master. At the end of the first year the young Confucian became frustrated at failing to know all about Zen. The young Confucian approached and accused the Zen Master of hiding knowledge about Zen. The young Confucian considered the Zen Master to be an expert who's task it was to explain the details of Zen. The Zen Master told the young Confucian that a Master is a facilitator and guide, not an expert. A Zen Master has no expert knowledge to hide. The next day the two walked together on a mountainside. At one point the Zen Master stopped by a flowering shrub and asked the young Confucian to smell its blossom. The young Confucian smelt the blossom. Then the Zen Master asked the young Confucian what the smell was like. The young Confucian provided a lucid account through many different metaphors. 'There,' the Zen Master said, 'now you see that I have nothing to hide from you.'

Satori is an intuitive 'looking into' in which we discover one's self. Knowing the essence of things is to know one's self. To understand one's self is to know one's self, moment by moment. Life is living. To know *satori* is to know the spirit of Zen. To know the spirit of Zen is to begin to be aware of systemic thinking at a most fundamental level.

Essence of systemic thinking

Systemic thinking, then, is not something that can be explained easily and understood comprehensively. It is not recommended to rush into rationalisation of this sort. Very quickly we will lose touch with the notion of wholeness in a trivialised account of its so-called properties. Many textbooks that deal with systemic thinking make this mistake. They explain the world in terms of systems and subsystems, what a system is and how a system behaves. An account in these terms does to systemic thinking what analysis does to *satori* – it strips it of all essential meaning.

Systemic thinking begins with an intuitive grasp of existence. I was struck recently by two books rich in systemic intuition – one by Thomas Berry and the other by Peter Reason. Berry in his book *The Dream of the Earth* writes of a systemic existence in a mood of spiritualism as he observes that, 'we bear the universe in our being as the universe bears us in its being'. Berry on page 132 remarks that, 'The two have a total presence to each other and to that deeper mystery out of which the universe and ourselves have emerged.'

In response to Berry's thoughts, Reason in his book *Human Inquiry in Action* observes that the human race is not an alien species suddenly transported to this universe and deposited on Earth. In a quite literal sense, human beings come from Earth. Because of this, Reason on page 13 says, 'phenomena as wholes never can be fully known for the very reason that we are part of them, leading us to acknowledge and respect the great mystery that envelops our knowing'. In other words, not only might you and I know of one's self and the world in terms of wholeness, as with Zen, but also our grasp of wholeness will be bounded, partial and subjective. For that reason alone our lives forever will be shrouded in mystery. Yet, as we will consider in this part of the book, in the mystery of living there might be a certain 'mastery' of the moment.

Between mystery and mastery

Seeking absolute mastery as reductionism and science do, misses the point of human being. It turns the magic of mystery in our lives into the misery of failed mastery over our lives. The point is that complexity emerges which the human mind is no master over. In fact, the human mind is both the creator and the subject of complexity, not an externally appointed master over it and all its parts. Balancing mystery with mastery means living somewhere between the hopelessness of the belief that we are unable to understand anything and, at the other extreme, the naivety of the belief that we can know everything. Human beings in this way know of and learn within the unknowable. Thinking systemically thus demands an overhaul of concepts and approach in current use in 'management and organisation', beginning with the practitioner's ever present guiding lights, 'problem' and 'solution'.

10 The demise of problems, solutions and normal organisational life

Introduction

Reductionism is mainstream thinking that separates science – one form of study of things – from our lives and the world in which we live – the things science purports to study. It sees practitioners and researchers as independent external observers of a world of separate physical, biological, and social objects. This leads people to think about phenomena as entities that can be fully appreciated as detached real things, behaving according to fixed causal relationships.

Science has in our minds fragmented the world and our lives. It has alienated so-called parts, like people, from the patterns and rhythms of life in which we participate. The richness and mystique of living is deflated to a mental model with an unrealistic and mind-blowing simplicity of the type, 'A caused B'.

An 'A caused B' rationality is a source of much frustration and torment in people's lives. If a difficult situation arises at work, then an 'A caused B' mentality sets up a witch-hunt for the person or people who caused the problem. For example, say Summaya is blamed for public criticism of Khalid, the CEO. Summaya is chastised for this and is punished as part of the solution to her insubordination. The problem is considered solved with the expectation that organisational life will return to a normal and comfortable existence.

Whilst Summaya could well have contributed to the so-called problem, she may feel disaffected since, as she sees it, she merely responded quite reasonably to actions of, say, Khalid and his immediate manager Taha. Yet Summaya has been blamed and found guilty in the kangaroo court of reductionism. Systemic thinkers, however, will appreciate that the problem will have emerged from the interactions of, in this case, Summaya, Khalid and Taha. Sadly for the Summayas of this world the blame mentality is consolidated in NIMO denial, that is, 'the cause of that problem was Not In My Office'. People, especially those like Khalid with formal power, may attempt to detach themselves from patterns of interrelationships and emerging difficulties to which they in fact have a systemic attachment and moral responsibility.

Scientists' and technocrats' obsession with reductionism has had and continues to have a dramatic and direct impact on social rules and practices emerging in social behaviour of the sort just discussed. If we start out thinking of one's self as an individual autonomous self, then we go on to separate parts from the whole, people from knowledge, and, consequently, so-considered problems from context. We employ language and observations like, 'I know that this person caused that problem.' Reductionist thinking directs people to seek solutions in terms of causal factors rather than through systemic awareness.

It is to be expected that people conditioned by the mental model of reductionism and causal thinking will find it difficult simply to flip over to a consciousness of systemic awareness. Reductionism and holism are two ways of thinking, which are poles apart. As Peter Senge has observed, challenging and changing mental models often involves a lengthy gestation period of learning. Cognitive processes do not operate in one way at one moment, then as a matter of routine operate in another way at the next moment. A mind-walk from pole to pole, however, may catalyse the learning process. Complexity theory, which is a strand of systemic thinking, has a mind-walk already mapped out.

From causal factors to systemic awareness

The message of complexity theory oozes out of the title of Ilya Prigogine and Isabelle Stengers's book *Order Out of Chaos*. The idea is that the great complexity of the interrelated world, which may be experienced as chaotic, has some observable order and coherence to it. This notion of order may be sifted out of the debate surrounding and targeting reductionism.

As previously stated, reductionism attempts to establish causal laws. The laws are deterministic in the sense that they are fixed and have so far withstood attempts to refute them. With knowledge of fixed laws, behaviour of the natural and social world is thought to be predictable. If so, then it is possible to alter one variable to control another. Control of the natural and social world to improve the human condition as with Enlightenment thinking is an extension of this way of thinking. Its application through technology has achieved 'progress'. However, 'progress' has its costs, such as pollution of the environment and dehumanisation of the workplace. Such counter-intuitive consequences might be attributed to science's misunderstanding of behaviour in the natural and social world.

Systemic thinking argues that behaviour is most usefully understood as the result of loops where variables are interrelated. The impact of Summaya's actions on Khalid may feed on to Taha, which may feed back to Summaya. To understand the behaviour of Summaya, it is necessary to grasp the feedback dynamics of the loop between Summaya, Khalid and Taha. Feedback clearly is a key concept here.

There are two main forms of feedback. One produces stable equilibrium, called *negative feedback*. The other leads to instability, called *positive feedback*. Since loops are still considered driven by laws that hold between variables – they are fixed – the term deterministic feedback system is used to depict them. The behaviour described by Senge's systems archetypes is of this kind. In some circumstances there are random terms in the laws, so the term probabilistic feedback system is employed to depict the behaviour that results. The two types of behaviour, however, turn out to be quite similar.

The next question that arises, with these systemic representations in place, is how come we are still largely unable to predict and control the natural and social world? For example, why is it not possible to predict long-term weather behaviour or sort out organisational difficulties once and for all? We have to look to books like *Complexity: The Emerging Science at the Edge of Order and Chaos* by Mitchell Waldrop for a possible reply.

One key insight into complexity is that dynamic behaviour is capable of producing unexpected variety and novelty through spontaneous self-organisation. This is where a complex of variables interrelates with multiple feedback, which spontaneously creates new order. Spontaneous means that what emerges is not predictable. Behaviour flips between positive and negative feedback producing simultaneously unstable and stable conduct. There is production of order of a changeable, diverse, and unpredictable kind. Emergence is unpredictable because it results from details of dynamics that are inherently unknowable to the human mind.

A favoured illustration of complexity theorists is concerned with weather patterns and begins with the image of a butterfly in the Amazon rainforests. The butterfly takes off flapping its wings, creating air movement. A highly localised pattern of air movement emerges. This local weather pattern interrelates with other ones, giving rise to a new emerging local weather pattern. A number of subsequent emerging and ever more global weather patterns three days later results in a hurricane in Hong Kong. If, however, the butterfly had flapped its wings at a different time or in a different way, then this may have led to a tornado in Texas. Complex behaviour is said to be dependent in this way on the detail of what happens. To fully explain behaviour entails knowledge of all such detail. So, with weather, there is an irregular pattern that can be described in general terms but, with detail of dynamics beyond our grasp, cannot be predicted beyond a few days. Even modern high-powered computer technology cannot get to grips with the immense complexity involved. This is despite our knowledge of deterministic and probabilistic laws that so far have withstood refutation.

Ralph Stacey in his book *Strategic Management and Organisational Dynamics* extends complexity theory into the social domain. The constitution of social laws he says is fundamentally different from laws in the natural sciences. Laws in the natural sciences are deterministic or probabilistic and persistently have withstood refutation. Laws of social behaviour on the other hand are expressed through social rules and practices and are 'agreed upon' by people, either wittingly or unwittingly. For example, what we call corporate culture is nothing more than people's behaviour shaped by written and unwritten rules and practices – be they about empathetic customer care or an aggressive sales pitch. Furthermore, Stacey points out, 'human systems' are different because human agents do not merely follow social rules and practices, they might wish to change them. 'Human systems' are adaptive. Social rules and practices are modifiable, not fixed. The nature of complexity is different in the social sciences.

'Human systems' involve many people, each with their own interpretation and experiences of social rules and practices that affect them. People therefore act in co-operation and/or in conflict. People learn in this way. Such a dynamic is suggested by Senge's disciplines of mental models and team learning. However, Stacey, apparently departing from Senge's ideology of harmony, emphasises the importance in and 'legitimacy' of political interaction. Political tension is important in the process of challenging mental models and facilitating team learning. Stacey explains the dynamic as follows. Individuals in an organisational environment detect an issue, build support around the issue forming a coalition. The coalition then endeavours to lodge the issue on the organisational agenda. If successful, the process may at some stage bring about changes to organisational rules and practices. Changes might be considered an emergence resulting from spontaneous self-organisation of interpretive beings around an issue. The dynamic is not directed by a central authority and does not result from formal rules and practices!

Of course, social rules and practices can and do endure. Distinct qualities of a society may last several centuries. Corporate culture may remain intact over a number of years. There may be a certain momentum that keeps things going in the same direction for some time, irrespective of changing circumstances – which might be thought of as 'the oil tanker syndrome'. Yet, 'human systems' are not ultimately predictable and cannot be dealt with in any commonly used sense of the term 'predict and control'. People are not supreme planners and masters over their own lives or anybody else's. Complexity is a source of great uncertainty that mainly prevents this, thankfully.

Complexity theory evidently holds mighty lessons for aspiring 'problem solvers'. Traditional 'problem solving' paints a picture of 'management and organisation' where problems can be identified, solutions located and implemented, and everything thus kept under control. Complexity theory testifies to a more realistic explanation. 'Problem solvers' must grapple with complex interrelationships and emergent behaviour that is inherently unknowable to the human mind. Let's face it, complexity theory locates a momentous 'problem' with the concept of 'problems'.

The 'problem' with 'problems'

Since the industrial revolution, management action has been conceived of as a linear process of 'problem solving'. Problems are thought about as if they are real things that can be separated out of a situation and solved. If a solution is achieved, then all other aspects of organisational life may be sorted out and returned to normal. However, this perception reduces situations rich in issues and full of tension, to an illusory problem that is considered solvable. The 'problem' with 'problems' as a concept is that it poorly represents social situations and misdirects people's actions.

More recently, processes of issue management have been introduced into practice. Management of interrelated issues is considered by some people to be far more relevant than any process of 'problem solving'. Issues rather than 'problems' do arise because people have different views and experiences of social rules and practices that affect them. Yet, issue management also runs into a quandary.

The 'issue' with 'issues'

Debating interrelated issues, aims to induce learning between people that nurtures a fuller appreciation of each other's mental models. However, it is all too easy to think that the full extent of interrelated issues can be unravelled and understood in this way. There are many factors discussed in the following chapters that prevent open and meaningful debate, such as intrapsychic, cultural, and knowledge-power forces. If people are not aware of these dangers, then they might think that consensus or an accommodation between views is relatively easy to achieve. People might set about securing shared vision without being fully equipped with an understanding of the nature of dialogical processes in which they engage.

So, the 'issue' with 'issues' as a concept is that it too is somewhat impoverished. It can misdirect people's actions in the following way. Interrelated issues might be debated in what is understood to be dilemma free negotiation. Issues are thus considered to be soluble, rather than solvable. Tension is thought to dissolve in negotiation. However, negotiation may well be reflexive but it does not guarantee that people are sensitised to deep-rooted dilemmas that all too often emerge. In believing issues can be debated in a shared experience, negotiation de-emphasises the individual side of experience where dilemmas originate.

The 'dilemma' with 'dilemmas'

An idea contiguous with that of 'issues' is to characterise situations in terms of 'dilemmas'. Dilemmas arise because experience is somehow personal and so each person experiences issues in a different way. The nature of experience and interpretation is such that people can form wholly different and irreconcilable perspectives from friends, colleagues and associates. The value of diversity in personal experiences and perspectives may be reduced detrimentally if consensus or accommodation is pushed for too strenuously. Introducing the concept of dilemmas is meant to stimulate a thoughtful process of exploration of people's personal experiences and possible ways in which these can be preserved and shared in a constructive manner, all at the same time.

The 'dilemma' with 'dilemmas', of course, is that they are by definition insoluble. That is not to say people should be gloomy and resort to free lives made up purely of experience in which nothing is done with dilemmas. Free living, ironically, is defenceless and is likely to succumb to colonising power structures. Dilemmas might be reduced and controlled in this way. People, however, can try to do something positive to prevent this by encouraging deeper exploration of dilemmas and sensitive ways of approaching them. This is where systemic awareness and a resulting recognition of boundary judgements come to the fore. Boundary judgements and in particular the ethic of each judgement are so important to the argument of this book, that I have elected to deal with them in a separate chapter that follows.

11 Getting to grips with complexity

Introduction

The task of this chapter is to consider how anyone can in a fashion get to grips with a complex of interrelated and emergent issues and dilemmas. It is vital first of all to ensure that the reader fully appreciates the implications of complexity theory introduced in the last chapter for all forms of practice including, to employ traditional terms, decision-making, problem solving, and strategic planning. These forms of practice each develop firm views on future events. Generally speaking, we are supposed to learn all about our current situation, where we are actually going, where we intend to go to improve things, and how to make certain within a small margin of error that we get there. However, as Ralph Stacey points out in his book *Managing the Unknowable*, traditional strategic thinking holds an unquestioned assumption that we arrive in some future because someone intended it to be that way. If this were so, then *a priori* established intentions must extend over large numbers of interrelationships, through recurring emergence, over long periods of time into the future.

Complexity theory questions whether long term intended action is possible. It points out that the way things unfold is inherently unknowable to the human mind, emerging through spontaneous self-organisation originating from some distant detail, rather than advanced planning. The most we can do is to manage what is local, whilst appreciating the incomprehensibility of global complexity. Managing what is local entails continually considering outcomes that extend over a small number of interrelationships, very few stages of emergence, over only short periods of time into the future. This is what I mean by learning within the unknowable. We learn our way into a mysterious future.

Learning our way into a mysterious future calls for continuously revisiting what might be going on, what we are doing and achieving, and the way we are doing it. It is the essence of the process introduced in Chapter 18, 'Organisational learning and transformation'. People take up issue with social rules and practices and outcomes that are produced. This is a matter of ongoing experience, interpretation and learning. It leads to emergent outcomes rather than long range planning and fixed implementation. That is not to say that social rules and practices which are valued cannot, do not, or should not endure, just that they will not remain fixed *ad infinitum*. The rate of change will be context dependent.

The learning process is highly creative and adaptive, and eminently suitable to a systemic world as pictured in the last two chapters. It leads to relevant action 'here and now' in the face of what we can realistically and meaningfully appreciate, rather than 'fantasy land management', as Stacey calls it, of some invented future that almost certainly will not come about.

Some people consider everything hunky dory when they feel in command and reckon that all things are under control. According to complexity theory, however, any one who honestly believes that they have everything under control is seriously out of touch with what is going on. Any one who sets about achieving such control is badly mistaken in their aspirations.

There are two kinds of terminal result that might arise from a command and control mentality which practitioners need to be aware of. First, too much perceived certainty and agreement kills novelty and creativity, stifling adaptability, putting in doubt future survival in any guise. Second, rigid control might provoke a completely different response by creating uncertainty and disagreement that leads to doubt, suspicion and instability. The dynamic is dominated by negative political interaction leading to inefficiency, ineffectiveness, an experience devoid of meaning, unfairness, and a movement towards self-destruction.

What is needed, Stacey argues, is a bounded instability of recurring spontaneous self-organisation that generates novelty and creativity in a managed dynamic full of tension. 'Managed' here refers to leaders who exhibit a tendency to develop informal social groupings and who are motivators, able to harness energy from group members. They will help to clarify and allow challenge to social rules and practices and will recognise the needs of individuals, whilst appreciating the complexity of the whole within which members of the group are all interrelated. Leaders 'act local' whilst appreciating the impenetrable extent of global complexity.

Local action accepts that people can only attain a partial interpretation of events. This is what things are like within the unknowable. The question that now surfaces is how can we achieve any form of interpretation in a meaningful way? Addressing the question leads us to two dilemmas for systemic thinking that I first raised in Chapter 8.

Two central issues revisited

Interrelatedness as a key insight of systemic thinking leads us not surprisingly to discover that everything is interrelated with everything else. This raises a central issue for systemic thinking, that *systemic appreciation is an apparently ever-expanding activity*. Taken as such, it would appear that systemic thinking offers little of practical relevance. What of practical worth can be achieved if no limits are attached to the thinking process? We will think systemically forever and do absolutely nothing else.

Complexity theory adds to interrelatedness the further insight of emergence that arises from spontaneous self-organisation. It argues that emergence results from details of dynamics as pictured in the Amazonian butterfly illustration presented in the last chapter. (Detail here means origins of emergence, not Senge's detail complexity.) The total dynamic thus is even more complex according to complexity theory. So, any attempt at a comprehensive systemic representation is not only expansionary, it also gets people hopelessly lost in a labyrinth of interrelationships and recurring emergence. The further away in space and time we venture from our locality, the more mythical is our interpretation of things.

Systemic thinkers appreciate that they can only grapple with what is local to them. It is possible to proceed, but only by formulating a bounded appreciation in local terms. Systemic thinkers are consciously aware that such an interpretation is a partial and temporary view. Yet, there is a reward for assuming this stance. Systemic thinkers make contact with the spirit of C. West Churchman, his concepts, and the second central issue for systemic thinking.

Churchman asks, *who is to judge that any one bounded appreciation is most relevant or acceptable?* Each judgement is based on a rationality of its own that chooses where a boundary is to be drawn, which issues and dilemmas get on the agenda, and who will benefit from this. For each choice it is necessary to ask, what are the consequences to be expected in so far as we can evaluate them and, on reflection, how do we feel about that? As Churchman points out, each judgement of this sort is of an ethical nature since it cannot escape the choice of who is to be client – the beneficiary – and thus which issues and dilemmas will be central to debate and future action. The spirit of C. West Churchman becomes our moral conscience. A key principle of systemic thinking, according to Churchman, is to remain *ethically alert*. Boundary judgements facilitate a debate in which we are sensitised to ethical issues and dilemmas.

Boundary judgements

Boundary judgements are the core of Churchman's process by which an action area is temporarily created in a local context. Local, remember, refers to space and time. Space refers to things we are involved in and is not a geographical concept. Churchman criticised the traditional systemic view that boundaries exist in the natural order of physical, biological and social things. He argued that boundaries are mental constructs (mental models). Mental constructs determine what is in view and might be taken into account at the moment and what is out of view and thus excluded from consideration. A boundary judgement will therefore determine at this point in time the client, issues and dilemmas of concern, and purposes to pursue.

Boundary judgements are about ethical choice making and are value laden. Gerald Midgley pressed home this point in *Systems Practice* making reference to unemployed people. Drawing a boundary that excludes unemployed people from organisational analysis opens up the way for seemingly unproblematic discussion of efficiency and effectiveness. The ethic and likely issues for debate might include workers' survival in the market place, and/or the maximisation of profit to shareholders. If on the other hand unemployed people are included within a boundary judgement, then the dilemma of perpetuation of unemployment is likely to surface. The ethic here might be that all people should have equal opportunities for employment.

A boundary judgement is a choice that determines who is to be in the bounded action area and will benefit, and who is to be out and will not benefit. For this reason, Churchman in his book *The Systems Approach and its Enemies* stressed the importance of critique. Critique helps us to become more aware of the boundaries within which we live and operate. Critique in everyday situations involves listening to and responding to the viewpoints of one's worst enemies in reason. Enemies, Churchman points out, are in a sense and quite ironically our best friends – it is they who are most likely to help their intellectual adversaries to see the partiality and irrationality of their favoured boundary judgement and possible consequences relating to this. Or, as Alvin Gouldner more or less put it in his book *The Coming Crisis of Western Sociology* – as Norma Romm reminds me – we can learn if we listen to 'bad news' that does not conform to our bounded rationality.

So, a boundary judgement creates an action area that is both partial and temporary. There is nothing absolute or permanent about it. Yet, there remains scope for and value in deepening systemic appreciation of any action area. Deepening systemic appreciation is the theme of the next chapter.

12 Deepening systemic appreciation

In the last chapter we learnt more about C. West Churchman's notion of boundary judgements. A boundary judgement when purposely drawn sketches out an action area by suggesting who might be stakeholders, in particular clients, and alerts us to issues and dilemmas that become a focus of attention. This opens up a partial view on organisational life that is considered a helpful interpretation for now. Deepening systemic appreciation of the partial view adds content to the interpretation. The aim is to become better informed about issues and dilemmas leading to more relevant choices for improvement. The idea put forward in this chapter is to generate a rich systemic appreciation of issues and dilemmas of the action area in terms of insightful key categories of organisational settings.

The literature on 'management and organisation' is important in this endeavour, although in this book it is made sense of only within an appreciation of complexity theory. The literature provides many different angles on organisational settings. There is no one right way of categorising what has been written. Any form of categorisation is considered in the social sciences an *ideal type*. The intention of an ideal type is to stimulate debate, to generate insights and to enhance learning. The measure of utility will depend on the purpose to which the ideal type is employed and experiences of people using it in a range of different contexts.

The purpose of the categorisation offered in this chapter is to deepen systemic appreciation of any action area. The people who employ the categorisation are mainly practitioners. To date, the practitioners that I work with have experienced sufficient utility in the ideal type introduced below to support its continued use. The ideal type so far is found to be transferable across organisational contexts.

Organisational life might be made sense of in terms of the following four categories – systems of processes, of structure, of meaning, and of knowledge-power. The prefix 'systems of' indicates the desire to be systemic with respect to that category. The four categories help to locate types of issue and dilemma encountered in organisational life. *Systems of processes* is a category concerned with efficiency and reliability of flows of events and control over flows of events. *Systems of structure* is a category concerned with effectiveness of functions, their organisation, co-ordination and control. *Systems of meaning* is a category concerned with people's viewpoints on the meaningfulness to them of what is going on and choices of improvement strategies. *Systems of knowledge-power* is a category concerned with fairness in terms of entrenched patterns of behaviour where what is said to be valid knowledge and proper action, is decided by powerful groups. A guide to the application of each view of any action area is offered in subsequent chapters.

A cynic however might persist with the criticism that the chosen categorisation is somewhat arbitrary. A matching reply might point out that it is no less informed, for example, than a library cataloguing system. It is both useful and insightful to catalogue books on 'management and organisation' through the four-category schema proposed in this chapter, as it is to catalogue books through the Dewey decimal schema. Indeed, it would be an interesting exercise to reorganise books on 'management and organisation' in the local library employing the four category schema. A ratio comparison can be made between the total number of books that fall into each category. My impression of the literature on this score is suggested in Figure 12.1. Volumes covering the management of processes are much greater in number. Here is one insight that the ideal type most obviously points out. It is an important insight that reflects the current obsession in management practice with efficiency and reliability of organisational processes. Systemic thinking, however, treats each of the four categories with equal concern.

Deepening systemic appreciation by employing the four categories can be likened to opening up four windows on an action area. Looking through each of the windows results in four different impressions of organisational

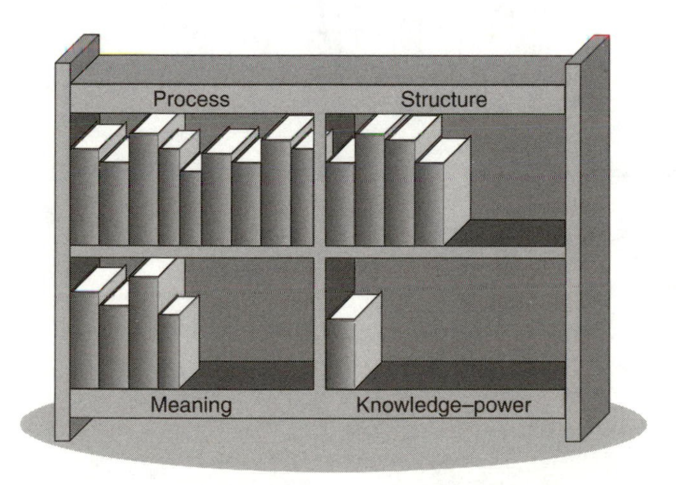

Figure 12.1 'Four windows' categorisation as a bookshelf

issues and dilemmas. The knack of deepening systemic appreciation is to keep in mind that issues and dilemmas, which each impression draws attention to, are interrelated. A holistic, not reductionist, appreciation is sought. Furthermore, each person will arrive at a unique appreciation. Sharing their appreciation allows participants to enjoy the perspectives of other people and to engage in an activity of generative learning, as Senge calls it, whereby systemic appreciation continues to deepen.

The 'four windows' metaphor in a sense facilitates the painting of a lifescape of an action area. It works rather like the following general illustration. Imagine you are in a four-sided room, each side with a window. One window affords views over farmland, another pans over a forest, another looks out to sea, whilst the remaining window frames a port and a busy dock. Each window opens up your vision to one aspect of a complex activity surrounding the room. In concert, the four views come together in a panoramic picture of the lifescape. A holistic perspective of the interrelationships between farms, forest, port and sea is formed in this way. Another person positioned in a different room will see a contrasting lifescape. Exploring the contrasting views may lead to generative learning. Sharing views may enrich each person's systemic appreciation of the complex surroundings.

The process of sharing views is so far reaching that a separate chapter deals

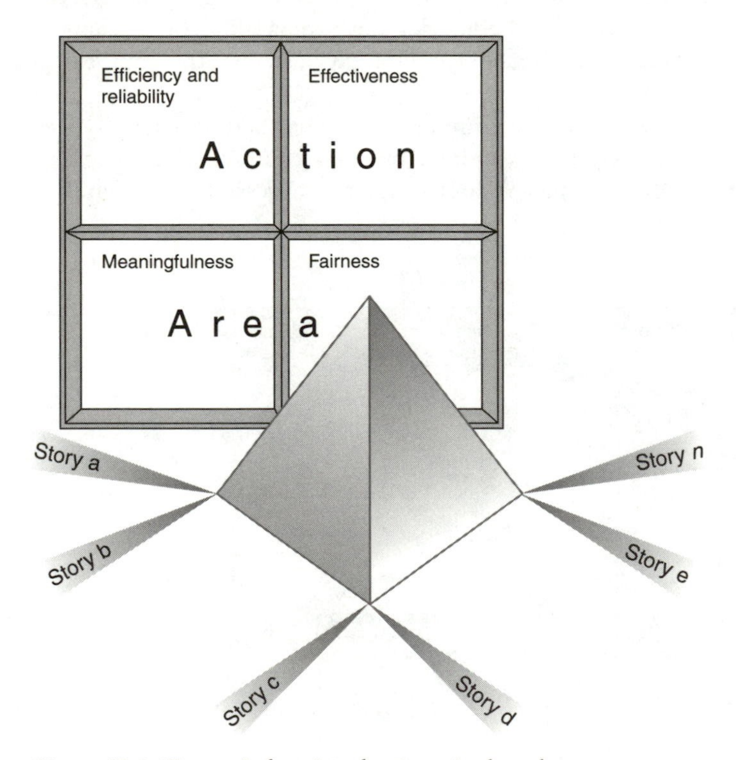

Figure 12.2 'Four windows' and prismatic thought

with it (see Chapter 17). The process is likened to the effects of a prism. A prism refracts white light leading to an explosion of colours in many different directions. Sharing views can have this effect on systemic appreciation leading to an explosion of ideas in many different interpretations.

At all times it must be kept in mind that deepening systemic appreciation concentrates on a bounded action area. The action area is a partial and temporary view of an organisational setting that is considered most helpful for now. However, deepening systemic appreciation culminating in an explosion of ideas in many different interpretations is at the same time testing the acceptability of the boundary judgement. Practitioners are advised to remain flexible enough to accept challenge to any boundary judgement they have made and to redefine their perspective if called for. For example, an action area defined in terms of quality management has 'the customer' rather than shareholders as client, with many suggested improvements that need to be thought through. Customer here means anybody internal or external to the organisation who we provide with a product, service or information. The ideas in this chapter are pictured in Figure 12.2. Guides to aid investigation of any action area in terms of the four windows and the prism occupy the next five chapters.

13 Window 1

Systems of processes

What are processes?

Processes are ordered flows of events. In an organisational context, processes are the way in which work gets done – operational processes – and the way in which work is supported – management processes. A system of processes is all of the ordered flows of events undertaken for a particular activity. The extent of a system of processes is defined by boundary judgement, not by the traditional notion of an organisation's boundary that separates consumer from worker. The aim of looking through this window is to be systemic with respect to processes – to explore the bounded span of processes.

Two central concerns about systems of processes to which we wish to remain alert are efficiency and reliability. Efficiency means to work without any unnecessary waste in time or resources. Reliability means dependable and accurate performance. When looking through the window on systems of processes, we therefore consider whether there are possibilities for improvement to the efficiency and reliability of operational processes and/or management processes.

Process maps

The view through the window on systems of processes can be made clearer by formulating process maps. These maps act as a model of organisational activities. They represent in terms of processes what is done, who does what, whom is responsible for what, and when things are done. Activity-based maps make clearer how much time and/or money is spent on an activity, and hence through simple calculations how efficient it is. They also locate duplication, redundancy, convolution and breaks in processes that might be the cause of unreliability.

Figure 13.1 is an example of an activity-based map. Events are shown as rectangles. Decisions are shown as diamonds. Arrows point out the direction of the flow of events. Notice that the flow contains loops and shows that systems of processes are cyclical, not linear. There are symbols positioned on

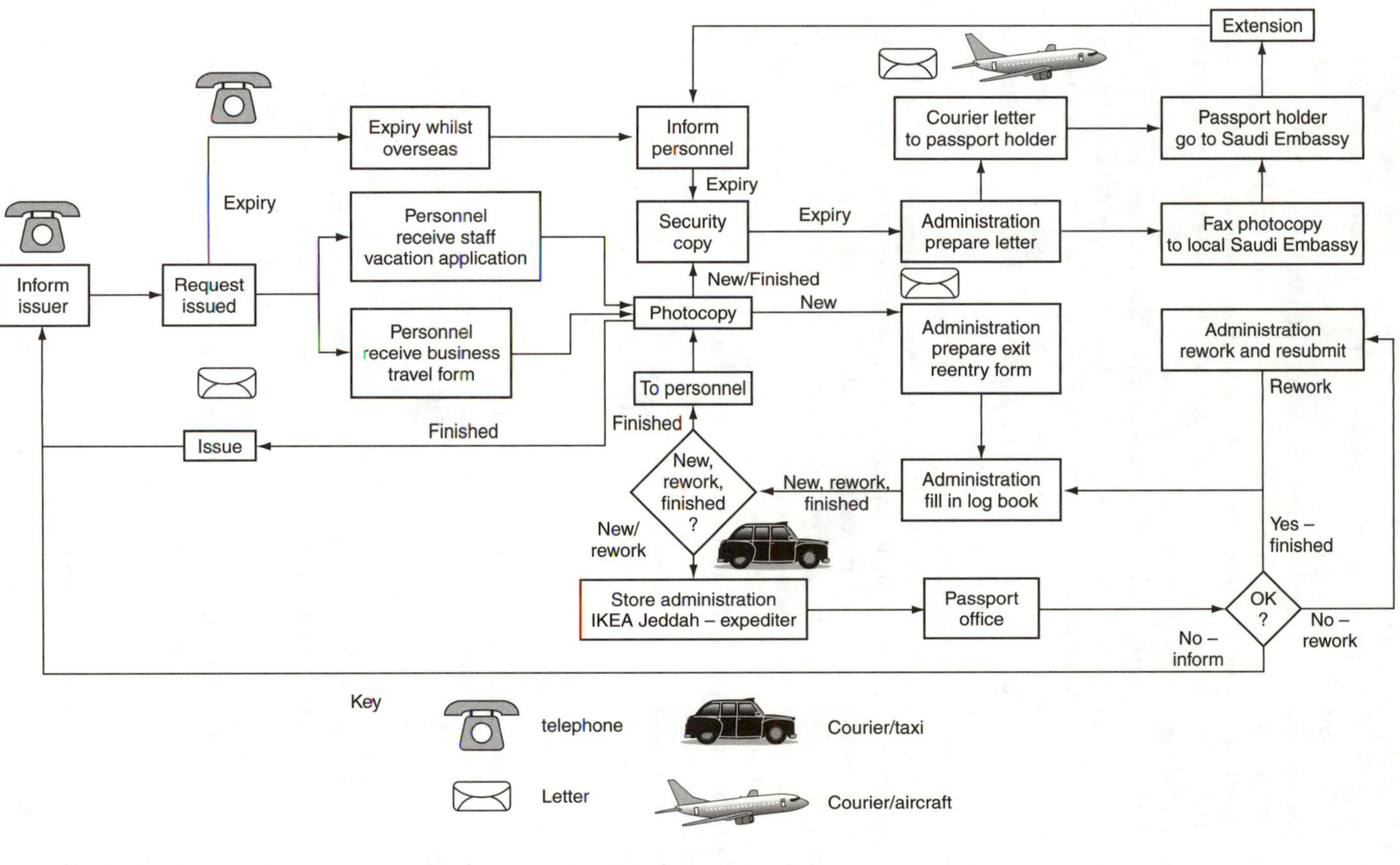

Figure 13.1 Activity-based process map: exit re-entry visa, IKEA (Saudi Arabia)

the map that indicate the kind of actions taken for certain events. Annotations such as envelopes and telephones indicate how time is consumed.

Each activity may be measured either for cost or time. A best case and a worst case measure are taken for each event. The total sum of the best cases or the worst cases for each measure across all events yields respectively a financial and a temporal range within which the system of processes is currently operating. A most likely case can also be calculated for each event and thus for the whole system of processes.

Activity-based process maps are knowledge tools that render an activity-based description of an organisational context. They are educational tools that facilitate learning about work that is done. They are tools that can guide implementation of improvement strategies by indicating what might be the effect of changes to processes in a particular organisational area, or in the organisational context as a whole. Thus, process maps support choice making about process design and process improvement.

Activity-based process maps may be employed to raise fundamental questions about activities. That is, why they are carried out in the way that they are, or, indeed, why they are carried out at all? A 'walk through' a process map by the people who carry out the tasks raises at each step the question, why do we do this? Accordingly, reflection on processes generates learning and may stimulate a breakthrough in thinking. A breakthrough is a realisation that activities might be carried out in a wholly different way, or not at all, which is likely to redefine the rules and practices of 'the industry' in a transformational improvement. Failing this, it may be possible to locate opportunities for incremental improvement in processes.

Improvement of efficiency and reliability

A possible spectrum for improvement of organisational efficiency and reliability of processes is shown in Figure 13.2. It illustrates a wide scope of options. At one end of the spectrum is continuous incremental improvement. At the other end of the spectrum is radical change and quantum improvement. Each extreme is flagged by a contemporary management strategy that typifies the intent. Kaizen's central principle is continuous incremental improvement, whilst business process reengineering's central principle is radical change. These two strategies are discussed a little later. Lying between these extremes is a range of possible improvement strategies. Improvement strategies are categorised in the next section yielding further understanding about ways in which process improvement might be achieved.

Categories of improvement

The following four categories usefully identify the main kinds of approach to process improvement. The first is in fact labelled *process improvement*.

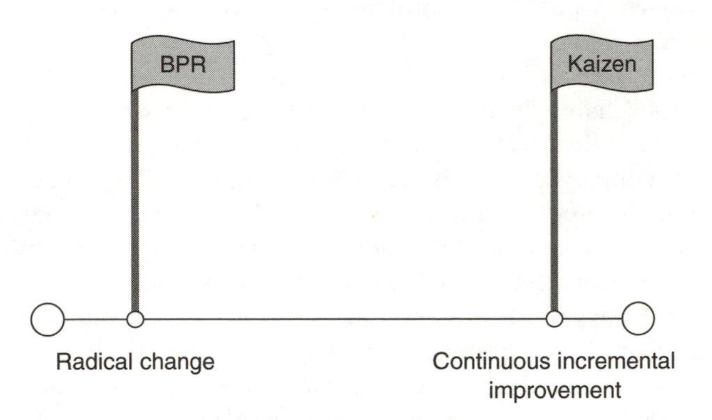

Figure 13.2 Improvement of efficiency and reliability

Aspects of a system of processes are considered to be inefficient and/or unreliable and are recognised as in need of enhancement. The second is labelled *process redesign*. An entire system of processes is regarded as in need of augmentation. The third category is labelled *business reengineering*. All systems of processes within the action area specified by boundary judgement are thought to be in need of reform. The last category is labelled *process transformation*. Here, the supposition is that radical improvement through transformation of the bounded systems of processes offers much potential. These categories suggest a spread of strategies designed especially for improvement of organisational processes.

Strategies for improvement

The literature of 'management and organisation' is full of ideas about improvement of process efficiency and reliability. Two well-known contemporary management strategies have already been mentioned – kaizen and business process reengineering.

Kaizen is associated with the writings of Imai as well as Ishikawa. These people are two of the so-called quality gurus that Japan has produced. Kaizen is relevant to the first three categories of improvement introduced above. Quality management is about meeting agreed customers' requirements, at lowest cost, first time every time. Groups of people negotiate with their customers to agree upon requirements. Customer means any person or group of people, internal or external to a bounded action area, who we supply with a product, a service, or information. Here again, we see that processes extend beyond traditional organisational boundaries. Agreed requirements are compared to actual provision and any failure to meet requirements is noted and acted upon. Projects are set up that aim to improve processes enabling consistent provision of what is promised (Phil Crosby's definition of quality). Reliability is established and efficiency is secured. This approach is pursued in unflagging fashion, delivering continuous incremental improvement.

Business process reengineering is normally associated with Michael Hammer and James Champy's book *Reengineering the Corporation: A Manifesto for Business Revolution*. Hammer in his seminars explains it succinctly – it is 'starting over'. In this sense business process reengineering is relevant to the fourth category of improvement called process transformation. Reengineering enthusiasts liken transformation to 'breaking the china'. The symbolic shattering of what is in existence refers to a defunctionalisation of organisational ways of life, followed by a reconstruction built on the basis of a small number of core business processes. The name of the game is simplicity. The minimum number of steps to achieve the purpose of each core business process is sought. Sophistication is a calamity in reengineering. It is not clever, it just adds time and cost. It decreases efficiency and most often makes no further contribution to reliability and may even hinder it.

Discussion

One of the tasks and benefits of looking at systems of processes and considering potential improvement strategies is to address what can be learnt about the improvement strategies themselves. There are issues and dilemmas associated with each one. Kaizen for example proposes continuous incremental change. But that might be slow off the mark and offer opportunities for competitors to leap ahead. It might also result in tinkering around with things in different organisational domains unless projects are well co-ordinated. Keeping momentum going might pose difficulties. Ultimately, the logic underpinning the way work is done is not fundamentally challenged by kaizen with consequent limitations on learning.

Business process reengineering, which can be applied to all types of organisation, does put in question the logic of systems of processes, or indeed the lack of it. However, in so doing it recommends radical change. This might instigate fear in advance of change and organisational trauma as a result of change. These unintended consequences can occur because huge improvement in efficiency smacks of downsizing and outsourcing (or to be politically correct, rightsizing and rightsourcing). Also, in becoming ultra-efficient now, that is, keeping things very simple, we might be sacrificing our flexibility to change in the future. Perhaps what is seen to be necessary in terms of short term organisational efficiency will turn out to be debilitating in terms of long term organisational effectiveness? These and many other issues and dilemmas relating to process efficiency and reliability form an important part of choice of improvement strategy.

Each unique boundary judgement will define client, purpose, and issues and dilemmas for discussion. Choice of whether or not we opt for improvement in process efficiency and/or reliability, and where on the spectrum for improvement we might lodge thinking, therefore results from boundary judgements. It makes no sense to think that an approach to process improvement can be lifted off the shelf, ready made. Rather, it is the task of people to engage critically with the options available and to be informed by them. People make choices according to what is known about the organisational context and strategies for improvement as seen through the window on systems of processes.

Choice of improvement strategy, however, is made in the light of what is learnt by employing all four windows, and prismatic thought about the way issues and dilemmas are accounted for through a panoramic view. It must be in the front of one's mind, at all times that issues and dilemmas transcend the four windows and only rarely will be adequately framed by one of them. Hence, equal attention is paid to each of the four windows before an improvement strategy is chosen and implemented. This systemic view is developed through the next three chapters.

14 Window 2

Systems of structure

What is structure?

Structure refers to organisational functions and various forms of co-ordination, communication and control. A structure is a set of rules and procedures that organise management support around operational activities and within the operational activities themselves. It is, in short, the organisational arrangements. A system of structure is the entire set of rules and procedures that span the action area defined by boundary judgement. Structural rules and procedures may well extend beyond traditionally conceived organisational boundaries. An important consideration with structure is to be alert to issues and dilemmas of effectiveness. Effectiveness means to achieve successfully things we set out to do. Possibilities for improvement of management support in terms of organisational effectiveness are therefore sought.

Improvement of effectiveness

A possible spectrum of improvement for organisational effectiveness is illustrated in Figure 14.1. It suggests a range of options in terms of the strength of emphasis placed on rules and procedures. At one end of the spectrum formal structure is strongly emphasised, meaning that a comprehensive formulation of rules and procedures spells out exactly what is to be done and who will be responsible for what. Bureaucracy is located at this end of the spectrum. At the other end of the spectrum Mintzberg's adhocracy finds its place. Here, arrangements are informal with specification of a minimum number of rules and procedures. Alternative structural arrangements can be made sense of in terms of this spectrum.

Diagnosis and design

Systems of structure are sometimes misunderstood only to represent tools for blueprint design. A blueprint design might be of considerable value say for a new venture. A blueprint design may offer a possible redesign of an

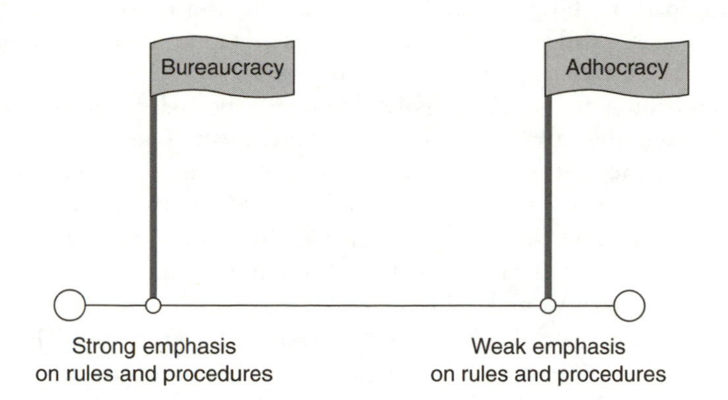

Figure 14.1 Improvement of effectiveness

existing organisational arrangement if dramatic changes are sought and considered feasible. However, in these terms a blueprint is a preconceived off-the-shelf model awaiting construction. There is another role that models can perform. They might be used as a diagnostic tool seeking to locate ineffectiveness and points for improvement rather than acting as a blueprint design.

Diagnosing organisations employing one or more structural arrangements helps to surface issues and dilemmas about effectiveness. Each structural arrangement proposes a structural logic about what are essential qualities of effectiveness. One or more of these logical arrangements may be employed to diagnose the action area for possible structural flaws. Flaws can be thought about as ineffectiveness in arrangements that make difficult achievement of things we set out to do. Of course, one logic will locate one possible account of structural flaws, whilst another logic will suggest another possible account. Which one, or ones, are considered most insightful will depend on context. And context is a matter of interpretation. One interpretation might see benefit from a formal arrangement of rules and procedures much more so than some other ones. An exploration of types of structural arrangement as they relate to an action area will generate dialogue and facilitate making judgements on this score.

Strategies for improvement

A healthy and quite diverse set of ideas about effectiveness to do with systems of structure is found in the literature of 'management and organisation'. The system of structure familiar to most people, at least through practical experience, is bureaucracy. Bureaucracy is one of several structural arrangements that are founded on a traditional hierarchical view of organisational life.

Bureaucracy is in its essence the establishment of lines of authority.

Authority is said to be both rational and legal. The aim is to give people clear roles and tasks. Rules set out exactly what is to be done by whom. People follow rules rather than instructions. Rules are diverse and are categorised according to types of issue that are expected to arise. Two very general categories are 'controls' and 'sanctions'. The hierarchical design for bureaucracy initially was *tall*, with many levels of management and supervision. More recently the notion of a *flat* hierarchy has attracted attention, partly because it reduces overheads by slicing out layers of management, but also because it claws back on the extent of rules that are considered necessary to make things work.

An alternative to tall or flat hierarchy is *democratic hierarchy*. This is Russell Ackoff's invention detailed in Chapter 5. The idea, as you may remember, is to establish rules for greater participation through a board structure. Organisational members operate at three levels, rather than just one. There is greater involvement for individuals in the activities that directly affect them.

A clearer break with traditional hierarchical thinking is found with the *organic idea*. Ludwig von Bertalanffy's open systems theory that is explained in Chapter 3 offers a classic impression of the organic organisation. Emphasis is placed on rules of function rather than rules of authority. Vertical linear control is replaced by a focus on interrelationships of subsystems and feedback control dynamics. A focus on the relationship between the whole activity and its external environment is another key difference. Important organic concepts include goal attainment, steady state, adaptation and survival.

Stafford Beer's *viable system model* discussed in Chapter 4 significantly develops the organic concept. He recognises five main management functions – operations, co-ordination, control, intelligence and policy. The first three are found in the original organic concept. They are the autonomic operations, which means in biology the subconscious element of an organism's brain that deals with routine matters. The significant addition made by Beer is the conscious element, which introduces intelligence and policy making. It is this that brings on the structure from merely an adaptive one to a proactive one designed to influence its own future. Rules and procedures set out to achieve effective communication between the five management functions and an external environment. Ultimately, the aim is to secure organisational viability.

Each of the strategies for improvement summarised above is concerned to establish rules as a priority. *Adhocracy* that was introduced by Henry Mintzberg is a minimalist approach to structure and rules. The main thrust is to create an informal arrangement where people simply know what is expected of them. They have a brief and decide how best to achieve it. Informal relationships evolve between people, each learning who does what, the services they can expect from each other, and to trust that this will happen. There is considerable scope for creativity and transformation.

A *community-type arrangement* is one that operates according to cultural rules and practices, not technical procedures. People become members of an organisational activity because they can identify with its values and purpose. There is often a charismatic leader at the helm. Cohesion is attained as long as organisational members share the same values and work towards the same purpose. People play particular roles, but muck in when the need arises. Work gets done because of commitment to values and purpose rather than as a result of formal rules. Of course, there are pros and cons for each of these structural arrangements, some of which are set out in the following discussion.

Discussion

The bureaucratic way has survived for many decades as the most common form of structure. It provided an answer during the industrial revolution to a change in the character of organisations. Small tightly knit organisations making products in modest numbers were increasingly replaced by large factories engaged in mass manufacturing which demanded mass employment. A bureaucratic approach suggested a manager–supervisor–worker hierarchy to cope with the scale of things. A clear division between people's roles as well as their activities was established through sets of rules. This left very little ambiguity about the work to be done. Everyone knew where he or she stood, including the client. For these and other reasons the bureaucratic approach is still with us today.

Bureaucratic management also has received its fair share of criticism. One of the main concerns is that the strict rules operating in a vertical manner makes communication long and slow. This reduces flexibility. It also means that people have to seek higher authority for things they want to do. Responsibility is held at the top. People at lower levels in the hierarchy easily become alienated and demotivated, which kills innovation and creativity.

The counter-idea of a flat hierarchy aimed to overcome some of these difficulties. Removing layers of management and supervision brings the decision-maker closer to the decision domain. It should speed up things. Difficulties experienced by organisations trying to flatten include information overload. People's span of control may become so wide as to become unmanageable. Also, the hierarchy as a feeder for middle and senior management is dismantled. The future managers of the organisation are disposed of. Such short-term gains in cost savings may seriously threaten long term needs of viability. The flat hierarchy initiative consequently hit significant difficulties and lost favour.

The democratic hierarchy attempted to preserve the benefits of hierarchical management mentioned above. At the same time it offered a way of increasing people's participation in decision-making of direct concern to their working lives. The board structure reduces alienation and encourages creativity and innovation. It does all of this without demanding structural overhaul that may give rise to organisational trauma. Yet, it sticks with hierarchy and suffers from being inward looking and, some might argue, not systemic enough.

Organic thinking certainly has a systemic quality to it. It gained some favour in the 1950s and 1960s as an alternative to the more mechanistic hierarchical approaches. Yet, it too was to suffer much criticism. To begin with, organic thinking suggests that an organisation has a harmonious structural existence with fixed goals in its parts. The roles of a heart and a kidney for example do not change in the lifetime of a person. The survival of the person depends on smooth co-ordination of these organs. Conversely, human organisations and the groups they comprise tend to be full of tension and have ever-changing purposes. The biological metaphor misses this point.

Stafford Beer's viable system model goes some way to address these and other related concerns. It recognises the need for local and changing goals. Yet it emphasises harmony between parts and possibly undervalues tension that can be the source of much creativity and transformation. Beer's team syntegrity paves the way towards addressing these concerns. Furthermore, Beer's viable system model is conceived of as representing real systems in the world. Just as a zoologist might look for organisms roaming around jungles, with Beer and indeed other organic thinkers, social scientists might look for real organisations operating in human made jungles. Yet, a human organisation to be more accurate is in its essence a set of rules and practices that operate primarily through cognitive processes. It is the coming together of minds in co-operation and/or conflict, rather than a distinct construction out there in the real world. It is in many senses a cultural and/or political phenomenon, not a physical entity.

Both adhocracy and community organisation emphasise the cultural dimension. Technical procedures give way to social rules and practices. Adhocracy as an informal structure creates space in which decisions can be made quickly by those closely involved in issues and dilemmas. It allows for an environment of creativity in which staff are often highly motivated. However, it loses certain benefits of a formal structure. Missing are clearly defined expectations and career structures. Some people may experience tension in the ambiguity as they experience things. The issue for debate here is freedom of space to do things versus clarity in what is expected of a person and how progress is to be measured. Similar observations might be made about community organisation.

Systems of structure provides another window through which to appreciate issues and dilemmas of an action area. Yet, we can make systemic sense of the action area only by thinking in terms of interrelationship of issues and dilemmas as understood by looking through all four windows at the same time. For example, systems of processes flow within systems of structure. The two cannot be separated as if they were siamese twins each with potential for a separate existence. They share along with systems of meaning and systems of knowledge-power vital qualities essential to the integrity of the whole. Subsequent chapters amplify this point.

15 Window 3

Systems of meaning

What is meaning?

Meaning arises from people's cognitive processes and the way that, for each person, their cognisance defines their relationship with other people and the world. Cognitive processes might be conceived of in terms of values, norms, ideologies, thought and emotion, coherence and contradiction. A person's actions and utterances cannot be made sense of without reference to this texture of what they think. *Values* are intrinsic desires and motivators. *Norms* underpin what is considered to be normal and acceptable behaviour. *Ideologies* are sets of ideas about how things should be. *Thought and emotion* refer to what a person thinks and how they feel about that, as well as the impact that feelings have on what a person thinks. *Coherence and contradiction* are qualities of 'validity' in cognitive processes. All of these things are key in making an adequate interpretation of what a person says and does.

Cognitive processes constitute meaning that may be shared in some way between people and yet remains somehow personal to individuals. Systems of meaning that people employ may coexist and adapt in relative harmony and/or degrees of conflict. That is, systems of meaning may yield cohesion in cultural ways of living and/or tension arising from disagreement, perhaps leading to coalition building and political interaction. Appreciation of what people mean and the temperament of their coexistence are therefore of central interest when seeking 'agreement' on improvement strategies.

What is meant by agreement?

There are perhaps three types of agreement explored in the literature of 'management and organisation' that are considered by one faction or another to be desirable and/or feasible – consensus, accommodation and tolerance.

Consensus is the idea that people can or will form strong agreement on what needs to be done and how to do it. Consensus is the linchpin of traditional planning, decision-making and problem solving. It is also drawn upon in contemporary management strategies including Senge's learning organisation. The notion of consensus, however, is increasingly recognised as undesirable and unlikely. It is undesirable because it epitomises assimilation and in the worst cases acts as a form of oppression. It is undesirable since it threatens our very survival by reducing diversity of thought needed to fuel creativity and transformation. Ironically, in achieving alignment through consensus in a learning organisation, one result might be to restrict organisational learning.

Consensus also may be unlikely. Reflection on the last section reminds us of intricacy in the texture of meaning people ascribe to things. It is incredible to think that people's values, norms, ideologies and so on, can be uniform and unvarying within any population. Even in circumstances where there is strong cultural cohesion, in a marriage of meaning amongst people, there still remains individual experience and interpretation that will forever remain unique. People's experiences cannot somehow be made one and the same. Consensus, surely, is nothing more than a theoretical construct and perhaps an undesirable one at that?

If, as argued above, difference characterises individual experience, interpretation and opinion, then it will be more realistic to seek to establish an *accommodation* between people. This idea is rehearsed in Checkland's soft systems approach. Seeking accommodation can be likened to finding some common ground whilst preserving other differences in opinion. Common ground is a higher level understanding where people find agreement on things to do. Although not ideal for any individual when measured against their values, norms and ideologies, an accommodation may represent an adequate way of proceeding. Organisational members might accept that it is worth giving up some of their individual needs in order to preserve the integrity of the whole and the benefit to them that this might return. Furthermore, individual needs are not sacrificed forever when establishing an accommodation between people. They remain in the background and may re-enter the process of negotiation and re-negotiation.

A stronger view on the dangers of assimilation and the desirability of diversity challenges even moves towards accommodation. Why not preserve and celebrate all differences? Why not harvest the positive worth of what emerges from an existence where tension is accepted as a norm? Why not indeed? Perhaps common sense when applied to understanding society might suggest *tolerance* as the most suitable way forward? Yet, to achieve toleration would involve a transformation of mainstream management thinking that would be both demanding to achieve and stressful to maintain. This is not a good enough reason to dispose of toleration; simply a red flag signalling a warning about its difficulties. We should remain mindful that toleration as a view of agreement is a product of postmodern thought that is only just beginning to gel in management writings.

The three possible types of agreement introduced above are depicted in Figure 15.1. This diagram shows each type of agreement as it handles only

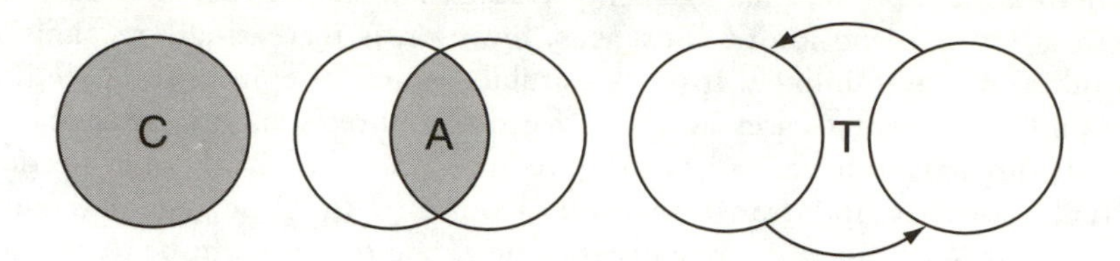

Figure 15.1 Three possible types of agreement: C = consensus; A = accommodation; T = toleration

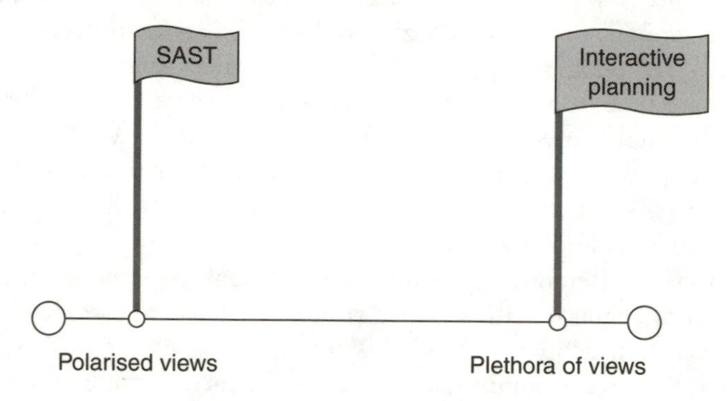

Figure 15.2 Improvement of meaningfulness

two different viewpoints. In reality, there may be many viewpoints at play in the arena of debate. Strategies for improvement will need to take that into account.

Improvement of meaningfulness

A possible spectrum of improvement in terms of meaningfulness is illustrated in Figure 15.2. Two forms of disagreement mark out the ends of the spectrum. 'Polarised views' is positioned at one end of the spectrum. Here I have located strategic assumption surfacing and testing (SAST) as a relevant strategy. At the other end of the spectrum 'plethora of views' is sited. Approaches like Ackoff's interactive planning and Checkland's soft systems methodology are relevant when a plethora of views is encountered. Moving along the spectrum from polarised views towards a plethora of views indicates more and more diversity in views. The type of agreement that is sought will be influenced by the amount of diversity in views. The following strategies for improvement help to facilitate thinking about systems of meaning, diversity of views, and a relevant type of agreement to aim for.

Strategies for improvement

One approach to handling polarised viewpoints is Mason and Mitroff's *strategic assumption surfacing and testing* (SAST). The approach recognises that people sometimes cluster together in support of one view or another. This can be likened to coalition building as understood by complexity theory. Views may then become polarised. Different systems of meaning come into tension with each other through coalitions in conflict. People, however, may fail to appreciate fully the texture of their own meaning systems or, indeed, systems of meaning underpinning another view with which they apparently disagree. This is a recipe for unproductive exchange between people whose opinions do not meet. People simply talk past each other. In this sense, trying to pin down the counter-view(s) is akin to handling a slippery fish. SAST asks, what can be done to bring polarised viewpoints into meaningful engagement? (See Chapter 21 for an illustration of SAST in action.)

The way forward suggested by SAST is for people who are supporters of each polarised view to group together. Employing a series of procedures offered by SAST, each group then surfaces and tests assumptions it is making in the belief that its preferred viewpoint, or let us say strategy, is going to work. These assumptions are otherwise hidden and remain unquestioned. The group will learn about and improve their strategy. Next, each group challenges the other's preferred strategy in terms of assumptions located in the counter-view(s). This exposes each strategy to the most severe of tests by its 'enemies', isolating unfounded assumptions and, on the basis of this, exploring ways in which the strategy might break down, or be improved, if implemented. In every sense this parallels Senge's desire to challenge mental models and to learn from so doing. If operated in a constructive manner, SAST's adversarial discourse is geared up to generate learning between groups that results in a synthesis, which, by definition, is greater than the sum of its parts.

SAST may operate well when there are two, three, or perhaps even four different strategic intentions in play. The greater the diversity of views, however, the more unwieldy the process becomes. Managing more than three or four groups with SAST's set of procedures quickly becomes less than productive. There is a need to explore many different views in a manner that channels people's concerns towards meaningful learning. Here we may turn to Ackoff's interactive planning or Checkland's soft systems methodology. Detailed accounts of these approaches are written up in Chapters 5 and 6 respectively. Broad principles will suffice here. In fact, the principles of the two share similarities that I suggest can be presented as one.

Interactive planning and *soft systems methodology* each offers a cycle of learning and understanding. The cycles can be thought about as having three phases. The first phase encourages learning about the real world. Interactive planning learns by way of scenario building, whilst soft systems methodology learns in terms of, for example, rich pictures. The second phase is about constructing ideal systemic models. Interactive planning explores ideal visions and ideal systemic properties for these, whilst soft systems methodology constructs a number of ideal conceptual models. The third phase compares ideal systemic models to whatever appreciation is made of the real world. Interactive planning constructs strategies to close the gap between what might happen and what we want to happen. Soft systems methodology generates an agenda for improvement through debate. The aim in each case is to explore many different mental models, to generate innovative ideas that promise improvement, and to conceive of ways in which the change proposals might be implemented.

Not surprisingly, there are many issues to take into account when seeking to establish agreement between people. Some of these are discussed below.

Discussion

The idea that lies behind each of the strategies for improvement discussed above is to attain clear expression and transparency of thought in a process of learning and understanding. Different systems of meaning are explored with the aim of achieving some form of agreement. Yet, a number of questions must be raised. How clear and transparent are resulting expressions? On what basis is agreement achieved? Has there been genuine learning and understanding? These questions are addressed when problematising forces that distort the way ideas eventually become consolidated in strategies. Three types of force are important here – intrapsychic, cultural and political.

Intrapsychic forces are described in the work of Argyris and Schön. Peter Senge pays much attention to what this partnership has to say. He recognises spontaneous, tacit theories-in-use that shape discussion and dialogue. You may remember from Chapter 2 the concern that Senge has about defensiveness and smoothing over, and the way these inhibit the challenging of mental models. Whichever improvement strategy is chosen from those reviewed above, the danger is ever present. So, there is a need to problematise intrapsychic forces within each approach, perhaps by adopting the recommendations of Argyris and Schön's action science? Although taking away a certain amount of spontaneity from the process, as William Foote Whyte pointed out in *Participatory Action Research*, action science does attempt to achieve a more open, meaningful and rigorous debate for everyone involved.

Cultural forces shape people's cognitive processes. That is, they influence mental models that a population of people share and often employ without knowing. Cultural forces are an extremely potent, albeit invisible, form of control system. Each of the improvement strategies summarised above helps people to make more visible mental models and hence to challenge cultural forces. However, this does assume conditions are ripe for open and meaningful debate, which may not occur if political forces operate in an unproductive fashion.

Political forces may enter the process of decision-making. In fact, complexity theory admits that a political dynamic is inevitable, but only desirable if encouraged as a constructive part of creativity and transformation. If a political dynamic is negative and is allowed to fester, then what emerges might be less than the sum of its parts. This must be so because learning is constricted. Time is wasted. A negative political dynamic can be most destructive. For example, in such circumstances SAST actually helps opposing sides by arming them, making a ruinous engagement increasingly likely. Sensitivity to political forces therefore is crucial. Yet, there is little of note said on this matter by Ackoff, Checkland, Mason and Mitroff or, indeed, Senge.

There are further questions to be raised about participation and representation. For example, who is to participate? Who is to decide who is to participate? And in large organisations, how can representation be arranged that is both meaningful and fair to everyone affected by decisions that are made?

Some real benefits are on offer if the dangers discussed above are handled carefully. In my view, what really counts is that which emerges from the means of getting to an agreement, rather than the end agreement itself. For example, people learn about each other's roles, ways of working together, and the whole within which they participate. True, the agreement itself is valuable if carefully considered by following the means of one approach or another. However, it is what emerges from the means that is likely to possess an enduring quality.

Perhaps the most insidious danger of all forces is systems of knowledge-power. This was purposely excluded from the above discussion for separate treatment in the next chapter. It is fundamentally a phenomenon related to, but distinct from, what is called organisational politics. It is not about micro-political interaction as such, but macro-social configuration according to who holds power and decides what is valid knowledge and action. Systems of knowledge-power are covered in the next chapter, which opens up the last of the four windows.

16 Window 4

Systems of knowledge-power

What is knowledge-power?

Knowledge-power is the idea that people in positions of power determine what is considered to be valid knowledge and consequently valid action. It points to a measure of fairness in the way things are done. Marx and Engels expressed this concern as we have already seen in terms of class structure in *The Communist Manifesto* as follows: 'The ruling ideas are forever the ideas of the ruling class.' Linda Alcoff and Elizabeth Potter in the introduction to *Feminist Epistemologies* unveil dominant knowledge produced and authorised by people in privileged political, social and economic positions. They, in effect, argue that nowadays the notion of 'ruling class' would benefit from wider interpretation. There are many forms of entrenched patterns of social relationship that privilege some people often at the expense of others. Alcoff and Potter come up with the following examples – race, class, sexuality, culture and age. To these I would add disability, the expert scientist and management hierarchy. The main aim of this chapter is to sensitise the reader if necessary to issues and dilemmas of knowledge-power as they enter into 'management and organisation'.

Why problematise knowledge-power?

Looking through the window of knowledge-power problematises what is seen through the other three windows. When looking at systems of processes and of structure, we question the fairness of designs. That is, we spotlight who in fact benefits from efficiency of processes and effectiveness of structure? If a design is not investigated in this way, then it is possible, or more likely probable, that the design will be built without question on ideas of privileged people. This may disadvantage and/or alienate other people. It will carry through entrenched patterns of organisational and social behaviour. The same is true about decisions that are made in the process of managing forms of conflict arising from interaction between people's systems of meaning. Decisions are likely to consolidate ideas of people in privileged positions. Let us consider some possible systemic consequences of letting things perpetuate in this way.

Entrenched patterns of behaviour in the workplace may affect the efficiency and effectiveness of designs. Formal power such as found in management hierarchy may only appear to be the driving force behind the implementation of a design. There remains potency in possible subsequent actions taken by people affected by the implementation. Complexity theory applied to the social domain suggests a complex of interrelationships and spontaneous self-organisation of people that formal power barely recognises and may find difficult to handle. Micro-political interaction can lead to the formation of coalition(s) around issues and dilemmas that arise because of the intervention. A coalition may become influential. Influence might result in significant loss in efficiency and effectiveness. One tactic against formal power, which people may bring into play, is subtly to refuse to operate designs to their potential efficiency or effectiveness. In fact, thought about in this way, designs offer only potential efficiency and effectiveness. What is actually achieved, or not, may result more from results of micro-political interaction of people who are affected, than from formal plans of powerful people involved as designers and decision-makers.

The more formal power is exerted, the greater the level of micro-political interaction which is likely to result. The greater the level of micro-political interaction that results, the more likely it is that formal power will be undermined. Then formal power is exerted again, feeding a cycle of negative conflict. This sort of negative conflict may be perpetuated and indeed accentuated wherever there are knowledge disparities. (The reader might like to consider which of Senge's systems archetypes characterises this dynamic?)

Negative conflict becomes increasingly likely the greater people's awareness of their plight. In many locations, people's awareness has heightened as they come to know their rights in terms of 'natural justice' and grow in confidence that change is possible. In other places, movements are afoot to raise awareness in terms of fairness. There are some groups of people who are more vulnerable than other groups. In such cases the dominance of existing order may prevail for extended periods of time. Actively building coalitions with influence may be the only way to stimulate change and create a new order. A catalyst for social transformation might be necessary. Strategies focusing on fairness may be essential.

The question here that privileged people might ask themselves is, is it worth the bloody hassle? Why not seek to create a fair environment of knowledge equals in which political interaction is directed in a constructive way as discussed by complexity theory, that is, in a process of learning, creativity and transformation?

In any case, there is the oft-neglected issue of the ethics of decisions and designs. Irrespective of the impact of people's micro-political actions on efficiency and effectiveness, there still stands the question concerning how you feel about things in terms of fairness. Ask yourself the following questions. What is your emotional reaction to the possible outcomes that might result from decisions and/or designs you are considering endorsing? Are you contributing to the kind of world in which you wish to live? Are you contributing to the creation of a world order that could one day yield decisions about you that you would consider unfair? How would you feel if your friends, sisters and brothers, mother and father, children or partner, were subjects of the decision or design? Can you justify your power and money, say, against what this costs in terms of other people's helplessness and poverty? Do you care? Should you care? Do you have the will to act in a way that might contribute to social transformation? Problematising knowledge-power dynamics deepens appreciation of efficiency and effectiveness and further sensitises people to the ethical nature of designs and decisions.

Problematising knowledge-power

A potentially productive place to begin problematising knowledge-power is through gender studies, in particular the feminist literature. The area is well researched and has generated wide-ranging discussion of more general relevance. Linda Alcoff and Elizabeth Potter in the edited book *Feminist Epistemologies* make clear that issues their contributors raise are not limited to, or do not reduce to, gender studies alone. Knowledge-power issues they discuss cast insight into many other forms of entrenched patterns of social behaviour.

The systemic quality of Alcoff and Potter's publication in this regard comes through with force. They say that gender and indeed any other form of knowledge-power, 'cannot be adequately understood – or even perceived – except as a component of complex interrelationships with other systems'. There is a plethora of ideologies at work in the production of knowledge. Furthermore, in the same volume Bat-Ami Bar On explains how feminist thinking questions Marx's single axis of privilege around class. (Although I note that Marx was concerned with the plight of women.) She envisages a more complicated social grid that raises questions on the relationship between the multiple underprivileged groupings. For example, the social grid from a feminist perspective would comprise feminist approaches such as black, cultural and lesbian issues. The notion of systems of knowledge-power is in line with these findings of feminist researchers.

Lorraine Code sees knowledge, and I would say designs and decisions that result from knowledge, as an artefact of a privileged group. A group generalises its interests and neglects and suppresses interests of others in the process. This is not systemic. It is a form of reductionism. Feminism is concerned for example that what emerges in western countries from the social grid (systems of knowledge-power) serves the interests of a small group of educated and usually prosperous white men. Social arrangements

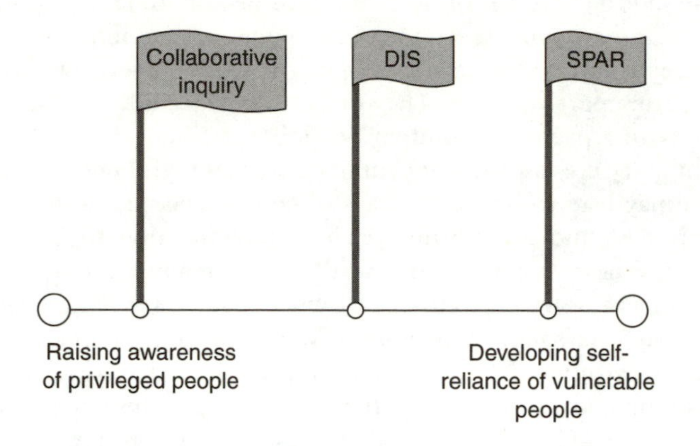

Figure 16.1 Improvement of fairness

in science conform to this pattern if my review of six most influential systemic researchers is anything to go by. In addition to this, inquiry into racism might locate privilege in the dominance of an ethnic or tribal grouping. Studies on disability strongly suggest that the voice of disabled people is muted and thus not taken into account in plans for the future. Each axis of privilege points to every other axis and to similar types of concern.

Improvement of fairness

A possible spectrum for improvement in terms of fairness is shown in Figure 16.1. It suggests a range of needs. One extreme of the spectrum is marked by the need to emancipate privileged people from their ideologies and power structures that lead to unfair treatment for less privileged people. This prepares the way for privileged people to participate more openly in dialogue. Collaborative inquiry works along these lines. At the other extreme of the spectrum is the need to unshackle underprivileged people from impoverished conditions that result from dominant ideologies and power structures. This involves development of self-reliance of underprivileged people. Self-reliant participatory action research (SPAR) operates in this way. The central region of the spectrum suggests that certain strategies for improvement such as dialogical intervention strategy (DIS) address to some extent both forms of setting free. A range of strategies that addresses fairness is discussed in the next section.

Strategies for improvement

Peter Reason's *collaborative inquiry* aims to emancipate the privileged and powerful people from ideologies that they pursue, in order that they become better able to respond to the needs of disadvantaged people. In *Participation in Human Inquiry and Action*, Reason explains collaborative inquiry as a way of training people and on the way developing the community towards a consciousness of future participation. The aim is to free up both individuals and the community in a process of mutual development.

Collaborative inquiry creates the opportunity for meaningful encounters. These encounters may lead to improved ways of co-existence. Reason talks of 'greater effectiveness and greater justice'. I understand that to include efficiency and effectiveness sought in an ethically aware manner. To achieve this ideal, it may be necessary explicitly to problematise power dynamics.

Collaborative inquiry encourages people to frame and reframe reality in successive cycles of learning. Learning here is a process that challenges conventional wisdom and entrenched patterns of living. The experience may be very uncomfortable for some people and an end result is not guaranteed. The mutually agreed focus might be any one or more of the axes mentioned earlier, for example, gender, disability, and/or management hierarchy.

At the outset, collaborative inquirers agree upon the focus of learning and introduce their knowledge and ideas on the matter. They then agree how to proceed, including recording and interpreting one's own and each other's experiences. The collaborative inquirers engage with their experiences in an attempt to become freer in their perceptions about the matter in question. They reassemble as a group on occasions and share experiences in the context of the inquiry. This may result in a conclusion of the process, or reframing the question, in another round of learning.

In contrast to collaborative inquiry, Fals-Borda and Rahman in *Action and Knowledge* seek to nurture the *self-reliance* of people who are underprivileged or disadvantaged. This supports underprivileged and disadvantaged people as they strive to attain independence. It may begin a process of social transformation. The idea amongst other things is to preserve diversity in ways of living and to arrest the onslaught of assimilation. This is most often presented as a macro-social argument, but may be applied to organisational life. The ultimate goal in any case is for underprivileged people to grow in self-confidence and become knowledge-equals. People become aware of their capacity to transform relations of knowledge.

Action may involve awareness raising, which aims to establish authentic people's movements. Another possibility is self-development through socio-economic initiatives. A third idea is to renegotiate ways in which support is received through hierarchical relationships, in organisational or state contexts, diminishing people's dependency on so-called higher authorities.

Dialogical intervention strategy, presented by Hölscher and Romm in *Development is for People* (edited by J.K. Coetzee), is an explicit form of knowledge production. It is relevant to formal and informal educational environments. It may involve privileged and/or underprivileged people. The approach aims to uncover interaction that lacks dialogue, including –

conclusive consensus, accommodation without wide-ranging exploration of alternatives, manipulation and/or elimination.

An issue(s) of concern in society is/are chosen by an investigator. Again, issues might relate to a number of axes of knowledge-power recognised by Bar On. Other participants then join a dialogue about the issue(s) in an exploration of ways in which people see things. The investigator consolidates arguments presented. There may be further dialogue reflecting on the consolidation of people's experiences. The aim is to develop the practice of receptivity to counter-positions. All involved then seek to institutionalise new practices in the form of accountable action.

These three strategies for improvement of fairness not surprisingly raise many issues for further discussion. Some key concerns are examined below.

Discussion

Strategies for improvement in fairness seem to present as many dilemmas as issues dealt with. To begin, there is the question of investigator or facilitator bias. What safeguard is needed to prevent the value system of a change agent from replacing a dominant ideology? How does the change agent know when/if they are making an imposition? In any case, are the people involved equally prepared to enter into and influence dialogical processes? This might question both whether they want to be involved and whether they are capable of getting their contribution across? How do we know any of this? And how can we cope with things we do know?

Another dilemma is the ethics of raising awareness. What if transformation is thought to be unrealistic? Raising people's expectations, and we might say aspirations and hope, can simply result in accentuation of frustration. Or, perhaps, some local change possible now may very well be reversed later on by a greater power. What if social transformation ultimately fails? Does anyone have the right to suggest a gamble with other people's emotional well being in this way?

Then there is the question about how far anyone should go to achieve social transformation. Is it enough to raise awareness? Is there a need to support action? When does this become subversive? Is subversion desirable? Is it acceptable? What options exist other than subversion that set out a preferable course of action? When is enough enough? And, in the end, how can social transformation be evaluated? There are of course many more questions that can be raised, and perhaps should be raised. I am sure that the reader's own experiences will point to some of these.

Whatever, there is no short-cut when it comes to knowledge-power. There is no quick fix. There is no instant satisfaction. Yet, engaging in questions like the ones just raised may reveal that improvement simply cannot be reduced to and measured in terms of efficiency and effectiveness. It will not work from anyone's point of view, whether it is because of unrealised potential in efficiency and effectiveness, or unfair consequences of biased action.

This chapter introduces the last of the four windows that facilitate the generation of insights into any action area. Each window offers one perspective, yielding one set of insights into issues and dilemmas of any particular action area. The next chapter extends the window metaphor with the idea of prismatic thought. Prismatic thought encourages development of panoramic views of the lifescape of an action area that opens up thinking about relevant ways of achieving improvement. It is prismatic thought that paves the way for a meaningful choice of improvement strategies.

17 Prismatic thought

Introduction

The previous four chapters each offer a window to open up on any action area. An action area, remember, results from boundary judgements. The windows help us to appreciate issues and dilemmas pertaining to systems of processes, of structure, of meaning, and of knowledge-power. Looking through all four windows at the same time sets the scene for panoramic views of the lifescape of the action area. However, this is not an objective view of some bit of reality around us. Rather, it is the basis of a possible interpretation of things from our viewpoint. Each interpretation might be considered an image of the action area (after Gareth Morgan's *Images of Organisation*). Creativity and transformation of thought in this regard may be of considerable value in generating a most informed and relevant image. I am referring here to a sort of prismatic thought.

What is prismatic thought?

Prismatic thought is a metaphor for creative and transformational thinking. To appreciate the metaphor it is instructive to rehearse what a prism is and how it works. Without being too technical, a prism is a piece of transparent material having parallel polygonal ends, with a number of rectangular surfaces meeting them at right angles. Amongst other things, these physical characteristics of a prism are used to split light into its component colours by double refraction, once on entering the prism and again on leaving it. Prismatic thought, then, might be considered the transformation of what is seen through the four windows, realising bursts of colourful creation through stories, metaphor and diagrams. Each type of creation offers a possible way of imaging an action area. A diversity of interpretations generates a wide range of possible images. What is considered to be the most plausible image is then employed to guide the choice of an improvement strategy. This concept is developed below.

Creativity and transformation

It is quite likely that in the process of thinking through boundary judgements and deepening systemic appreciation, images of the action area begin to form. The task of prismatic thought, through dialogue, is to develop these images and to bring forth new ones. In so doing, we facilitate what Senge calls generative learning. It is a mode of learning that challenges existing mental models and, in effect, creates a conceptual space in which a new order of thought might emerge. It is a part of learning within the unknowable.

Existing mental models prevail in everyday living for a good reason. A feature of complexity people routinely face is masses of information about this and that, and seemingly every other thing. Well established modes of thought help us to make rapid sense of what is going on. Everyday thinking is essential to the smooth handling of everyday living. Unfortunately, when it comes to 'management and organisation', everyday thinking can restrict learning to a superficial level. Significant emerging issues and dilemmas in the action area can and do suffer neglect. Everyday thinking then becomes a conceptual trap.

Conceptual traps capture all of us most of the time. They are built on assumptions that shape the way things get done. In 'management and organisation' it is easy to be deceived by a predominant view of leadership style, organisational structure, or approach to strategic management. These assumptions normally are not challenged and tested. Things keep getting done in the same old way.

The knack of creative and transformational thinking is, as Russell Ackoff suggests on the cover of this book, to yield many different views of the same thing and the same view of many different things. It is in the nature of systemic thinking to so do. The aim is to challenge assumptions, to provoke new thoughts, and to generate unexpected insights that have high intrinsic value to the participants.

There are two kinds of learning with prismatic thought – idea generation as well as image generation that I have already mentioned. Idea generation comes up with ideas about the complex of issues and dilemmas, which ones are most pressing, and makes suggestions about why this might be the case. Idea generation may seed new thoughts that can be developed into images of the action area. That is, we move from a list of ideas to whole pictures of the action area. It is only with whole pictures that we may begin to get to grips with both detail and dynamic complexity. Approaches to idea generation and image generation are introduced below.

Idea generation

There are many approaches known as creativity enhancing techniques that propose ways of generating ideas. I suspect every reader of this book will have encountered *brainstorming*. The idea is to create a congenial environment for creative thinking and to follow a process that surfaces many ideas about some named task. The task might focus on unearthing issues and dilemmas or thinking up ways of tackling them, or both. Every idea of every person is in the first instance considered potentially a good idea. Every person is taken to be a good idea generator and is encouraged to contribute.

The way people are encouraged to participate may take several forms. Each form has its own label. For example, apart from brainstorming as such, there is nominal group technique and the 'why?' approach. Brainstorming tends to involve free flowing debate where ideas generate more ideas, with someone capturing all of the ideas on a flip chart. Unfortunately, the voice of some people may not be heard, perhaps for reasons introduced in Chapters 15 and 16. So, *nominal group technique* adds structure to the process. People might be asked to sit silently and to write down their ideas about the named task. The anonymous ideas are then circulated and may trigger off thoughts in the minds of other participants, which are added to the list of ideas. The ideas are then set out on a flip chart and, if there are very many, the sheets of paper are pasted around the walls for all to see. A computer program may be employed to organise ideas and to structure them according to some named relationship such as, will idea A lead to the achievement of idea B?

At some stage the idea generation process will open up into free debate. The *'why?'* approach asks idea generators to direct the question 'why?' to their ideas. For example, why will this idea lead to that preferred improvement? The answer is then subjected to the question 'why?' again. The question–answer–question cycle may continue for half a dozen times or more. In this way ideas begin to undergo critical investigation. Every form of brainstorming in due course encourages dialogue of one sort or another about ideas. Dialogue is the source of and usefully may be cultivated into image generation.

Image generation

Images are whole pictures of an action area, not just a collection of ideas. They depict key issues and dilemmas of an action area and animate them in a dynamic story about what is going on. One way we can attempt to make sense of things in terms of images is through *metaphor*. A metaphor is the application of a descriptive form to an object or action to which it is not literally applicable.

On first encounter, the notion of metaphor may seem a radical approach to creative thinking, asking people to learn to think on a completely different plane from everyday reasoning. This is not so. The title of Lakoff and Johnson's book, *Metaphors We Live By*, reminds us that making sense of our experiences through metaphor is an everyday mode of understanding. For example, to say 'we aim to grow and diversify our enterprise in order that it survives' is to employ a biological metaphor. This statement makes sense of organisational aspirations in terms of biological functions. We employ metaphor all the time to help make sense of things, to express ourselves, and to direct future actions.

The skill of applied metaphor is an accomplished one in a wide range of art forms. Metaphor is frequently the essence of novels, films, plays, lyrics, cartoons and photographs. The aim is to target our experiences through thought and emotion and to develop these into whole images of some new and often unfamiliar context.

The skill can also be an accomplished one in 'management and organisation'. The skill may be likened to that of an athlete. All healthy people are able to run and on occasions will do so, but some people train and can run much faster or longer than those that do not. Equally, you can train in the use of metaphor and become better at it. By the way, training in running is a metaphor for training in metaphorical thinking! Here are a few tips for training in metaphor.

Choose any metaphor. You will probably find that people in your life employ metaphor albeit very loosely, offering you an excellent starting point. Do some preliminary thinking about the metaphor you choose. Work out its attributes and characteristics, and the dynamic that it represents. In Senge's terms, what is its detail complexity and dynamic complexity? Think about how these may represent stakeholders, the way they interrelate and the behaviour that you witness. If your thinking with metaphor does not begin to create a meaningful image, then try out another one. Whatever happens, do not get bogged down in detail. Allow yourself to be inspired by images that are created.

Next, make some tentative decision about what you think is happening using images and insights generated by metaphor. Ask yourself why you think this is happening. Consolidate thinking with a most plausible opinion about issues and dilemmas that need addressing. Then compare images and insights surfaced by different metaphor. Ask if insights generated by each metaphor are equally helpful. Ask how successful each metaphor is in creating an image that resonates in your mind with the context of inquiry. Ultimately, you need to choose a most plausible account of events and then think through what this implies in terms of improvement strategies that might be implemented.

In this section of the book I have discussed systemic thinking in terms of *how things might be*. Systemic thinking, however, suggests that we also need to learn in two other modes. We also need to create images of *how things ought to be*. We then need to learn about the process of change, from *how things might be to how we think they ought to be*. These three interrelated modes of learning are at the heart of the approach of this book, that we move on to consider in the following section.

Approach

18 Organisational learning and transformation

Introduction

In the last section of the book, I introduced the concept of *learning within the unknowable*. The nub of the argument is that the complex nature of the world in which we find ourselves is unknowable to the human mind. The world comprises many, many interrelationships. The dynamic is characterised by spontaneous self-organisation. Thus, it is only possible to get to grips with things that are local to us in space and time. Local in space means, 'things that we are immediately involved with'. Local in time means, 'not very far into the future'. We therefore know of the unknowable, manage within the unmanageable, and organise within the unorganisable.

This argument of complexity theory casts doubt over the claims of traditional strategic planners. It is doubtful whether results that happen today are those intended any length of time ago. It is inconceivable to think that we can plan over any great span of interrelationships or very far into the future. The more that we try to think global rather than local, the more we experience the resistance of complexity.

Systemic thinking offers a particularly profitable way of gaining meaningful insights into things that are local to us in space and time. First, boundary judgements help people to formulate viewpoints about issues and dilemmas experienced in their lives. It reminds us of the ethics of our choices. Each viewpoint is partial and temporary. Second, deepening systemic appreciation facilitates construction of incisive insights into each viewpoint. In this way, we learn within the unknowable.

The current and two subsequent chapters suggest how learning within the unknowable can yield organisational learning and transformation. This chapter that concentrates on choosing and implementing improvement strategies is about learning with scenarios. Scenario building is remoulded from its traditional form to incorporate boundary judgements and deepening systemic appreciation. Whilst this approach is primarily written for organisational learning and transformation, it is revisited in the appendix to this chapter in a way that shows its relevance to Senge's discipline of personal mastery. The next chapter explores evaluation of the results of improvement strategies and how to enhance their positive impact. The last chapter in this section reviews the relative merits of instrumental action and experiential action when it comes to organisational learning and transformation. To begin with, let us turn to learning with scenarios.

Learning with scenarios

Scenario building is a widely employed approach that purports to investigate possible and probable future events. It often forms part of strategic planning. For example, statistical forecasting techniques such as Monte Carlo simulation calculate probability-based scenarios. Russell Ackoff in his book *Redesigning the Future* constructs scenarios to investigate 'the future an organisation is already in' as part of idealised planning. De Geus in his book *The Living Company* recalls how he and former colleagues at Royal Dutch/ Shell incorporated scenario building as a routine element of strategic thinking. Gareth Morgan in *Images of Organisation* draws upon organisational metaphor to script plausible stories about an organisation's past, present and future. Colleagues chatting in the corridor about their corporation's future are loosely building scenarios. Scenario building enters strategic thinking in many ways for many different purposes.

A traditional approach to scenario building sets out to forecast the future and to plan for it. A scenario is constructed and risk analysis is undertaken within this future. Risk analysis aims to characterise the range within which the future is likely to evolve. This can be likened to shining a torch into the dark – the beam becomes wider and dimmer the further ahead it shines, as does the probable range of future organisational events, yet we can still see ahead of ourselves reasonably well and plan accordingly. Plans and contingencies are made for that foreseen future. In some cases, scenarios, plans and contingencies, are worked out in great detail.

An influential social philosopher, Alasdair MacIntyre, comments with scepticism in his book *After Virtue* that scenario building faces formidable complexity. He says that scenarios of the sort just described very rapidly become inaccurate. They become more and more uncertain and increasingly useless. Ironically, the criticism might continue, the more detailed the scenario, and hence its supposed credibility, the less probable it is that the scenario will demonstrate any notable degree of accuracy.

Complexity theory recognises MacIntyre's criticism of a traditional approach to scenario building. However, MacIntyre does not spot, as does Senge for example, the value of scenario building for learning organisations. Here, the aims and benefits are considered to be quite different. Instead of planning for and attempting to secure the future, we become mentally agile with respect to change and learn our way into an unknowable future. The following list sets out some key aims and benefits of scenario building as it facilitates learning into an unknowable future.

- People are better informed about the sorts of event that occur.
- People are better informed about the way events occur.
- People are more alert to issues and dilemmas that they face.
- People learn how to challenge their mental models – their mental agility is kept fit and they learn how to learn.
- Scenario building develops means that endure, rather than ends that rarely come true. It builds new working relationships between people as well as team coherence.
- It facilitates relevant local decision-making.
- It can be applied to personal vision as well as to forms of agreement that underpin shared vision.
- It provides a focus on learning about interrelatedness and spontaneous self-organisation.
- It supports managing within the unmanageable and organising within the unorganisable.
- It encourages learning within the unknowable.
- It guides organisational learning and transformation, whilst recognising that this is always built on a partial and temporary view of reality.

What is meant by 'improvement' is briefly explained below.

Improvement

Improvement is an aspiration that is context dependent and thus can only be defined locally. It is stakeholder based and relates to clients, and issues and dilemmas relating to those clients. Improvement is defined within the action area that comes into focus through boundary judgements and deepening systemic appreciation. What is to be improved is decided upon as part of the process of organisational learning and transformation.

Overview of process

The structure of the process of learning a way into the future benefits from Russell Ackoff's idealised planning. Its essence, however, is more congruent with C. West Churchman's critical systemic thinking. Some of the content mirrors Royal Dutch/Shell's participatory approach to strategic planning, Werner Ulrich's critical systems heuristics, and Joseph Juran's project-based approach to quality management. The structure, content and essence operate within an awareness of complexity theory. The basic process set out below comprises *three lines of learning, or questioning*.

- *Explore the current action area*. Where might we be heading?
- *Draw forth shared vision*. What ideal would we really like to work towards?

- *Projects to achieve shared vision.* How might we change direction towards what we would ideally like?

Scenarios are constructed for each one of these three lines of questioning. Each line of questioning is a reflective counterpart to the other two in the sense that they inform each other. Scenarios are built by employing boundary judgements and by deepening systemic appreciation. Scenarios have many forms, including storytelling, different types of diagram, as well as metaphor. Initially, scenario building helps people to learn about the possible need for transformation. Scenario building also helps to constitute in organisational consciousness a will to change. In any case, the overall aim is to draw out and expand upon people's knowledge and experience, and to inform organisational learning and transformation.

A diagrammatic view of the process is now offered. It aims to illustrate the circular and systemic nature of the process. It highlights the learning and transformational qualities of the process. It makes clear that the process is about learning a way into the future.

Diagrammatic view of process

The following figures illustrate how the process operates in real life.

Figure 18.1: *Establish a timeframe* over which improvement strategies might be implemented and evaluated. Here, five time steps are shown, although no time units are given. Units are determined in the unique context of improvement strategies. Normally, time step 1 approximates the future as far ahead as we dare to guess events. How far ahead this is thought to be will depend to some extent on the momentum built into the way things are currently done. Over time we aim to achieve organisational learning and transformation.

Figure 18.2: *Explore the current action area.* What might we be faced with, say, over the next three time steps?

Figure 18.3: *Draw forth a shared vision.* What ideal would we like to achieve, say, over the next three time steps?

Figure 18.4: *Projects to achieve a shared vision.* How might we close the gap between what we might be faced with and what ideally we would like to achieve as we see things at the moment? What projects will most likely help to close the gap by making improvements that we currently desire?

Figure 18.5: *Explore the current action area.* After one time step has elapsed, reconsider what we might now be faced with, say, over the next three time steps.

Figure 18.6: *Draw forth a shared vision.* Reconsider what ideally we would like to achieve, say, over the next three time steps.

Figure 18.7: *Projects to achieve a shared vision.* Reconsider how at the moment we might close the gap between what we might be faced with and what ideally we would like to achieve. Review and update existing projects.

Figure 18.1 Learning a way into the future (1)

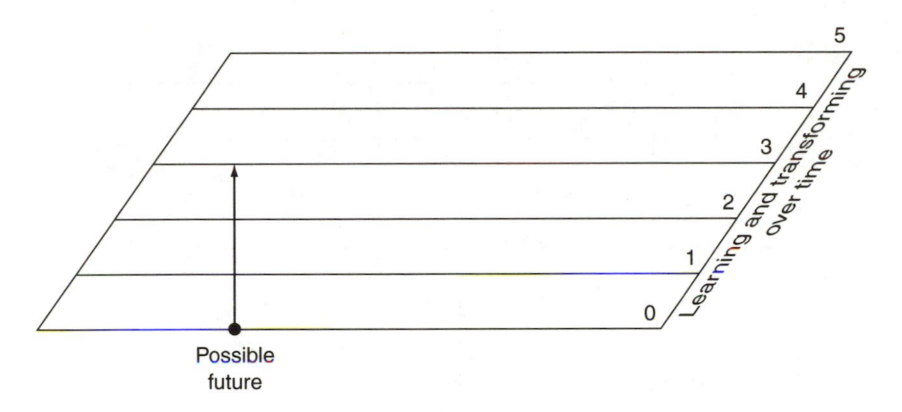

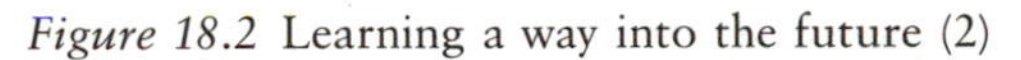

Figure 18.2 Learning a way into the future (2)

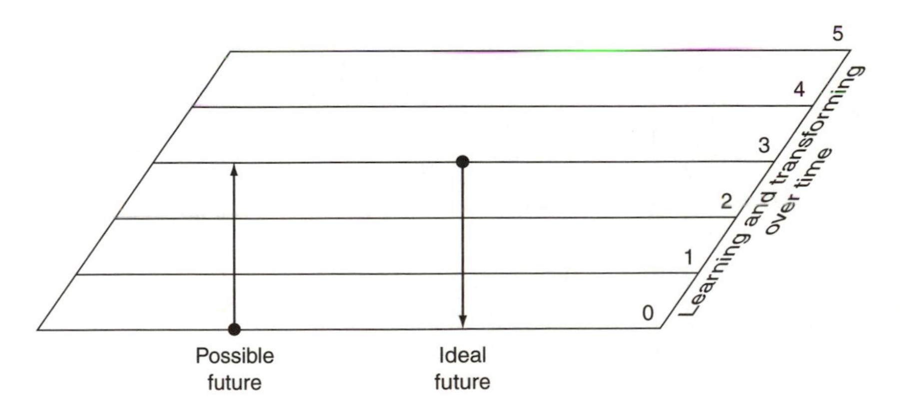

Figure 18.3 Learning a way into the future (3)

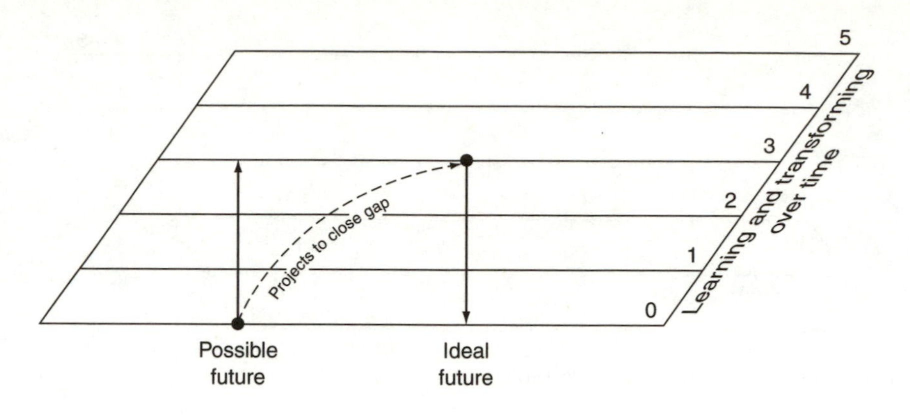

Figure 18.4 Learning a way into the future (4)

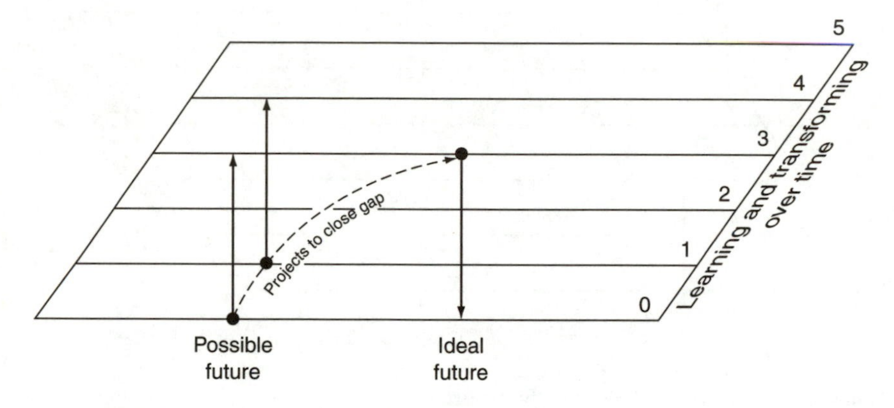

Figure 18.5 Learning a way into the future (5)

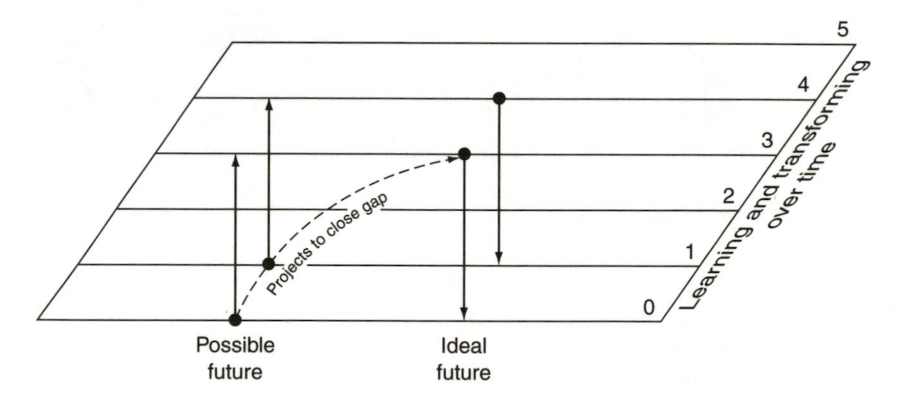

Figure 18.6 Learning a way into the future (6)

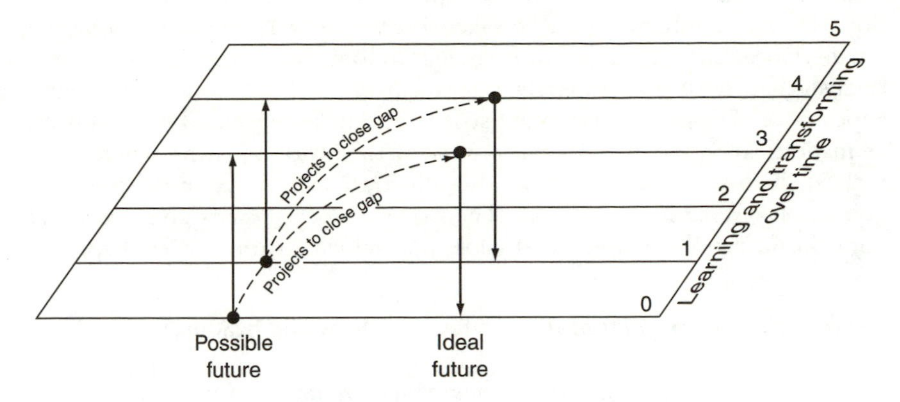

Figure 18.7 Learning a way into the future (7)

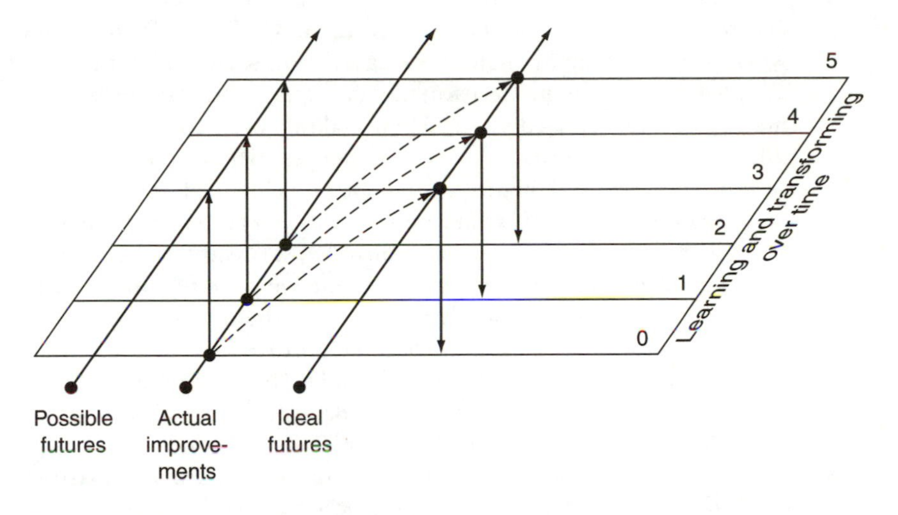

Figure 18.8 Learning a way into the future (8)

Terminate redundant projects. Formulate additional projects, if any, that will most likely help to close the gap and make improvements that we currently desire.

Figure 18.8: The process moves on another time step (and so on). A detailed account of the three lines of questioning is set out in the next section.

Inside view of process

The three lines of questioning just illustrated in diagrammatic form may be represented as a coherent set of procedures for organisational learning and transformation. However, the procedures set out below are only a suggestion. They certainly must not be taken literally as a recipe to be followed. Furthermore, the account below is subject to limitations imposed by written English that, most unfortunately, forces a linear write-up and instrumental appearance. The process as I practise it is very definitely circular, not linear, as made clear in the diagrammatic view of the process just presented. The cyclical quality of the process is also illustrated in an extended practical animation offered in Chapter 21. The presentation below is given in bullet point form, details of which the reader can relocate from earlier chapters.

Explore the current action area: where might we be heading?

Learning in space: appreciating things as we are involved in them

- Undertake boundary judgements to explore the current action area.
  - Who are the stakeholders? Werner Ulrich in his book *Critical Heuristics of Social Planning* drew upon C. West Churchman's work and came up with four categories of stakeholder that are adopted here – client, decision taker, expert and witnesses. The first three are involved in decision-making over core issues and dilemmas of concern. *Clients* are people whose purposes are served. Purpose and hence actual client is defined by measures of success. *Decision takers* are people who can change the measure of success. *Experts* are people whose expertise influences/shapes decision takers. The *witnesses* are people who are not involved in the making of decisions but are affected by the intended results of decisions. However, they may become involved in shaping what happens by actions they choose to take, for example, through political interaction leading to spontaneous self-organisation, and the lodging of new issues on the organisational agenda.
  - Surface the core issues and dilemmas of concern to the existing client that are central to current decision-making.

Learning in time: how things might unfold

- Deepen systemic appreciation about what we might be faced with and explore where we might be heading.
  - Establish a timeframe over which scenarios relating to issues and dilemmas are to be thought through.
  - Look through all four windows – past, present and future.
  - Undertake prismatic thought – past, present and future. Write a story/scenario and/or work out a metaphor and/or draw diagrams and/or pictures about what we might be faced with, in terms of interrelatedness and spontaneous self-organisation.
    - What sorts of event occur in your account?

    - Why might these events occur?
    - What kind of issue and dilemma are you alert to?
    - Is the account ethically justifiable?
    - What kinds of thing need improving?
- Check the logic and plausibility of each account.
    - Is the account internally consistent?
    - Prepare other accounts.
    - Compare accounts.
    - Question the plausibility of each account.

Draw forth shared vision: what ideal would we really like to work towards?

Learning in space: appreciating things we would like to happen

- Undertake boundary judgements to explore alternative action areas and what ideal shared vision we would like to work towards. Also, encourage people to influence shared vision with their personal vision (see the appendix to this chapter).
    - Who ought to be the stakeholders? Reflect on the four categories – client, decision taker, expert and witnesses. The first three are stakeholders you think ought to be involved in decision-making over core issues and dilemmas of concern. *Clients* are people whose purposes ought to be served as defined by measures of success. *Decision-takers* are people who ought to be able to change the measure of success. *Experts* are people whose expertise ought to influence/shape decision takers. The *witnesses* are people who will be affected by decision-making but not involved in it. However, they may become involved in shaping what happens by actions they choose to take, for example, through political interaction leading to spontaneous self-organisation, and the lodging of new issues on the organisational agenda.
    - Surface what will be the core issues and dilemmas of concern to the client that you think ought to be central to current decision-making.

Learning in time: how we would like things to unfold

- Deepen systemic appreciation about the ideal shared vision.
    - Establish a timeframe over which ideal scenarios relating to issues and dilemmas are to be thought through.
    - Look through all four windows as if in the ideal future. What ideal properties can you see?
    - Undertake prismatic thought as if in the ideal future. Write a story/scenario and/or work out a metaphor and/or draw diagrams and/or pictures about the ideal future, in terms of interrelatedness and spontaneous self-organisation.
        - What sorts of event occur in your ideal future?

    - Why might these events occur?
    - What kind of issue and dilemma are you alert to?
    - Does the account allow for people's personal vision?
    - Is the account ethically justifiable?
    - What kinds of thing would you aim to improve?
- Check the logic and feasibility of each account.
    - Is the account internally consistent?
    - Prepare other accounts.
    - Compare accounts.
    - Question the feasibility of each account.

Projects to achieve shared vision: how might we change direction towards what we would ideally like?

Learning in space: appreciating things we need to get involved in

- Define and choose projects to change direction towards what ideally we would like.
    - These might arise through coalition building around issues or dilemmas and consequent spontaneous self-organisation. Leaders who appreciate the value of learning within the unknowable will encourage this kind of dynamic.
    - What is to be improved?
    - What is meant by improvement?
    - Define each project.
        - What is the aim of the project?
        - Who is responsible for the project?
        - What is the timespan of the project?
        - What is the timetable for the project?
        - What resources are required for the project?
        - How will the project be evaluated (see next chapter)?
    - Choose projects for implementation.
        - Which projects are likely to have an immediate impact and which ones are for the long term?
        - Which projects are expected to have a tangible impact and might be catalysts to change? Which ones are anticipated to have a more subtle impact but could lead to deep-rooted change?
        - Apply the Pareto principle – which 20 per cent of the projects promise to achieve 80 per cent of the improvement that is sought? These 20 per cent are known as the vital few. The remaining 80 per cent are known as the useful many.
- Undertake boundary judgements to explore and enhance each project.
    - Who would be the stakeholders? Reflect on the four categories – client, decision taker, expert and witnesses. The first three would be

involved in decision-making over core issues and dilemmas of concern as projects are implemented. *Clients* would be the people whose purposes are served by the projects as defined by measures of success. *Decision takers* would be the people who can actually change the measure of success. *Experts* would be the people whose expertise influences/shapes decision takers. The *witnesses* would be the people who are not involved in the making of decisions but are affected by implementation of the projects. However, they may become involved in shaping what happens by actions they choose to take, for example, through political interaction leading to spontaneous self-organisation, and the lodging of new issues on the organisational agenda.
  - Surface the core issues and dilemmas of concern to the client most likely to become central to decision-making during the lifetime of the project.

Learning in time: how we might encourage things to unfold

- Deepen systemic appreciation to enhance each chosen project.
  - Establish a timeframe over which each project relating to improvement of issues and dilemmas is to be thought through.
  - Look through all four windows at each project.
  - Undertake prismatic thought as if implementing each project.
    - Write a story/scenario and/or work out a metaphor and/or draw a diagram and/or picture about project implementation in terms of interrelatedness and spontaneous self-organisation.
    - What sorts of event might occur if the project was implemented?
    - Why might those events occur?
    - What kind of issue and dilemma does this make you alert to?
    - Is the account ethically justifiable?
    - What kinds of thing are to be improved?
  - Check the logic and feasibility of each account.
    - Is the account internally consistent?
    - Prepare other accounts about project implementation.
    - Compare accounts.
    - Question the feasibility of each account.
  - Implement chosen projects.
  - Undertake systemic evaluation for each project that is implemented (see next chapter)?

Step on to evaluation

If we purport to be implementing improvement strategies, then for the process to be meaningful we have no option but to evaluate the impact of chosen projects. Omitting or opting not to do this means learning is unnecessarily curtailed. We do not learn our way into the future. Instead, we are swallowed up by the unknowable. The next chapter suggests a process to facilitate systemic evaluation of projects under way. (May I remind you that the following appendix (18.1) revisits Senge's discipline of personal mastery in the light of the approach of this chapter?)

APPENDIX 18.1: INDIVIDUAL LEARNING AND TRANSFORMATION

Adaptation of the above process can assist in creating a structure for Senge's discipline of personal mastery. The diagrammatic view can be seen as a picture of a lifelong journey. The lifelong journey comprises a recurring cycle of three types of scenario building as set out below.

The first scenario is an appreciation of one's current reality. A truthful account is essential. The second scenario is thinking about intrinsic desires – one's ideal future. Techniques from *The Fifth Discipline Fieldbook* such as 'drawing forth personal vision' may be employed here. The third scenario addresses how to close the gap between one's current reality and one's intrinsic desires. This will involve setting up projects in one's life, whilst managing the inevitable creative and emotional tension, as well as structural conflict that Senge warns of.

At the end of one time step, all three scenarios are revisited. One's current reality will have changed. One's intrinsic desires may well have moved on. Projects in life therefore might be revisited and adapted where necessary, or terminated, whilst new projects might be started. This whole process is repeated again and again throughout one's lifelong journey. The journey can be illustrated by making reference to the figures initially presented and discussed in the section called 'Diagrammatic view of process'.

- Figure 18.1: *Establish a timeframe* over which your personal vision might be implemented and evaluated. Here, five time steps are shown, although no time units are given. You must decide the duration of time over which to implement your personal vision. Normally, time step one approximates the future as far as you dare guess events. How far ahead you choose to consider things will depend to some extent on momentum built into your current reality. Implementing personal vision amounts to your learning and transforming over time.
- Figure 18.2: *Explore your current reality.* What might be your current reality, say, over the next three time steps?
- Figure 18.3: *Draw forth personal vision.* What ideal would you like to achieve, say, over the next three time steps?
- Figure 18.4: *Projects to achieve your personal vision.* How might you close the gap to achieve your personal vision as you see things at the moment? What projects will most likely help to close the gap and begin to make the improvements that you currently desire?

- Figure 18.5: *Explore your current reality.* After one time step has elapsed, reconsider your current reality, say, over the next three time steps.
- Figure 18.6: *Draw forth personal vision.* Reconsider your personal vision, say, over the next three time steps.
- Figure 18.7: *Projects to achieve your personal vision.* Reconsider how at the moment you might close the gap to achieve your personal vision. Review and update existing projects. Terminate redundant projects. What additional projects if any will most likely help you to close the gap and to make improvements that you currently desire?
- Figure 18.8: The process moves on another time step (and so on).

19 Systemic evaluation

Introduction

Systemic evaluation is an integral part of any endeavour that purports to be concerned with improvement strategies. The process outlined later on in this chapter suggests how to evaluate action under way by facilitating learning and understanding about the impact of projects implemented. The process operates in a support role with the aim of enhancing the positive impact of the projects and dealing with counter-intuitive consequences. It aids reflection on actions taken and in this way opens up opportunities for new issues and dilemmas to be considered. It also asks whether chosen improvement strategies are still valued. Evaluation therefore plays a central role in keeping all concerned people informed about the consequences of projects and helps them to learn their way into the future. It facilitates learning within the unknowable. A number of key concepts are reviewed below before outlining a possible process for systemic evaluation.

Formative and summative evaluation

Evaluation generally speaking is either formative or summative. These two approaches may be co-joined in a comprehensive ongoing systemic evaluation. *Formative evaluation* is normally associated with the processes of decision-making, problem solving and strategic planning. The aim here is to generate information about each project in progress. Information produced is used to enhance the impact of each project in terms of specified improvement, for as long as that is still valued.

Summative evaluation is normally linked up with accountability or research. Summative accountability assesses how well certain individuals or groups measure up to some specified standard. Summative research on the other hand reflects back on projects that are well under way or that have concluded. It seeks to consolidate what has been learnt through the process of implementing the project. The findings are transferred into future improvement strategies either locally or elsewhere. Summative research, rather than summative accountability, is of greater interest to the approach of this book. The focus therefore is on formative evaluation and summative research, and the ways in which these in tandem can impact upon improvement.

Measurement of improvement

Formative evaluation as outlined below is directed towards issues and dilemmas surfaced when looking through all four windows on the action area – systems of processes, of structure, of meaning, and of knowledge-power (as interpreted through prismatic thought). Each one of these helps to locate different possibilities for improvement. They also suggest a range of measures sufficiently diverse to cope with the multidimensional character of project implementation. Four types of measure are therefore considered.

- Measures of efficiency and reliability of systems of processes.
- Measures of effectiveness of systems of structure.
- Measures of meaningfulness of agreement in the context of systems of meaning.
- Measure of fairness of systems of knowledge-power.

These measures must be considered alongside each other as expressions of an interrelated and emergent dynamic. Measurement of any sort, however, is not straightforward. A discussion of measurement theory is warranted. The following presentation builds on ideas Ewart Carson and I put forward in *Dealing With Complexity.*

Measurement theory

Measurement is the process by which numbers and labels are assigned to aspects of an organisational or societal context. It is carried out in such a way as to represent the context in line with clearly defined rules. *Rules* define the nature of data construction as well as manipulations that are permissible to perform on the data. Manipulation of data aids its interpretation and subsequently transformation into a useful format – it aids learning – which is fed into the evaluation process.

Data may be of a quantitative or qualitative form. *Quantitative data* is usually constructed when essentially technical issues are under scrutiny, such as efficiency and reliability of processes, or effectiveness of structure. *Qualitative data* is normally constructed when human related issues are being evaluated, such as meaningfulness and fairness. There are many forms of formal arithmetic manipulation that can legitimately be carried out in the interpretation of quantitative data. The process of interpretation of qualitative data, however, tends right from the start to be through dialogue, which is highly subjective. It is crucial that the exact nature of constructed data is understood so that only legitimate manipulations and interpretations are made. The *scales of measurement* propose four categories of data and permissible ways of treating data ascribed to each category.

Scales of measurement

There are four distinct scales of measurement – nominal, ordinal, interval and ratio. This categorisation is quite easy to remember with the mnemonic NOIR. Each one is reviewed below. The rules or logical properties of the scales of measurement are set out in the appendix to this chapter.

Nominal scale

Nominal measurement occurs when aspects of the situation are labelled in a classificatory or nominal manner. Data that is constructed is classified and members of each nominal group are then said to share an identity. The process of classification may be clear cut, or subjective and open to debate. Subjective classificatory tools include metaphor and analogy.

In clear-cut classification the logical properties recorded in the appendix of this chapter are considered to hold. In subjective processes like metaphor or analogy, the logical properties ask 'what if' rather than suggest 'what is'. Clear-cut classifications include 'boy or girl' (gender-age classification) and the scales of measurement (classification of data). Subjective classifications include, from earlier in the book, library categories and the 'four windows' metaphor.

Ordinal scale

Ordinal measurement involves ranking aspects of the situation. Constructed data is compared and ranked by employing a standard of comparison. The process of ordering, like nominal measurement, may be clear cut or subjective and open to debate.

Similar to the nominal scale, in clear-cut classification the logical properties recorded in the appendix to this chapter are considered to hold. In subjective processes the logical properties ask 'what if' rather than suggest 'what is'. Clear-cut classifications might include Moh's scale of hardness of minerals where mineral A is ranked as harder than mineral B if A can scratch B, but B cannot scratch A. A subjective and debatable ordinal measure is a person's ranked table of favourite movies.

Interval scale

Interval measurement is where aspects of a situation are ranked and the interval between each ranking is known precisely according to a scale of intervals. The choice of zero on an interval scale is arbitrary; that is, it has no absolute meaning. The nature of zero is the main distinction between the interval scale (arbitrary) and the ratio scale (natural).

An example of an interval scale is a thermometer where zero is arbitrary. The equally spaced intervals do not have comparable magnitudes determined by the number of times the one contains the other. For example, 10°C is not twice as hot as 5°C. Arithmetic manipulation is permissible conditional on preservation of the ranking and relative differences. For example, a linear transformation that multiplies by a constant preserves both ranking and relative differences. All common statistics are therefore permissible.

Ratio scale

Ratio measurement operates with a scale that has a natural zero. Thus, any two intervals on the scale have comparable magnitudes expressed by the number of times the one contains the other. Weights, lengths and quantities, are examples of ratio scales. Measures on the ratio scale can be investigated and interpreted through any mathematical or statistical technique.

When data are interpreted it is vital that only legitimate manipulations are performed according to the logical properties of the appropriate scale of measurement. This warning must be heeded in particular in the social sciences where measures are very often subjective and nominal or ordinal. Interpretations based on data not suitable to the logical properties of a manipulation are subject to the GIGO criticism – 'Garbage In, Garbage Out'. Evaluation that falls to the GIGO criticism facilitates a false learning about, and misunderstanding of, the impact of actions taken.

Perhaps before proceeding further, I should clarify why the term *data construction* is used in this text in preference to data collection. The point is that data is not waiting out there in volumes to be reaped like corn in an autumn harvest. The evaluator enters into a process that constructs data, rather than collects it. Data is the product of a process of investigation.

There is a diversity of data construction approaches that reflects the scales of measurement discussed above. In the social sciences these range from quantitative approaches that employ an instrument of data construction like physical measurement and structured surveys, to qualitative approaches where the evaluator is the primary instrument of data construction. Qualitative approaches tend to work towards the nominal end of the scales of measurement, whilst quantitative approaches at least in the first instance operate towards the ratio end. Four categories for data construction instruments are considered in this chapter.

- Physical measures.
- Surveys.
- Ethnography (writing about the people).
- Documentary analysis.

Physical measures

Physical measures are measures of physical things. They tend to be associated with products and processes. In the manufacturing sector, measures of product and process support production and process control. There is an extensive literature on this activity that extends into quality control. Quality here means producing the product consistently according to an agreed specification.

The initial aim of quality control was to *get rid of poor quality product*. This meant taking samples of the product at the end of the manufacturing line and, when faulty product was located, identifying and dealing with the cause of the fault. According to the Japanese quality guru, Ishikawa, this might relate to materials, methods, manpower (*sic*) or machinery. Most manufacturing companies now aim to *get rid of poor quality from the product*. This involves building into the manufacturing line measurement of critical factors of product and process. Faults are picked up at the location and time that they occur. Corrective action then can be taken. Measurement continues for example in manufacturing with storage, delivery and servicing. Indeed, necessary measures are derived for the whole system of processes.

Physical measurement extends into the service sector. It is particularly pertinent for paper-based processes, say, in the insurance and financial sectors. However, it is possible to represent any service as a system of processes and start to evaluate it.

Discussion so far has focused on reliability. Measures taken help to evaluate how well a product or service matches up to specification, or what is promised. Another important measure is efficiency. Efficiency means minimising unnecessary waste. It can be measured by ratio comparison between inputs and outputs, such as average unit cost and labour cost per unit.

Effectiveness goes hand in hand with efficiency. Effectiveness is about achieving chosen tasks. Stafford Beer in his book *Brain of the Firm* argued that effectiveness might be measured in terms of what is actually achieved, what we are capable of achieving, and what our potential effectiveness might be if we went about things in a different way. Comparison can be made between these three measures yielding several indicators of effectiveness. An example is actual time taken to get a new innovation into production, what we were capable of, and what our potential could be if we were to redesign the product innovation cycle. Interpretations of data for reliability, efficiency and effectiveness, are fed into evaluation and reassessed within the categories of meaningfulness and fairness.

Validity of physical measures is a matter largely to do with reliability of the measurement instruments. Instruments can pick up so called background noise that distorts and makes erroneous the measure. An example here is background radiation affecting measurement of low levels of radioactivity. Steps must be taken to recognise and filter out background noise. It is also important in physical measurement to recalibrate instruments at regular intervals to ensure that they are not introducing error. This is commonplace with medical instruments. For example, solutions manufactured at standard concentration are put to use to recalibrate instruments that measure concentration.

Surveys

A survey is a designed evaluation. A survey is used to sample people's views about issues and/or dilemmas of concern. It draws comparison between large numbers of respondents from a population, indicating how people feel overall about certain issues and/or dilemmas. A *population* is a group of people to whom results apply. There are two types of survey – questionnaire and interview. Questionnaires can be distributed to very large numbers of people, say through a postal or email facility, but frequently achieve a response rate rather less than 50 per cent. Interviews, on the other hand, are resource intensive, but interviewers do get straight to the categories of respondent of particular interest.

A *questionnaire* is a document setting out a formulated series of questions about an issue of concern. Questionnaires often seek ordinal responses. To this end they employ a Likert scale to record people's opinions and to facilitate comparison. A Likert scale usually provides seven (or five) options for each question. If the question asks whether you agree with some statement, then '1' might be strongly agree and '7' might be strongly disagree, with '2 and 3' and '5 and 6' catering for people with softer opinions, and '4' for those who feel neutral about the issue.

Questions may simply focus on categories such as age, sex, and role. Categories are used to segment data, which facilitates comparison. Questions might be open ended, encouraging people to respond without pre-set categories, or may employ ordinal scales to direct them. Responses to open-ended questions are analysed by the evaluator who seeks to uncover themes and lines of response. This process is called coding. *Coding* renders categories by which data is constructed and analysed.

There are many issues to take into account in *questionnaire design*. Questions must be devised and ordered in a way that encourages people to respond. Layout and format are crucial in this regard. Wording must be carefully chosen to eradicate ambiguity. Words that respondents might not understand are best avoided. Questions must not force respondents to give an answer that they do not feel happy with, either because their preferred option is missing, or because they have an ethical difficulty with any issue or dilemma of concern. Many of these worries can be addressed by *piloting* a questionnaire and improving it accordingly. This can be supplemented by using knowledgeable referees to evaluate the questionnaire.

Interviews involve face-to-face questioning. Skills of the interviewer therefore come into play and need to be considered. Communication and consultation skills are critical. Interviewers may need to prompt the interviewee for an answer. They may need to probe for a fuller answer. Risk of distortion on data construction arises because the interviewer might direct too forcefully when prompting and probing the interviewee.

Interviews can be categorised into four types. A *structured interview* has a standardised schedule with closed questions, where responses are pre-coded. A *semi-structured interview* has a mixture of open and closed questions that allows the interviewee greater flexibility to respond. An *unstructured interview* sets out areas for discussion allowing the interviewee to define the way the topic is discussed. *Group interviews* involve a number of people in discussion on a specific topic, introduced by a facilitator, held most often with a view to examine group dynamics in response to issues and dilemmas. Choice of type of interview depends on the evaluation question, the kind of data required, and the resources available. As with questionnaires, interview strategies will be piloted and improved. Responses to open-ended questions will be coded.

Surveys of all kinds have a number of common factors. To start with, evaluators must select respondents. It is rarely possible to construct data from the complete population. *Samples* are therefore required. The aim is to make whatever group is studied representative of the population. There are several ways to approach sampling, such as straightforward random sampling or stratified sampling. *Stratified sampling* segments a population into relatively distinct groupings. The choice of sampling approach again will be shaped by the purpose of the evaluation and resources available.

Data analysis is a search for significant differences, correlation and/or association, rather than causation. Univariate analysis explores each variable separately. Bivariate analysis explores relationships between two variables. Multivariate analysis is also possible. Computer software is available to make easier these and other forms of statistical manipulation, for example, SPSS (statistical package for the social sciences) is available at most universities and for the personal computer. Ideally, these findings are fed into further dialogue with respondents to encourage systemic reasoning.

Validity of data construction and analysis is of central concern. First of all, the GIGO uncertainty must be addressed. Data must be fully understood in terms of the scales of measurement and permissible manipulations that may be performed. Beyond this, evaluators must be on the look out for unknown and possibly unseen factors influencing findings. Also, correlation and association might be accounted for in a number of different ways, each of which requires discussion and comparison.

Ethnography

Ethnography is effectively an approach to anthropological study. The evaluator learns about people by entering people's everyday lives and writing about their own and other people's experiences. The evaluator attempts to capture people's points of view on issues and dilemmas of concern. Events are documented and insights are generated through the interpretation of the events. A diary might be kept. Themes are drawn out and recorded for further discussion. The extent to which an evaluator is involved will vary, from being a full member of a project team, to an occasional visitor on a watching brief.

Several issues surface with ethnographic evaluation. For example, is participation and observation to be overt or covert, which would be more effective, and what are the ethical implications of undercover evaluation? With complete participation, will the evaluator lose their 'objectivity' as they become immersed in issues and dilemmas and participate in choices? How can the evaluator's personal experiences usefully enter into the wider process that evaluates the impact of improvement strategies?

Documentary analysis

Documentary analysis investigates all forms of documentation relevant to the evaluation. There are two ways in which documentary analysis is carried out. The first is *factual data* gathering to supplement statements made in interviews or observations made by evaluators. This may be used in support of survey work or ethnographic investigation. The second concentrates on *how things were said*, rather than *what was said*. Whichever, it is important to draw upon and to make comparison between many sources, to enhance confidence in observations made. The whole effort may become difficult if access to sources is restricted due to the confidential and sensitive nature of its contents.

Triangulation and recoverability

There are two more important aspects of validity of evaluation to take into account – triangulation and recoverability. *Triangulation* attempts to overcome the deficiencies of any one approach to evaluation by combining a number of them and capitalising on their respective strengths. The idea is that no single approach is always superior. Each has its own unique strengths and weaknesses. This leads to method triangulation involving a variety of data sources and evaluators. Their combination, it is argued, will help to reduce bias and improve the validity of any conclusions drawn.

Whichever approach to evaluation is employed and whatever conclusions are drawn, it is important that *recoverability* is taken seriously as an issue. Peter Checkland and Sue Holwell (1998 on page 18) in *Systemic Practice and Action Research* argue that one aim of action and indeed, we might add, evaluation is to proceed in such a way that the process followed, 'is recoverable by anyone interested in subjecting the work to critical scrutiny'. This means documenting the thought processes and models that enabled people to do their work and to draw their conclusions. I offer some personal observations on recoverability in the case study in Chapter 21 that, in tune with complexity theory, suggests limitations to what can be recovered and known.

Process of evaluation

The process of evaluation suggested below has both formative and summative elements to it. The two are co-joined to form the basis of a comprehensive ongoing systemic evaluation – the output of the one is an input to the other. The process is described below. It is subject to the confinements of written English, that is linear and systematic, but the process is most helpfully interpreted as circular and systemic. Formative evaluation and summative research are presented in that order.

Formative evaluation

- Formative evaluation is undertaken on each project generated through the process of organisational learning and transformation, which is introduced in the previous chapter. Evaluate each project. Make sure you are clear about which people are chosen as stakeholders, in particular as clients, and thus what issues and dilemmas come to the fore. Be clear about what is to be improved and what improvement means. These are all central matters to both project implementation and evaluation. They provide a reference base for both activities. However, it must be kept in mind that the output of organisational learning and transformation operates within a bounded view of things that we know is both partial and temporary.
- Choose measures that are considered of central importance to tracking and evaluating the impact of the project. These might be considered *critical success factors* for the project. Employ the 'four windows' metaphor to consider what measures, if any, are required for the following categories.
    - Measures of efficiency and reliability of systems of processes.
    - Measures of effectiveness of systems of structure.
    - Measures of meaningfulness of project improvements.
    - Measures of fairness following project improvements.

  Each measure is just one expression of a whole dynamic. The measures together attempt to track changes to the lifescape in which projects are implemented. It is thus very important to keep in mind the interrelated and emergent nature of the lifescape and which aspects of these the measures reflect, which of course remains a matter of interpretation.
- Locate sources for data construction for each chosen measure. This involves thinking through the most likely sources for data construction that will allow chosen measures to be usefully investigated.
- Define the nature of data to be constructed in terms of the relevant

scales of measurement. Declare what are permissible manipulations and interpretations of the data to be constructed. This is where the lessons of measurement set out earlier in the chapter are fully taken into account. The aim is to ensure that formative evaluation avoids the GIGO criticism.

- Choose the types of measurement instrument required for data construction. Put together measurement instruments where necessary. Validate measurement instruments. This process can be time consuming. Time is well invested however. The aim is to ensure that data required is actually constructed by the measurement instruments, avoiding spurious measures. Again, it is important to avoid GIGO criticism.
- Decide on the frequency of measures to be taken. Ensure that the time period for measurement is congruent with the gestation period of the improvement strategy.
- Decide how data is to be stored. Like other forms of storage, the idea here is to keep and preserve the data. Data is often widely used, so it must be stored in such a way that its details as far as possible are conserved. *Recording sheets* are useful in this regard. A recording sheet aims to store constructed data in an easy to understand format. A possible procedure for making a recording sheet is set out below.
    - Indicate clearly the purpose of data construction.
    - Estimate the quantity of data.
    - Design the recording sheet.
- When making a recording sheet, always bear in mind the following points.
    - Make sure the purpose is clear, not vague.
    - Ensure that entries can be made accurately.
    - Ensure that the recording sheet is not unnecessarily time consuming.
    - Ensure that the recording sheet is not unnecessarily complicated.
- Some examples of recording sheets follow.
    - Cause of defect – when inquiring into the cause of a defect, say in a manufacturing process, a record is kept of the number and types of cause of defect.
    - Frequency of occurrence – when administering a questionnaire, the number of respondents for each question and each possible answer are tallied and recorded.
    - Diary – when undertaking ethnographic evaluation, a story of events and an interpretation of events is kept in a diary.
- Construct, store, manipulate, compare and interpret data. Make whole system interpretations of the impact of improvement strategies. Ideally, explore findings with a representative set of stakeholders. The role of an evaluator is to construct data for dialogue and to facilitate dialogue, not to make expert judgements about improvement. A key matter of concern here is to keep asking if project implementation is in all senses ethically justifiable.

- Decide how to present the findings.
- Feed findings into the continuing process of organisational learning and transformation. Recommend how to enhance positive impact and how to overcome counter-intuitive consequences that result from projects. Consider possible changes to improvement strategies. Consider the need to challenge assumptions about improvement strategies. For example, which people ought to be client? And, which issues and dilemmas thus ought to be addressed by projects?
- At all times in formative evaluation reflect on the way that people's knowledge and experiences are drawn upon to provide meaning to the process. This is not a task necessarily to be reported on. It mainly reminds people that they are not simply following a method. The method, if effective, guides people through their knowledge and experience and draws it into the process of evaluation.
- Feed experiences of choosing, implementing and evaluating improvement strategies and projects into summative research.

Summative research

- Reflect on the experiences of organisational learning and transformation as well as formative evaluation. Reflect on each 'stage' of these processes.
- Model two things.
    - Organisational dynamics that result from changes that come about through organisational learning and transformation.
    - Actual processes of choosing, implementing and evaluating strategies and projects for improvement that led to the changes.
- Consider the transferability of each model to other domains of application. Consider in particular where and when they might offer potential models on which action might be based.
- Feed findings into current formative evaluation with the aim of enriching the experience of evaluation.

An oft neglected issue

I have just described a possible process for systemic evaluation in somewhat instrumental terms, that is, rather like a method. The process of organisational learning and transformation covered in the last chapter can also be reduced to a method by instrumental minded practitioners. I must, however, remind the reader of the importance of knowledge and experience as part of the activity. The next chapter takes issue with purely instrumental interpretations of any approach and suggests a need to enrich method with knowledge and experience. (May I remind you that the following appendix (19.1) sets out the logical properties of the scales of measurement introduced in this chapter?)

APPENDIX 19.1: LOGICAL PROPERTIES OF THE SCALES OF MEASUREMENT

The rules or logical properties of the nominal scale are as follows:

- Reflexivity – either A = A or A < > A.
- Symmetry of equivalence – if A = B, then B = A.
- Transitivity – if A = B and B = C, then A = C.

The rules or logical properties of the ordinal scale are as follows:

- Irreflexivity – A is not > or < A.
- Symmetry of equivalence – if A = B, then B = A.
- Asymmetry of order – if A > B, then B is not > A.
- Transitivity – if A > B and B > C, then A > C.

The rules or logical properties of the interval and ratio scales are as follows:

- Symmetry of equivalence – if A = B, then B = A.
- Asymmetry of order – if A > B, then B is not > A.
- Commutation – if A and B are real numbers, then A + B = B + A and A * B = B * A.
- Association – if A, B, and C are real numbers, then (A + B) + C = A + (B + C), and (A * B) * C = A * (B * C).
- Substitution – if A = B and A + C = D, then B + C = D; and if A * C = D, then B * C = D.
- Uniqueness – if A and B are real numbers, then A + B and A * B respectively produce a single real number.

20 Instrumental and experiential action

Instrumental thinking in practice relies on method to establish and achieve purpose. Experiential thinking, on the other hand, encourages people to reflect on their knowledge and experience as a means of shaping future actions. Not surprisingly, comparison between instrumental action and experiential action locates points of controversy. For example, there is disagreement over what precisely is the relevance of instrumental thinking. Some people consider that instrumental thinking is a desirable way of living. Other people prefer that limits be placed on the domain of application of instrumental thinking.

By far the dominant view is that instrumental thinking is relevant to all types of activity, including decision-making, problem solving and strategic planning. This bent insists that methods can just as meaningfully tell us what to do with people's lives as they can with technical operations. The quest apparently is to identify the most potent methods and to popularise them in management practice – hence the rise of gurus in modern times.

Supporters of the counter-view are adamant that instrumental thinking must be restricted to technical activities. For example, instrumental thinking is instructive about how to maximise efficiency in physical industrial processes. Instrumental thinking in the form of quality control is often considered successful when applied in this way. However, the relevance of instrumental thinking is lost in the social domain. Social relationships are about ways of living and working together. There is no method that can be instrumental in directing people's relationships with each other in a wholly meaningful way.

Method can remind people of their experiences and knowledge that they have about life and ways of working together. Method cannot embody experience and knowledge of those things. It cannot somehow contain and transfer over to people, experience and knowledge of life and ways of working and living together. These are things that are internalised by the experience of working and living together, which generates learning and understanding. Valid action sets out to stimulate discourse about people's experiences so that they can think through what is meaningful to them. Unacceptable action is seen in obsessive attempts to translate dialogue into methods for instrumental purposes. Instrumental thinking, so the argument goes, is mixing up ideas about working and living together in a meaningful way, with how to do some particular thing. Instrumental thinking becomes method for method's sake, which is an absurdity.

The argument against instrumental thinking holds wide-ranging implications for contemporary management. Instrumental thinking is considered to lack relevance other than to technical issues. This strongly suggests that the hundreds if not thousands of management books that might be classified under '*n* steps to nirvana' simply misunderstand the nature of social contexts. Gurus and their methods as well as fad surfing practitioners operate in 'fantasy land'. Practitioners seek golden messages from silver-tongued gurus and consultants.

Rehearsed above are two extremes of a debate surrounding instrumental and experiential thinking. A balanced approach however can replace this either/or attitude. A balanced view holds that some parts of people's co-existence can be handled meaningfully through instrumental questions. Following dialogue about different aspects of living and ways of working together, people might find it helpful to draw up or to choose some existing relevant instrumental thinking, like a method, that proposes guidelines offering a possible way to proceed. The challenge is to strike a balance so that ways of working and living together do not became wholly instrumentalised, or conversely left redundant as experiences locked up inside people's minds.

The discussion of this short chapter facilitates thinking about a possible mode of practice. The mode of practice aims to establish ways in which a balance can be struck between instrumental thinking and the experience people have of ways of living and working together. Balance here is the emphatic point. It emphasises the need to balance the richness and mystery of experience with the guided 'mastery' of instrumental action. This message was made known in Chapter 9 and has been alluded to ever since. It is taken forward into the practical animation offered in the next chapter.

Practical animation

21 Local Area Policing (LAP) in York, UK

Introduction

This practical animation offers an account of my involvement in the implementation of local area policing (LAP) in York Division of North Yorkshire Police, UK, in the three-year period 1994 to 1996. LAP is an initiative that switches emphasis from shift-based policing to geographical-based policing. The following account is in fact an extensive chronicle about organisational change that aims to involve you in the storyline. Although the organisational context is policing, it is my experience that the greater part of the illustration typifies organisational issues and dilemmas that I encounter everywhere. Hopefully, the chronicle will resonate with your experiences whilst drawing forth the message of systemic thinking and complexity theory.

The work that I undertook with York Division is most suitably described as ethnographic. I was encouraged by the Management Group to become a participant as observer. In effect, I became a member of York Division. The duration of the LAP project made it inevitable that I would come to know the people and the situation well, indeed, intimately. So, for this practical animation, I find myself writing about the people, including myself.

The challenge that I face in writing about the people is exacting. There are many requirements to be satisfied. To begin with, I wish to produce an account that I find meaningful. It must also resonate with the experiences of my co-workers/co-researchers. However, a key purpose of this practical animation is to animate the concepts and approach introduced in this book. I need to present things in a way that is informative to you, the reader. Furthermore, I must attempt to build into the record below a degree of triangulation and recoverability. I will strive to strike a balance between these at times competing requirements. Others will judge how well this is done.

Also, I have tried to avoid presenting the practical animation as nothing more than a shallow *post hoc* rationalisation about how with intention we moved York Division from shift-based policing in 1994, to an improved LAP in 1996. I would like to think that some worthwhile improvement was achieved for the force and for the community of York. But there was no straightforward route or 'yellow brick road' to follow to a wizard 1996. I present events as they were in so far as one person's account is able to do so, and summarise a comprehensive assessment of which I was one of many evaluators.

The content of this chapter is set out as follows. First, I note an issue regarding recoverability that I became aware of with the LAP project. It suggests what I am able to tell you about events that happened. This is followed by a commentary that submits why LAP became an important issue in York Division. A sequential overview of major events comes next. (Major does not necessarily mean 'had the greatest impact'.) I intend for the overview to create in the reader's mind a sense of timing, scope and depth to the project. An account of the project is then given broadly within the structure of the approach to organisational learning and transformation outlined in the previous section of this book. The practical animation is rounded off with some reflections on my role as researcher.

Note on recoverability

A practical animation is a reflection of the past. Our appreciation of the past, as with the present and the future, is always partial. It might also be temporary, since further experiences and new appreciation influence knowledge of the past. The very act of reminiscing as a process of thought and emotion tends to concentrate recollection on occurrences that made an impression at the time – e.g. the sacred and the profane. Recoverability in social practice, then, is not like traceability in process control where causes of events may be located. Rather, recoverability as I have experienced it in the LAP project amounts to stories from the field, about what people did and why they did it, and what their experiences were like. Recoverability is a tenuous, albeit necessary, part of systemic practice. Recoverability as much as anything else is a form of learning within the unknowable that reflects on the past.

Emergence of an issue in York Division

Policing in the UK aims to operate within a doctrine of policing by consent. This means an unarmed police force working as members of the community, deriving their powers largely from democratic consent. Democratic consent makes the police force sensitive to public confidence and support. Despite or possibly because of these principles, the police force in the UK went through a turbulent period running up to 1994. A number of miscarriages of justice reached national prominence, shaking public confidence and trust in the police force as a whole.

In 1990 the police service conducted a major internal review called Operational Policing Review. It concluded that the service had lost direction.

Police in the main wanted to operate with flashing blue lights and to arrest criminals. A hard edge to policing cut through the community's experience. This was at variance with what the community actually wanted. They wished for police officers to work with the community and generally to be better oriented to local needs. The police force recognised it was 'out of sync' with the public that it served.

At the same time the police force came under increasing scrutiny through Government initiatives. These included the Audit Commission, the Citizen's Charter, and the Police and Magistrates Court Act. The Government of the day was committed to a cut in the level of public expenditure as a proportion of Gross Domestic Product, which reduced resources available to the police force. In the mean time, recorded crime had risen considerably.

So, the situation in 1994 was that the police force operated according to a doctrine of policing by consent, was under pressure through proliferating workload, had its confidence rattled by adverse high profile publicity, and faced growing financial scrutiny by a Government committed to cutting public sector expenditure. Forces like York Division were stretched by a massive increase in the level of service required in the face of growing social upheaval. Developments in policing were desperately needed.

This matter became a key concern in the UK police force and the idea of LAP entered the organisational agenda. The Management Group at York Division through the facilitation of its Commander, then Superintendent Steve Green, began to consider the possibilities offered by LAP. A Steering Committee was formed representing all main stakeholders of York Division (which included 'outsiders'). An outline of the major events that followed in terms of my involvement is presented below.

Major events of the project

The following overview is a sequential account of major events that followed formation of the Steering Committee in York Division. It might help the reader to get a feel for the project as it unfolded. In any case, writing about the people is a kind of a diary and a part of an ethnographic diary might well be a record of certain events and dates. A deeper engagement with the events is offered in subsequent sections.

May 1994

- Superintendent Steve Green contacted me by telephone requesting support with the implementation of LAP in York Division.
- A briefing letter outlining the task was sent to me. I accepted the invitation.

June 1994

- An initial meeting was held with Superintendent Steve Green and Chief Inspector Malcolm Foster at Fulford Road HQ. The content and scope of the task was discussed. I was invited to join the LAP Steering Committee.

July 1994

- A meeting of the LAP Steering Committee was held. I did not attend due to a rib injury.

August 1994

- A meeting was held with Superintendent Steve Green and Chief Inspector Malcolm Foster to update me on events. They expressed concern that the process of implementation was dragging on and needed reviving. A key meeting of the Steering Committee was set up for October after vacation period. The aim was for me to get things going.

October 1994

- A key meeting of the Steering Committee was held. The idea of a pilot scheme for the west area of York was agreed upon. Staffing what we named West LAP became a controversial issue dealt with through a focused dialogical process (discussed later). Further to this, an Implementation Team was set up to facilitate implementation. I was made responsible for the team. My co-researchers/co-workers working full time on the team were PC Helen Smith and Sergeant Roger Smith (PC means Police Constable).
- The next day there was a divisional policy meeting where the pilot scheme was endorsed. I explained the mode of implementation proposed by the Steering Committee for LAP. Quite simply, PCs were to co-create LAP in a process that involved design and implementation. PCs co-created for the area that they nominated to work in (following some agreeable reshuffling to even out resource distribution). I also attended my first Community Liaison Group meeting in the evening.
- Two days later I held a meeting with Sergeants. There was much useful discussion that strengthened the plans for implementation days.
- In the last week of October things moved on apace. The Implementation Team spent two days each with four groups of PCs designated to West LAP. These became known as implementation days. The PCs came up with possible designs for West LAP operations. The designs then went to the LAP Commander (Inspector level) for consolidation and tuning. The LAP Commander's consolidated and tuned prototype was subsequently discussed with PCs. The few alterations that the LAP Commander

recommended were accepted. These largely became necessary because there were co-ordination issues between all four LAPs as well as budgetary issues not fully taken into account in the PCs' plans. On the last day of October West LAP was launched.

November 1994

- The Management Group met with the Implementation Team to consider issues of co-ordination. The tentative date for full implementation in York Division was brought forward from 1 April 1995 to a confirmed date of 6 February 1995.
- The Implementation Team held a briefing with Detective Inspectors from the Criminal Investigation Department.
- The Implementation Team proposed evaluation forms for the implementation, which were endorsed by Superintendent Steve Green. He gave the go-ahead for a full-blown evaluation. West LAP evaluation began. Phil Green from the University of Hull joined the Implementation Team to support evaluation.
- A surgery was held with West LAP PCs. A surgery is an unstructured discussion of events. This led to revamped shift arrangements.

December 1994

- A surgery was held with West LAP PCs, Sergeants and the LAP Commander. Evaluation questionnaires were circulated to all members of York Division.
- North LAP implementation days.

January 1995

- East LAP implementation days.
- CID implementation day (one day).
- City/Core implementation days.
- The Implementation Team reviewed LAP implementation.

February 1995

- The Implementation Team prepared an executive summary of LAP implementation. This was presented for information and feedback to the Management Group.
- Senior Management implementation day.
- Implementation of LAP in North, East and City/Core areas.
- The Implementation Team met with the Management Group and representatives of Corporate Development Unit from Regional HQ, who

wished to explore some concerns about certain aspects of implementation (mentioned later).

March 1995

- Second round of evaluation questionnaires circulated to all operational members of York Division.

April 1995

- Implementation of LAP across North Yorkshire Police, of which York is one division. The York Division Implementation Team offered some guidance.

June 1995

- Third round of evaluation questionnaires circulated to all operational members of York Division.

August 1995

- Surgeries held with all four LAP areas in York Division.

September 1995

- Surgeries held with all four LAP areas in York Division.
- Annual strategic review with all senior officers of York Division. Presentation by the Implementation Team as evaluators. Revisions to the LAP project were formulated following discussion and further interpretation of the results of evaluation. The Implementation Team had finished its work and was disbanded. Phil Green with myself continued evaluation.

December 1995

- Fourth round of questionnaires circulated to all members of York Division.

June 1996

- Fifth round of questionnaires circulated to all operational members of York Division.

September 1996

- Annual strategic review with all senior officers. Presentation by Phil Green and myself as evaluators. Further ideas for improvement were agreed upon and the next stages of development in York Division were discussed, i.e. 'beyond LAP'. Issues that began to dominate included effectiveness of communications between Area Divisions, like York, with Regional HQ.

The above presentation gives a calendar account of major events. This provides a working background for the rest of the animation. The next section captures organisational changes that came about broadly in terms of the learning and transformation framework introduced in Chapter 18.

Initial reflections on the project

The main aim of this section is to picture the LAP project in terms of Figure 18.8, a diagrammatic view of the process of learning a way into the future. The diagram can be usefully laid over the calendar of events retold above. This produces an annotated picture of organisational learning and transformation that is shown in Figure 21.1. The following discussion expands on the annotations.

Annotation A

As stated, by May 1994 Superintendent Steve Green and the Management Group at York Division had thought very seriously about what they might be faced with in the light of proliferating workload, adverse high profile publicity, and growing financial scrutiny. In addition to this, they reckoned that the shift arrangement encouraged reactive and piecemeal policing. Ownership is therefore difficult to facilitate, grassroots or community policing is not possible, and less competent officers are covered by the next shift. Furthermore, anonymity with the public was inevitable.

Annotation B

A theme began to emerge about what the Management Group would ideally like to achieve. This comprised a version of LAP that met LAP principles. LAP surfaced from both Government directives and messages from the community, but reflected an increasing desire amongst senior police officers to move towards a community-based approach to policing. LAP in very broad terms was chosen as policy for York Division, but the question of implementation was yet to be resolved. In May 1994 I was asked to participate in thinking this one through and maybe to become actively involved.

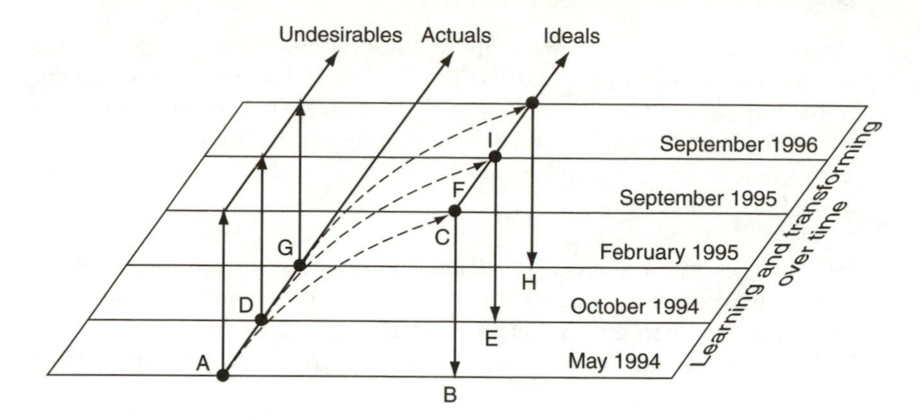

A Undesirable consequences of shift-based policing
B Ideal style of policing based on LAP principles
C LAP implementation process – Management Team and Steering Committee
D Shift-based policing not tenable
E PCs' designs for West LAP
F Pilot launched for West LAP
G LAP considered to be improvement on shift-based policing
H PCs' designs for City/Core LAP, East LAP, North LAP
I Implementation of LAP throughout York Division

Figure 21.1 Learning a way into the future with LAP

Annotation C

I explained to the Management Group the way I would wish to proceed. It was crucial to realise that LAP was not an end point in itself. As I saw things, LAP was no more than an agenda of issues and dilemmas to be introduced to the workforce now, with the aim of facilitating learning all round about what actions might be taken. This meant explaining the Management Group's thinking to everyone involved. For example, what did they think might be happening to policing today and where did they reckon policing ought to go? What did it mean to employ principles of LAP? Through these and other questions, a dialogue would be facilitated in which people would participate, contextualise, contribute, challenge, generate, learn, and even be transformed. This meant that senior management had to create space in which the workforce could enjoy every opportunity to learn a way into the future. We are talking here of a vision of leadership coming from complexity theory that Ralph Stacey introduced in his book *Strategic Management and Organisational Dynamics*.

So, in May 1994 we were at the start of the LAP initiative as seen on Figure 21.1. The project to achieve LAP began with the formation of a representative Steering Committee. As the project proceeded its details began to be worked out. Through a process of accommodation seeking between its members, the committee proposed a geographical arrangement with four LAP areas.

Annotation D

The Steering Committee consolidated learning about shift-based policing and its limited role in the community. This was a more detailed account of the Management Group's view given in Annotation A.

Annotation E

An Implementation Team was formed. The Implementation Team took the ideas of LAP to the PCs in each of the four LAP areas and asked them to enter into dialogue about the current situation and the possibilities for LAP in the circumstances. Formal sessions were arranged through implementation days. The PCs were encouraged to employ boundary judgements, look through the four windows, and be creative in a process of prismatic thought, although these precise terms were not employed. PCs were asked to think about who is the current client and who ought to be client. LAP was introduced as one view of who ought to be client, i.e. the community. The content of the dialogues is discussed in the next section. PCs went on to design operational policing in terms of LAP, in the four designated areas. The result was four LAPs each with an approach to policing contextualised to local needs. The only constraints placed over the PCs as designers were budgetary and the need for co-ordination between LAP areas (e.g. co-ordination of LAPs for special events like football matches and visits by royalty).

Annotation F

The West LAP pilot was launched in October 1994.

Annotation G

Evaluation began in December 1994.

Annotation H

PCs in City/Core LAP, East LAP and North LAP, designed operational policing for their LAP areas at implementation days, led as ever by the Implementation Team.

Annotation I

LAP was implemented across the rest of York in February 1995.

No further annotations are given on Figure 21.1, except to note the September 1995 and September 1996 reviews that are discussed below.

A review of LAP implementation by senior management was held in September 1995. The review was largely based on information generated by the evaluation. The project was endorsed in the main, although some concerns were raised. In particular, as evidenced by the evaluation and further interpretation of its findings by dialogue at the review meeting, one of the LAP areas was regressing significantly from LAP ideals. (Evaluation is discussed at length a little later.) In particular, PCs in one LAP area felt that the culture of empowerment that was part of their shared vision was not happening. It was discovered that two Sergeants had chosen to disregard the PCs' design and managed things as they chose to. Gentle but effective action was taken to remedy the situation. Evaluation made a real contribution to learning about the complex change process under way by yielding possible insights into people's as well as organisational behaviour. The LAP project was reformulated and another phase of implementation began. Evaluation continued.

A further review was undertaken in September 1996. Many aspects of LAP operations had been established at this point in one way or another. However, LAP in action had moved on considerably from the Management Group's first visualisation of it in 1994. No one could have predicted the diversity in outcomes that we witnessed. And now it was time to move on. A new agenda of issues began to surface. Discussion at the review increasingly swayed towards what were perceived to be new challenges such as internal communication between Divisions of North Yorkshire Police and Regional HQ. The LAP project had facilitated a period of learning into the future, but now I observed that LAP as an agenda for debate was increasingly taking a back role. A new era of learning was beginning to emerge. I remember observing this process of issue surfacing and coalition formation with fascination. There it was, complexity theory apparently happening before my very eyes. If only I had more than mere words by which to convey to you my thoughts and emotions at that stage.

Many other occurrences of spontaneous self-organisation mark the complex journey from 1994 to 1996. Many issues and dilemmas surfaced with coalitions building around them. Some fizzled out whilst others were successfully lodged on the LAP agenda. These resulted from people's involvement and experiences, not as an intended result of my facilitation or Steve Green's aspirations. In the next section, I discuss some of the details that lie behind management's involvement in LAP implementation, 1994–1996.

Management Group's deliberations

So, the project began in 1994 with the Management Group at York Division organising themselves around issues pertaining to LAP. They considered in some detail the client served by shift-based policing, and what might happen if shift-based policing was allowed to prevail. Put bluntly, shift-based policing evolved in such a way as to make police officers the client. The purpose was to perpetuate a family structure and for the family to become self-sufficient. It was an inward looking mode of thinking about the organisation and its running. In von Bertalanffy's terms, shift-based policing came close to being a closed system for a while. Shift-based policing operated routines without adequate regard to the changing economic and social context in which policing as such was immersed.

Looking through all four windows at the Management Group's deeper appreciation reveals important insights about shift-based policing. Operational processes and organisational structure were arranged around four groups who in an 8-hour shift policed the whole of York. One shift took responsibility for one 8-hour slot. Three shifts therefore covered each 24-hour period. Having four shifts made space for each shift to take time off. Each eight-hour shift operated according to set procedures managed through a control room. The control room received calls from the public, prioritised them, and requested police officers on duty to attend the incidents. Co-ordination and communication between shifts was minimal. Chief Inspector Malcolm Foster reckoned that this shift system amounted to part-time policing. Inevitably, policing was highly reactive, with each shift largely handling incidents in isolation from other shifts.

The divisional culture, or meaning systems, evolved largely because of the structural arrangements. Each shift became like a family with a unique family way. Members supported each other, welcomed new members, said farewell to departing members, and occasionally experienced the death of a colleague on duty and mourned for them. Many of the officers socialised together. Policing operated as much through family-style relations between officers as it did by formal procedures. However, the relationship with the Management Group could not have been in starker contrast. The management structure created an organisation like a paramilitary bureaucracy. The ruling ideas were forever the ideas of the most senior management. So, a degree of dependency but also suspicion existed between operational staff and senior management. At the same time, civilian staff felt like second class citizens. (These windows of thought are summarised in Figure 21.2.)

The Management Group did not formally undertake prismatic thought, but they intuitively came up with many stories that helped learning about what might happen. These included stories with the following themes.

- Stern Government action if the police force did not begin to respond to economic and social change.
- Public dissent targeting the police force with high profile media coverage.
- A police force dashing about in manic reactive style with decreasing effectiveness.
- Rapidly rising stress and sickness levels amongst operational officers.
- In time, organisational crisis and collapse.

Efficiency and reliability	Effectiveness
Procedures are operated through the control room leading to piecemeal and reactive day-to-day policing	A shift structure leading to fragmentation between shifts; poor communication and control with little adaptation or learning
Meaningfulness	**Fairness**
Shifts like families each with its subculture – tension between operations and management – civilian staff feel alienated – anonymity with the community	The ruling ideas are forever the ideas of management at the very top

Figure 21.2 Management Group's four windows view of shift-based policing

The Management Group explored possible ideals for an improved future, concerned as they were with imaginable undesirable scenarios for York Division. Superintendent Steve Green was strongly in favour of empowerment and proactive policing. The LAP initiative with its source in Government provided a vehicle by which that might happen.

It is essential to realise that LAP was not just another initiative about policing. It raised in the mind of many officers the issue of the boundaries of policing. This is a hoary old dilemma that has attracted much coverage in newspapers, broadcasts on contemporary affairs and the agendas of politicians. The kind of questions raised in these early stages were formalised and introduced later into the PCs' planning exercises, so that every person involved at all levels in the division had had to deliberate on the boundaries of policing. Questions raised by the Management Group included the following:

- How should the division relate to its stakeholders and the communities in which it operates?
- How should information on stakeholders' perceptions of the division be obtained and made use of?
- How should the organisation relate to environmental, consumer and other specialist groups?

There was enough outcome from dialogue around these probing questions to fill up the pages of a specialist report in the area. The dialogue was diverging rather than converging. A few of the issues that surfaced are listed below for interest.

- Is policing about catching offenders or helping them to find a non-offending role in society?
- Is policing simply about employing allocated resources in the most efficient way to catch people who have offended?
- What can police officers or indeed the force itself do to unshackle offenders from conditions that lead to offences?
- What are the social roots of crime and what role should the police play in tackling these roots?
- What are the wider debates in society that policing rubs shoulders with and how do/should police officers participate in the debates?

There was widespread opinion that policing did need to re-examine its boundaries. Traditionally, force members had assumed that policing is simply about employing allocated resources in a most efficient way to catch people who have offended. The emerging climate of community and pro-active policing, however, put that purpose into question. Most officers recognised that effective policing required the force to get more involved in wider social debates. However, there was a resignation felt by many officers that the great squeeze on resources made it difficult to achieve even the essentials such as upholding the law. Wider involvement would be physically impossible. This is a realistic but sad conclusion since it suggests that the thrust of LAP might be undermined right from the outset. Any achievement that LAP can claim in terms of greater involvement with the community will be despite inadequate resourcing of the police. And there would be only limited involvement in wider social issues.

In the context of this debate about boundary judgements, the Management Group formed the following view of how things ought to be. In terms of structure and processes, York Division could be policed on a geographical basis. Four local areas were identified, each one with some degree of distinctiveness to it. For example, one LAP was City/Core where most tourist-related robberies and late-night brawls occurred. Instead of being a member of a shift, staff would support a region, like City/Core. They and their colleagues would be responsible for a designated region 24 hours a day. They would be encouraged to develop policies and procedures most appropriate to local needs, and here I do mean geographical needs. This would be coupled with a transformation in knowledge-power relations, breaking down entrenched patterns of management behaviour. A new system of meaning would shape organisational rules and practices, one that would lead to open management, devolution of authority, local management of

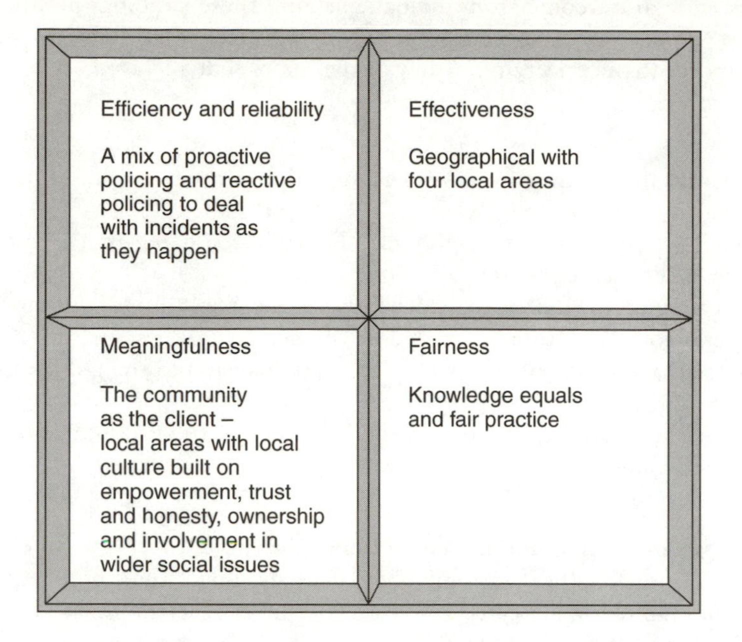

Figure 21.3 Management Group's four windows view of LAP

resources and so on. (These windows of thought are summarised in Figure 21.3.)

Again, formal prismatic thought was not undertaken although stories were told about LAP ideals and consequences of implementing them. The themes of some stories coming from the Management Group are given below.

- In the ideal world LAP would offer the community a policing style they felt comfortable with, creating an enhanced sense of security.
- Community policing would improve intelligence gathering and traditional measures such as arrests per constable.
- Ownership over an area would lead to a greater commitment of staff and pride in their work.
- LAP, however, needed the availability of more resources and would struggle without them.
- PCs and Sergeants may not respond positively to LAP. There is a deep suspicion separating management from the operational staff. There may be a need for internal marketing, or 'selling' to use Senge's terminology. (This I was to replace with 'co-creating' as recommended by Senge.)
- Shift families may feel they are being torn apart. The experience could be most traumatic. A representative Steering Committee might help to raise these concerns and consider ways of alleviating them.

The Management Group set up a representative Steering Committee to consider the possibilities for LAP and to prepare a way for implementation. The Steering Committee was soon in action. As stated, I joined this committee, but made clear that I saw my role as facilitating co-creation, not selling. To be honest, I was terrified of the role I had accepted and was not at all sure what contribution if any I could make. A breakthrough for me occurred some time into deliberations when 'I survived the risk' of suggesting and facilitating a dialogical process to handle a most contentious issue between members of the Steering Committee. The issue was about resource allocation. The committee organised into two polarised viewpoints creating a certain amount of conflict. The decision to be made was in effect the last step before the start of implementation. May I take a sidetrack for a while and tell you more about how we handled the polarised views?

Steering Committee engages in team learning

One of the most important resolutions made by the Steering Committee was to launch LAP with a pilot on 30 October 1994 in the west – one of four designated areas. This decision was made on 12 October 1994. Preceding this were many debates with arguments for a pilot scheme set against arguments for all four areas to be launched at the same time. The Steering Committee polarised into these two distinct camps. The majority of people were in favour of the pilot, including myself, yet two members, including a nominated LAP Commander, raised genuine concern about a pilot. The decision, however, began to swing towards the majority, partly because of the pressure of a majority and partly because the majority included the most senior officer present. No obvious or sinister use of power was evident, but the mental models institutionalised in the police force and still at work moved the decision towards the most senior officer. The following paragraph recounts a typical debate of the Steering Committee about the pilot.

All members of the Steering Committee agreed that the main aim of the pilot was to run a trial and then relay knowledge of the experience of LAP to the other three areas. However, the minority group argued, this would hardly be effective for York Division as a whole, unless police officers with experience in the LAP trial were re-deployed into the remaining three LAPs at the time they went live. Redeployment would allow for the fullest dissemination of knowledge and experience. The trouble with redeployment, the Commander of West LAP counter-argued, is that the good work done in establishing West LAP would be undone by fragmentation of the team at the conclusion of the pilot period. The retort of the minority group was that West LAP with all its experience would become York Division's jewel in the crown. The other three LAPs would forever be playing catch up. A degree of competitiveness and animosity crept into the debate.

I intervened and suggested that our discussion was not penetrating the real issues and dilemmas. For example, several matters raised by the minority group had not been adequately dealt with. All present agreed that some matters were being swept under the carpet and so consented to extend the meeting with a team learning exercise that I recommended. The process we adopted for testing the polarised viewpoints was strategic assumption surfacing and testing (SAST) that is introduced in Chapter 15. In fact, we put aside and extended our lunch hour to do this. I set up the rooms whilst several officers purchased sandwiches and drinks.

One strategy was to launch a pilot with no subsequent redeployment. The other strategy was to launch the pilot followed by total redeployment. The two groups formed in line with the strategy officers supported. Each group occupied a separate room in the first instance and followed standard SAST procedures. Missions were set, stakeholders named, assumptions about the strategy were surfaced and discussed. The groups then came together to engage in a constructive adversarial debate. A negotiated arrangement was agreed upon after a heated exchange. The decision was to go ahead with the pilot, but to manage carefully resources to benefit implementation of LAP in all four areas.

The group who stood for total redeployment was successful in arguing its point that all four LAP areas should benefit with experienced officers from the pilot. Subsequently, there was negotiation on the exact numbers of PCs and Sergeants to be redeployed. Each of the four LAP areas would be assigned a quarter of the officers from the West LAP pilot. The Commander of West LAP, as well as the minority group originally against the pilot as first conceived, and indeed everyone else present, were satisfied with the arrangements made. Although no one had achieved their ideal, each officer had learnt about the needs of each other officer and was prepared to accommodate for them in the final decision.

Perhaps the greatest value of this exercise was the in-depth understanding generated for all involved about LAP in York Division. Although as a Steering Committee we had discussed LAP extensively, our level of understanding paled to insignificance against that now attained through what amounted to generative learning as Senge calls it. Having to work out and defend a position on LAP (indeed any position) against the strongest attack that could be mounted from another group, substantially enhanced each participant's understanding of LAP as a policing strategy. This experience underlined for me the value of SAST as a tool with high potential for testing strategies and for generating learning about issues faced.

PCs develop shared vision

LAP implementation moved on. The Implementation Team held what were called implementation days with PCs. As stated, implementation began with a pilot called West LAP. Implementation was undertaken from the bottom up. Members of the LAP pilot were split up into four groups for manageability. Each group was tasked with designing the operation of West LAP.

Before this, however, I explained to all participants my role as facilitator. I was no expert in the sense made clear by the Zen Master to the young Confucian in Chapter 9. Rather, I was a guide with some expertise and experience in organisational change. I was there to facilitate and support. I ran through the Management Group's and the Steering Committee's thinking as covered above. The purpose of the preamble was simply to explain the ideas of LAP and why they had become important and lodged on the organisational agenda. In particular, I outlined the way the Management Group thought things were going and why LAP might be preferable. I introduced learning with scenarios recorded in Chapter 18 that I intended to work with as a means towards their learning and design work. In Senge's terms, I launched into a period of co-creating.

To begin with there was considerable resistance. One PC walked out after two minutes. Others were dubious about 'the promise' that the Management Group would endorse their work. Surely, all the Management Group would do is set up a committee to reject the proposals? I tried to convince PCs otherwise, but made a mental note that as soon as the PCs generated a substantial idea that they really valued, I would take this straight away to the Management Group for a stamp of approval. If the Management Group resisted the idea, then the LAP project essentially would be over for me. You will have guessed that I did not expect to see that kind of response from the Management Group.

The moment arose sooner than expected. The PCs felt strongly about an issue of co-ordination between LAPs that could at short notice deplete a LAP's resources. Decision-making on this matter would be 'outside their control'. The PCs wanted to suggest a procedure that provided each LAP with some resource protection. My tactic was to build a supportive coalition around the issue of 'confidence in the Management Group'. So, I organised a meeting that afternoon with the Management Group. The Management Group was relieved when I explained to them the purpose of the meeting, fearing I brought them bad news about implementation. An endorsement was readily given. The PCs' confidence grew, as did my credibility. Subsequently, the PCs in the main worked enthusiastically. At least, the voice of the dissenters was quietened. PCs more or less accepted after healthy debate the Management Group's scenario of what might happen. So, quickly they turned attention to conceiving a preferred future in terms of LAP principles rather than complaining about the future they might be heading towards.

PCs raised issues and dilemmas by looking through all four windows. They discussed shift arrangements, efficiency of intelligence feed-ins (LIOs), reliability of back-up teams, and effectiveness of structure coming up with a geographical arrangement within West LAP itself. They sought involvement in resource planning. They expressed a desire to increase the level of consultation between ranks, and for Sergeants as well as the LAP Commander to be more accountable to them in decision-making. The PCs spoke openly about the need for trust and honesty, vital in a profession where a PC's safety at any time may be threatened. And they recognised that crucial to the success of LAP was the ability to serve the community. More time was needed with the public. More information could be gathered in this way. The public should also experience a greater presence by the police force. An enhanced sense of security amongst the community of York might then prevail.

Each of the four groups of PCs generated ideas of this sort. Their designs were put forward to the Commander of West LAP. He was tasked with synthesising them and accordingly he proposed a prototype for further consideration. It was presented to the PCs and Sergeants of West LAP, discussed, amended and agreed for now. The acid test would be in the implementation of their ideas. Implementation started in October 1994. A similar process was followed for the remaining three LAPs and there are many stories that I could tell you if I had dared to extend this practical animation even further. In any case, the emphasis then shifted from choosing and implementing improvement strategies, to evaluating and maximising the impact of them.

Evaluation of LAP implementation

The Implementation Team began project evaluation in November 1994. Phil Green from the University of Hull joined the team providing an additional resource for design of measurement instruments and data construction. The following account draws extensively upon reports that we produced separately and in partnership. Norma Romm provided valuable feedback in the design of questionnaires.

Formative evaluation

Formative evaluation facilitated learning about LAP implementation. What improvement meant was determined on implementation days. In broad terms it meant responding to the community's needs. Improvement was specified for each of the four windows. The Implementation Team developed a system of measurement that got to grips with the PCs' notion of improvement.

Statistics for measures of efficiency of processes and effectiveness of structure were routinely recorded and readily available. They amounted to traditional quantitative policing measures widely used across constabularies. Measures of meaningfulness and fairness required further consideration. A suite of qualitative surveys was considered to be most appropriate. That is, we were concerned that data construction employing just one survey, or one type of survey, might give an unnecessarily distorted picture. A suite of surveys including kinds of questionnaire and interview would allow us to triangulate insights generated from several forms of study.

A questionnaire was designed for distribution to operational staff of York Division. We will look at it in some detail a little later. Each question was considered an indicator of change. The questionnaires were distributed on a regular basis to provide an indication of improvement (or not) over time. Our interpretation of the results of questionnaires was discussed with operational staff in surgeries. Surgeries were unstructured interviews, sometimes held on a group basis and at other times on a one-to-one basis. The aim here was to evaluate our interpretation of questionnaire results with operational staff, or to seek guidance about how to interpret certain indicators that we could not make sense of. Furthermore, ideas were generated at surgeries that could be fed back into the process of LAP implementation and operation.

The results of traditional measures, questionnaires and surgeries, were also fed into the annual strategic review in 1995 and again in 1996. Phil Green and I presented the findings to operational managers (Inspectors and above) who raised questions, suggested possible alternative interpretations and, in this way, came up with ideas about enhancing the impact of LAP. These ideas too were fed back to the LAP areas for consideration and possible action.

At the outset of the first evaluation in December 1994 only West LAP had changed from shift-based policing to LAP. We therefore categorised police staff into three segments – LAP police, divisional police, and civilian staff. A questionnaire was then designed for LAP police. It was modified for the other two segments. The December 1994 administration of the questionnaire also played the role of questionnaire piloting.

The questionnaire contained eighteen questions examining key principles of LAP. The questions might be considered critical success factors. Some questions focused on aspects of systems of meaning, including attitude and perception. Other questions probed systems of knowledge-power, in particular, changes to the management control in terms of fairness and people being knowledge equals. Space was provided for respondents to offer supplementary comments, or to elaborate on any specific answer. A Likert scale was used for each question. The structured approach aimed to provide a gauge of change, for each LAP area and by comparison between LAP areas. A copy of the questionnaire is given in Appendix 21.1 (at the end of this chapter).

As you can see, the questionnaire allowed for anonymity. The basic information sought was date, LAP area, and rank of the respondent. It was hoped that anonymity would encourage a full and honest airing of feelings and opinions with no stifling of viewpoints. All aspects of anonymity were considered. For example, asking about the number of years of service would have identified some of the respondents immediately and was therefore omitted.

One of the main aims of LAP is to enable greater contact between police and the community. Each police officer is supposed to get to know the locals and vice versa. So, the first two questions on the questionnaire examined the perceived usefulness of information from the public and from Divisional HQ concerning crime.

The next five questions address issues of empowerment and interaction between staff at different levels. They question the approachability and responsiveness of staff senior to the respondent. They investigate the level of opportunity staff have to negotiate issues and dilemmas with colleagues, senior staff and civilian staff. These questions were built around a sociological understanding of the term empowerment. Empowerment means the chances people have to enter into negotiation with other people. It does not mean local decision-making without wider consultation. That would mean the views of other people are not taken into account, and thus other people become disempowered. The fifth, sixth and seventh questions therefore explore people's opportunity to negotiate issues and dilemmas.

The next three questions elicited viewpoints of respondents about efficiency and effectiveness. This could then be compared to quantitative data available from traditional measures. The questions ask about effectiveness of policing, efficiency of resource use, and efficiency of use of the respondent's time.

Question 11 asks for an honest response of the respondent's view on their own receptivity to new ideas. More participation and dialogue at work resulting from implementation of LAP should according to its principles encourage a greater degree of receptivity. Question 12 asks about the level of enjoyment of work. Follow up questions could be raised to explore further this indicator. If enjoyment improved, then could this be a result of LAP? If enjoyment did not improve, then were there extraneous circumstances that accounted for lack in improvement? Question 13 asks about the fragmented nature of policing. LAP in principle gets rid of fragmentation resulting from shift-based policing. Question 13 therefore seeks to establish whether operational staff experience work more as a whole activity.

Questions 14 and 15 focus on responsibility. They ask how much responsibility the respondent has and whether it feels good or not. Question 16 asks the respondent about the level of stress they experience at work.

Question 17 asks in summary whether the respondent thinks that LAP is the most efficient and effective form of policing. That is, having experienced both shift-based and geographical-based policing, and taking into account any other style the respondent may know about, how does LAP fare?

The final question asks whether moral considerations enter into the respondent's way of work. This question aims to explore the officer's response to injustice. Would they act if they witnessed an injustice? The question in a sense indicates what police officers thought were the moral considerations of policing. At the end of the questionnaire, space is provided for general comments and suggestions for improvement of the questionnaire. A modified version of this questionnaire was administered to operational staff who still worked on a shift basis and to civilian staff.

The original aim was to distribute the questionnaire to all staff at all levels. In the event the questionnaire for police officers was distributed only to PCs and Sergeants in the December 1994 and March 1995 surveys. Subsequently the questionnaires were distributed to all levels. They were modified for the March 1995 evaluation with the removal of Questions 13 and 18 that were not properly understood by respondents. A new Question 13 was added to keep the numbering system in order and to raise an important issue about reactive versus proactive policing not included in the first questionnaire. For the March 1995 survey two unstructured questions were added. One inquired, what tasks were performed that the respondent felt were a waste of time? The other asked, what was the single biggest complaint the respondent had about their job? In June 1995 we added Question 20, asking the respondent whether they felt they gave other people the opportunity to participate with them.

The Implementation Team also designed a questionnaire for completion by each LAP Commander. It is reproduced as Appendix 21.2. It was in effect an information sheet that recorded quantifiable crime statistics for the preceding three months. This allowed for comparison to be made in trends of traditional policing measures.

The questionnaires generated a response rate of between 31 per cent to 41 per cent from police staff. This consistent and quite satisfactory response rate gave a reasonable level of confidence in drawing inferences from data construction. A mixed 10 per cent to 50 per cent response rate from civilians was less than satisfactory. There were only a small number of civilians, which made a wider range in response rate more likely. Results are summarised in a series of tables collected together in Appendix 21.3. The following discussion of the tables takes into account comments on the results made at surgeries and by senior management. The discussion only picks up on some points of interest for illustrative purposes.

The overall results for police respondents in the December 1994, March 1995 and June 1995 questionnaire surveys are recorded in Table 21.1. Remember, in December 1994 only West LAP was operational. All remaining officers were working shift-based policing. There appears to be a change in perception between December 1994 and March 1995 as follows.

- Increase in usefulness of both public and Divisional HQ information (Questions 1 and 2).
- Increase in approachability of immediate senior staff (Question 3).
- Decrease in responsiveness of senior staff to concerns of their subordinates (Question 4).
- Decrease in opportunities to negotiate issues with people of own rank, senior staff and civilian staff (Questions 5, 6 and 7 respectively).
- Virtually no change in perception of efficiency and effectiveness (Questions 8 and 9).
- Significant increase in efficiency of time utilisation (Question 10).
- Individuals felt more receptive to new ideas (Question 11).

- Virtually no change in work enjoyment levels (Question 12).
- Individuals felt that they had more responsibility (Question 14).
- Individuals enjoyed the feel of increased responsibility (Question 15).
- Stress levels decreased marginally (Question 16).
- Overall there was an increase in perception that LAP represented a more efficient and effective way of policing (Question 17).

The greater number of indicators suggested change in line with LAP principles. Notably, however, Questions 4 and 5 indicated a conspicuous decline. These are concerned with responsiveness and approachability of senior staff. They are crucial indicators of changes regarding empowerment and raised some genuine concern. Results from the June 1995 survey were eagerly awaited. The following changes in perception in June 1995 were received with guarded pleasure.

- Increase in approachability of immediate senior staff (Question 3).
- Increase in responsiveness of senior staff to concerns of their subordinates (Question 4).
- Increase in opportunities to negotiate issues with people of own rank, senior staff and civilian staff (Questions 5, 6 and 7 respectively).
- Increase in perception of effectiveness of policing (Questions 8).
- Further increase in perceived efficiency of time utilisation (Question 10).
- Small decrease in work enjoyment levels (Question 12).
- Individuals felt that they had even more responsibility (Question 14).
- Individuals enjoyed a bit more the feel of increased responsibility (Question 15).
- Stress levels decreased further (Question 16).
- Overall there was another albeit small increase in perception that LAP represented a more efficient and effective way of policing (Question 17).

In June 1995 there was an even stronger indication that changes were occurring in line with LAP principles. The only notable exception was enjoyment levels. Despite the decline, enjoyment levels, it should be noted, were significantly on the positive side. Also of encouragement was the result of the substituted Question 13 that indicated a perceived shift towards proactive rather than reactive policing as an efficient approach. The trend continued with December 1995 and June 1996 surveys (not shown in the tables in Appendix 21.3 since permission was not confirmed).

These inferences are drawn from data construction covering all police staff in each of the first three surveys (and beyond). The results may also be examined in relation to separate LAPs. Results of this type are given in Table 21.2. It is even clearer if you look at Table 21.2 that changes in West LAP were strongly positive towards LAP principles, at least for 12 out of 14 of the indicators. Taken as critical success factors the results were extremely promising with regard to PCs achieving their shared vision. For City/Core

LAP the results showed eight positive indicators out of the 14. However, for East LAP and North LAP the results showed only six positive indicators. The overall results discussed above hide these local differences. There was a need to investigate further City/Core LAP and, in particular, East LAP and North LAP.

The negative scores for Question 4 that asked about responsiveness of senior staff for East LAP and North LAP raised concern. Comments made at surgeries underlined the worry. Staff voiced a view that better leadership and supervision was needed. Subsequent investigation for one of these LAPs located the difficulty with two Sergeants who had chosen to flout LAP principles. They set and pursued their own agenda. The matter was dealt with sensitively, significantly alleviating the block they had created on progress towards LAP principles.

Negative scores for Question 17 indicated officers of East LAP and North LAP were not convinced by LAP as an approach to policing. Dealing with factors impacting on responsiveness encouraged a more positive answer as implementation progressed. Other possible influential factors were debated at surgeries and at annual review. These included pressing issues like a lack of resources necessary for officers to do their job adequately, which I mentioned earlier. LAP accentuated this difficulty since the policing style drew more heavily on basic resource utilisation. It was always my belief that under-resourcing significantly hindered LAP implementation. In any case, action was taken to enhance the impact of LAP in these areas. December 1995 and June 1996 surveys indicated significant improvements overall for East LAP and North LAP in line with LAP principles.

Evaluation involved interpretation of the mode and median as well as the mean. Table 21.3 is a record of mode and median results. Examination of Question 17 is of particular interest. Remember, this question asks about LAP in terms of efficiency and effectiveness. In December 1994, 15 of the 54 respondents rated LAP as negatively as possible making the mode '1' on the questionnaire. In March 1995, 11 out of 51 respondents rated LAP in this way keeping the mode at '1'. However, the mode became '4' in the June 1995 survey with 17 out of 66 respondents opting for it, whilst 11 respondents chose '1'. There was a hard core coalition of 11 or so officers with an entrenched antipathy towards LAP that persisted over time. The remaining officers evidently were swinging in favour of LAP, which began to legitimise LAP as an organisational policy. Note here that LAP as organisational policy did not occur as an end point in senior management's offices, but as a result of the means of organisational learning and transformation. It took some considerable amount of time to come about, and assumed its own look as the PCs shaped it and as results of evaluation were fed back into the process of change.

Quantitative statistics are summarised in Table 21.4. These were drawn from the Inspector's question sheet reproduced in Appendix 21.2. The first thing to note is the seasonal fluctuation in each of the measures. Even with results from December 1995 and June 1996 it was difficult to ascertain a clear picture of changes. The most notable improvement, however, was the rise in number of arrests per officer. This is clearly a measure of efficiency if we take crime clear up rate as one core objective of LAP. The measure climbs from 10.78 to 11.74 as 1995 progressed. This trend continued into 1996 rising to over 12 arrests per officer across York Division as a whole. The traditional measure triangulates positively with results of the questionnaire, which indicated that PCs experienced LAP as an efficient mode of policing.

In summary, the surveys signalled a considerable shift in officers' perceptions in favour of the majority of critical success factors as proposed by LAP principles. However, movement towards LAP principles was very strong in West LAP but much less so in particular in East LAP and North LAP. Evaluation brought this matter to light. It provided a focus for debate and informed action. Changes were made that enhanced the impact of LAP principles in all four LAP areas. Evaluation facilitated learning and transformation in this way. Resource limitations prevented us from undertaking direct survey work with the public. We were able to gather some feedback through the Community Liaison Group, by talking to PCs on the beat, and by keeping an eye on the results of Questions 1 and 2 from the questionnaire. The indications were satisfactory in so far as we could tell with these bounded insights. We will now move on to consider summative evaluation.

Summative evaluation

As said, implementation days were held with PCs from four LAP areas. The members of each LAP were split into four groups for the implementation days, easing manageability. Sixteen groups in all participated in the design process. Each LAP area came up with ideas unique to it and to its context. There were, however, a number of common themes that surfaced during the implementation days that we summarised for future reference. These were updated and enhanced through surgeries. The summary that resulted, which is reproduced below, amounts to a rationalisation of LAP generated by the PCs and to a lesser extent the Sergeants. It is a model that might be transferred for consideration to other divisions and other constabularies. It is indeed an example of summative evaluation.

- LAP demands a culture of trust, honesty, mutual commitment and flexibility.
- There are a number of desirable properties that LAP must achieve – ownership, devolution of authority, responsibility and accountability.
- There is a strong need for teamwork and co-operation. This refers to co-ordination within and between LAP areas.
- There must be flexible and adaptable shifts. It is important to balance operational needs with domestic/social needs of officers.
- Structuring within any LAP must remain flexible.

- An emphasis must be placed on updating the LAP team on developments, involving them in budgeting, and providing them with opportunities for consultation and feedback on their ideas.
- Foot patrol and use of bicycles are essential ways of attaining a high profile and access to the community.
- There needs to be formal access to the community that encourages greater involvement both ways, between the police and the community. Many ideas were proposed such as direct involvement of officers in community centres, friends associations, parish councils and schools.
- There is a good argument for full time and/or part time administrative support in each LAP area in the form of an office person.
- LAP teams must be given the basic resources necessary to do their job properly. Much is expected of LAP team members and so the teams justifiably expect basic equipment to be provided.
- Availability and establishment of adequate buildings is central to LAP team effectiveness.

Having presented an account of both formative and summative evaluation of the LAP project, I now wish to comment on my role as researcher.

My role as researcher

In this section I wish briefly to reflect on the way I perceived and handled my role as researcher or participant as observer. From the reading so far, you will have sensed that I purposely took an active role in LAP implementation. I did not present myself as an expert consultant, but neither did I pretend that I could enter into a neutral facilitation role. Two vignettes are presented below that are frank about how I felt in regard to ethical issues important to me and the way that I handled those emotions in my actions. The first vignette pictures the kind of relationship I experienced with the Management Group. The second vignette does the same for PCs.

Vignette 1

In my opinion, the Management Group broke with tradition and showed great foresight and an even greater courage in so doing. The police force is steeped in a tradition of command and control. Many careers are built on it. One 'mistake' in our actions with LAP and careers of the Management Group might fall by it. These colleagues of mine at York Division had families and mortgages, as well as their future career to worry about. I was conscious always that I would not have to live with the possible consequences of our actions, since my career at that time was firmly set in the university sector. I carried throughout the process of implementation of LAP a great sense of personal responsibility towards my colleagues in the Management Group.

Vignette 2

In the police force changes are made at senior level with very little warning. Indeed, this was to happen in York Division when Steve Green was promoted in 1995 to Regional HQ. I troubled over the possible consequences of change if a traditional management style were to be reinstated? I had encouraged each PC to believe in a new future, to work towards it, and to be committed to it. What if their hopes and expectations were dashed? What would be the impact on individuals? What would be the impact on the organisation? As I understand it, what was going on in my mind was imagination of a rapid boundary readjustment and an ethical alertness to the impact of this. So, I published and distributed across York Division details of the process we followed and the designs PCs came up with. The publication was a form of insurance for them and offered some security for the continuation of their work. They would be able to hold up the document as a receipt of their efforts and the promises made to them. In February 1995 Regional HQ sent a small team to raise their concern with me about the publication. I suggested that if they were serious in support of the changes in York Division, as they had previously stated, then the document should pose them no difficulties. The meeting was relatively short.

There are other pointers to the way I perceived and handled my role as researcher in the preceding text. For example, I reported a tactic where I took a substantial idea of the PCs for immediate endorsement by the Management Group to increase the PCs' confidence and my credibility. I mentioned that at the outset I was terrified of the role I agreed to take on. I could have mentioned the resurfacing of this terror at the start of the implementation days, at the launch of the West LAP pilot, and in a serious moment of friction between traffic police and myself in respect of resistance by their senior staff. In contrast to terror, there were numerous occasions when I socialised and had great fun with members of York Division.

In just about every sense I was living as a member of York Division. I was a political, an emotional, and a thinking contributor to organisational learning and transformation. I became a part of the complex of interrelationships from which York Division and its version of LAP emerged. Perhaps I made a positive contribution in the way I encouraged people to learn their way into the future, interpreting LAP principles, rather than delivering LAP as a non-negotiable fixed end point towards which all staff had to re-orientate themselves?

Having read my account of organisational learning and transformation through LAP in York Division, may I now ask you to reflect on the illustration through questions I raise below about the complex nature of what occurred? You may wish to raise your own questions?

Questions to ask yourself

A traditional way to round off a case study is to state what was achieved and then set out further work to be done. Instead of drawing my own conclusion, however, I would like you to draw your conclusions in terms of the concepts and approach of this book. Let us turn the above practical animation into a case study for your consideration. The following questions might form your case study guide. The index will help you to locate where in this book the concepts and the approach are discussed.

- How would you characterise the complexity of York Division in terms of the following?
  - Detail complexity.
  - Dynamic complexity.
  - Interrelatedness.
  - Predictability.
- See if you can employ Senge's systems archetypes to come up with one or more simple models of the dynamic complexity of York Division prior to LAP.
- What boundaries to policing are discussed in the practical illustration? Name the client and the purpose in each case. What measures of performance were or could have been used for each case?
- What issues and dilemmas of an ethical nature surfaced in the practical illustration? How did you feel about them?
- What were the main issues and dilemmas of shift-based policing as the Management Group saw things? Picture what they saw through the four windows, systems of processes, of structure, of meaning, and of knowledge-power.
- What do you think might have happened if shift-based policing had remained in place? Facilitate your thinking using prismatic thought. In the light of this thinking, would you say that there is any such thing as normal organisational life?
- What were the main issues and dilemmas of LAP as the PCs saw things on implementation days? Picture what they saw through the four windows, systems of processes, of structure, of meaning, and of knowledge-power.
- What role did formative evaluation play in the implementation of LAP? What might have happened without formative evaluation? Was formative evaluation employed as a control system or a learning procedure?
- What was the main source of thinking that gave substance to summative evaluation – management or operational staff? What does this suggest about summative evaluation?
- Did the Management Group manage over York Division, or did they manage within the unmanageable?
- Did the Management Group organise the totality of York Division, or did they organise within the unorganisable?

- What can you say you know about the unknowable in the context of this practical illustration?

APPENDIX 21.1: OPERATIONAL STAFF QUESTIONNAIRE

(Your name is not required. This information will be held as confidential and will be seen only by the consultant. Please answer all questions as accurately as possible by circling the number that you choose on the scales provided.)

Date: **LAP area:** **Rank:**

How useful are the following?

	Not useful						Very useful
1 Information from the public concerning crime.	1	2	3	4	5	6	7
2 Information from Divisional HQ concerning crime.	1	2	3	4	5	6	7

Please comment on the following.

	Not approachable			Very approachable			
3 Approachability of your immediate senior staff.	1	2	3	4	5	6	7

Comments:

	Not responsive				Very responsive		
4 Responsiveness of senior staff to your concerns.	1	2	3	4	5	6	7

Comments:

Opportunity to negotiate issues.

	No opportunity			Every opportunity			
5 With own rank.	1	2	3	4	5	6	7
6 With senior staff.	1	2	3	4	5	6	7
7 With civilian staff.	1	2	3	4	5	6	7

Comments:

	Ineffective					Very effective	
8 How effective do you think policing is?	1	2	3	4	5	6	7

Comments:

9 How efficient do you think policing is?
Comments:

Inefficient						Very efficient
1	2	3	4	5	6	7

10 How efficiently is your time used?
Comments:

Inefficiently						Very efficiently
1	2	3	4	5	6	7

11 Are you receptive to new ideas?
Comments:

Not receptive						Very receptive
1	2	3	4	5	6	7

12 How much do you enjoy your work?
Comments:

Very little						Very much
1	2	3	4	5	6	7

13 How fragmented do you think policing is?
Comments:

Not fragmented						Fragmented
1	2	3	4	5	6	7

14 How much responsibility have you got?
Comments:

Very little						Very much
1	2	3	4	5	6	7

15 How does responsibility feel?
Comments:

Bad						Good
1	2	3	4	5	6	7

16 How stressed do you feel?
Comments:

Little						Very
1	2	3	4	5	6	7

17 Do you think LAP procedures are the most efficient way of policing?
Comments:

Definitely not						Definitely yes
1	2	3	4	5	6	7

	Closed						Open
18 Are you open to moral considerations at work? *Comments*:	1	2	3	4	5	6	7

Have you any general comments or suggestions?

Do you think that this evaluation sheet can be improved?

Thank you for completing this evaluation sheet.

APPENDIX 21.2: INSPECTOR'S QUESTION SHEET

To be completed by the Inspector of each LAP area.

Please answer all questions as accurately as possible.

Date:
LAP area:
Number of personnel dedicated to your LAP area:

Please indicate for the preceding three months:

Response time:

No. of car crimes:

No. of violent crimes:

No. of burglaries:

Total no. of reported crimes:

No. of arrests per PC:

Clear up rate per PC:

- (i) Violent
- (ii) House burglary
- (iii) Burglary other

No. of LIO feed-ins:

Expenditure items.

Overtime in average hours per week:

Area fuel budget:

Area equipment budget:

If there has been a change in crime rate over the previous three months, then please suggest a reason for the change (e.g. significant number of recent arrests due to Christmas period).

Thank you for completing this information sheet.

APPENDIX 21.3 SURVEY RESULTS

Table 21.1 Overall mean results for operational staff questionnaire (December 1994, March 1995, and June 1995)

Question no.	*All police December 1994 (54 respondents) (LAP 18)*	*LAP police March 1995 (51 respondents)*	*LAP police June 1995 (66 respondents)*
1	5.28	5.36	5.17
2	4.06	4.45	4.29
3	5.06	5.22	5.37
4	4.11	3.92	4.20
5	5.92	5.47	5.60
6	4.31	4.28	4.44
7	4.08	4.06	4.16
8	3.75	3.73	3.95
9	3.55	3.49	—
10	4.00	4.18	4.38
11	5.30	5.75	5.68
12	5.24	5.22	4.98
13	—	5.37	5.17
14	4.70	5.08	5.43
15	5.37	5.72	5.77
16	3.85	3.75	3.64
17	3.18	3.48	3.52

Table 21.2(a) West LAP mean results for operational staff questionnaire (December 1994 and June 1995)

Question no.	*West LAP December 1994 (18 respondents)*	*West LAP June 1995 (21 respondents)*
1	5.39	4.95
2	—	—
3	4.28	5.76
4	3.78	5.10
5	6.28	5.43
6	4.18	5.10
7	3.39	3.52
8	4.12	4.62
9	—	—
10	4.06	4.10
11	5.67	5.76
12	5.17	5.43
13	—	—
14	4.83	5.29
15	5.67	6.19
16	4.17	3.43
17	3.71	4.24

Table 21.2(b) Divisional Police (December 1994) compared to City, East and North LAPs (June 1995) from mean results of operational staff questionnaire

Question no.	*Division December 1994 (36 respondents)*	*City LAP June 1995 (16 respondents)*	*East LAP June 1995 (15 respondents)*	*North LAP June 1995 (14 respondents)*
1	5.22	6.19	5.14	4.36
2	—	—	—	—
3	5.47	5.73	5.00	4.71
4	4.29	4.00	3.50	3.79
5	5.74	5.63	5.86	5.71
6	4.37	4.13	4.07	4.14
7	4.43	4.13	4.23	5.07
8	3.58	3.75	3.50	3.57
9	—	—	—	—
10	3.97	4.75	4.14	4.43
11	5.06	6.06	5.64	5.14
12	5.28	4.94	4.79	4.57
13	—	—	—	—
14	4.64	5.69	5.14	5.64
15	5.22	6.07	5.14	5.43
16	3.69	3.50	3.54	4.21
17	2.91	2.75	2.92	2.92

Table 21.3 Overall mode and median results for operational staff questionnaire (December 1994, March 1995, and June 1995)

Question no.	*LAP police Dec. 1994 (18 respondents)*		*Division Dec. 1994 (36 respondents)*		*LAP police March 1995 (51 respondents)*		*LAP police June 1995 (66 respondents)*	
	Mode	*Median*	*Mode*	*Median*	*Mode*	*Median*	*Mode*	*Median*
1	7 (7)[a]	5.5	4 (10)	5.0	7 (18)	6.0	5 (19)	5.0
2	7 (5)	5.0	—	—	5 (12)	4.0	4 (21)	4.0
3	4 (6)	4.0	6 (11)	6.0	6 (13)	5.0	5 (20)	5.0
4	4 (5)	3.5	4 (9)	4.0	5 (18)	4.0	5 (19)	4.0
5	7 (9)	6.5	7 (15)	6.0	7 (17)	6.0	7 (22)	6.0
6	4 (5)	4.0	6 (8)	5.0	5 (18)	5.0	5 (18)	5.0
7	2 (4)	3.5	6 (10)	4.0	6 (10)	4.0	4 (13)	4.0
8	4 (9)	4.0	4 (13)	4.0	4 (19)	4.0	4 (25)	4.0
9	4 (8)	4.0	4 (13)	4.0	4 (14)	4.0	—	—
10	4 (5)	4.0	5 (13)	4.0	4 (16)	4.0	5 (21)	4.0
11	7 (7)	6.0	6 (14)	5.0	6 (19)	6.0	6 (35)	6.0
12	6 (5)	5.0	6 (11)	6.0	6 (15)	5.0	5 (20)	5.0
13	5 (4)	5.0	6 (10)	5.0	6 (16)	6.0	6 (25)	6.0
14	7 (5)	5.5	4 (9)	5.0	6 (15)	5.0	6 (27)	6.0
15	6 (6)	6.0	4 (12)	5.0	7 (17)	6.0	6 (30)	6.0
16	5 (4)	4.5	3 (11)	3.0	4 (16)	4.0	4 (17)	4.0
17	4 (6)	4.0	1 (9)	3.0	1 (11)	3.5	4 (17)	4.0

Note

a The number of respondents who selected the mode is shown in brackets.

Table 21.4 Quarterly results for Inspector's question sheet for the period 1 August 1994 to 31 July 1995

	Three month period			
	1/8/94–31/10/94	*1/11/94–31/1/95*	*1/2/95–30/4/95*	*1/5/95–31/7/95*
No. car crimes	1,605	1,652	1,229	1,530
No. violent crimes	163	165	60	143
No. burglaries	1,456	1,571	1,139	1,272
Total no. reported crimes	5,224	5,140	4,483	4,887
LIO feed-ins	1,523	1,667	1,636	808
Total no. arrests	?	?	1,402	1,515
No. arrests per officer	?	?	10.78	11.74

Note:
A question mark has been inserted where an accurate figure is not available.

22 Reflections and key insights of systemic thinking

I was taught that concluding a book on 'management and organisation' normally is not very difficult. The task is to tie up, round off, and crystallise the argument. The book is reduced in this way to an island of thought on which the reader, if convinced, may build their future. With systemic thinking, conversely, comes an ocean of ideas that is a medium for many currents of thought that give rise to endless tides of appreciation. It is a way of thinking that sets out to erode islands of thought and certainly cannot be reduced to one. So, I am unable to offer you a conclusion as such. Instead, I urge you to see the image on the front cover of this book. And I urge you to listen to the echoes and re-echoes passing between the covers of this book. Then you will see and hear, again and again, that:

- We will not struggle to manage over things – we will manage within the unmanageable.
- We will not battle to organise the totality – we will organise within the unorganisable.
- We will not simply know things – but we will know of the unknowable.

I find these three paradoxes of systemic thinking mightily thought provoking. If they were embraced by human kind, then surely we would witness profound changes in the way we conceive ourselves as a species on planet Earth and the way we handle ourselves in everyday life. And the amazing thing is that the kind of transformation I am talking about has no need for or call to a 'religious conversion', just a humble awakening to the realisation that really we don't know very much about anything and actually never will.

Perhaps I could encourage you to reflect once more on systemic thinking through its key insights summarised below, which are extracted from the pages of *Rethinking The Fifth Discipline: Learning Within The Unknowable*.

- Systemic awareness begins with a spiritual appreciation of wholeness.
- Wholeness may be appreciated in terms of:
  - interrelatedness of events, and
  - spontaneous self-organisation leading to emergence and new order.

- Interrelatedness of events and spontaneous self-organisation in the natural sciences may be characterised in terms of:
  - deterministic and probabilistic feedback,
  - operating according to laws that so far have withstood refutation,
  - leading to emergence and new order.
- Interrelatedness of events and spontaneous self-organisation in the social sciences may be characterised in terms of:
  - adaptive feedback,
  - operating according to social rules and practices that people either wittingly or unwittingly agree upon,
  - that people might desire to change by forming coalitions around an issue in spontaneous self-organisation,
  - which may or may not lead to new order.
- Human existence is intrinsically unknowable to the human mind.
- We know of some things, but only those which are local to us in space and time.
  - In space – things that we are immediately involved in (not simply in a geographical sense).
  - In time – not very far into the future, or indeed the past.
- Beyond what is local to us is unknowable.
- What we do know is a matter of interpretation and is mysterious.
- We live all aspects of our lives between mystery and mastery.
  - There is mystery in the interpretive nature of what we know,
  - and in the unknowable that lies beyond our interpretation, yet
  - there may be a certain 'mastery' of the moment, and
  - living between mystery and mastery means learning one's way into the future.
- Mastery of the moment means that:
  - it is not possible to plan over a wide spread of interrelationships, through recurring emergence, far into the future; yet
  - it is possible to learn about what is local to us, that is,
  - it is possible to learn within the unknowable.
- Learning a way into the future in 'management and organisation' involves:
  - explicit awareness of the bounded nature of our designs and decisions,
  - explicit awareness of the ethical nature of our designs and decisions,
  - appreciation of optional designs and decisions in the local context of the action area, and
  - deepening systemic appreciation of issues and dilemmas that characterise designs and decisions.
- Systemic thinking challenges the following concepts of traditional 'management and organisation':
  - problem,
  - solution,

    - normal organisational life,
    - consensus,
    - medium and long term plans, and
    - prioritisation of ends over means.
- If systemic thinking has its way, then:
    - we will not struggle to manage over things, we will manage within the unmanageable;
    - we will not battle to organise the totality, we will organise within the unorganisable; and
    - we will not simply know things, but we will know of the unknowable.
- Systemic thinking in 'organisation and management' in essence is about being:
    - ethically alert,
    - critically reflective,
    - appreciating issues and dilemmas that we face,
    - exploring possible choices for action, and hence
    - may be known as critical systemic thinking.
- And, in humble reflection, let us know that really we don't know very much about anything and actually never will.

Further reading

Notes

† Indicates referenced in the text.
‡ Indicates republished by Wiley, Chichester in 1994.
# Indicates a journal publication.

1 Introduction

†Senge, P. (1990) *The Fifth Discipline: The Art and Practice of the Learning Organisation*, Century, London.
Stacey, R. (1992) *Managing the Unknowable: Strategic Boundaries Between Order and Chaos in Organisations*, Jossey-Bass, San Francisco.

2 Senge's *The Fifth Discipline*

Ackoff, R.L. (1981) *Creating the Corporate Future*, Wiley, New York.
Ackoff, R.L. (1994) *The Democratic Organisation*, Oxford University Press, New York.
Argyris, C. (1991) Teaching smart people how to learn, *Harvard Business Review*, 69, 99–109.
Argyris, C. (1993) *Knowledge for Action*, Jossey-Bass, San Francisco.
Argyris, C. and Schön, D. (1985) *Strategy, Change and Defensive Routines*, Ballinger, Cambridge, Mass.
Argyris, C. and Schön, D. (1991) Participatory Action Research and Action Science Compared. In, Whyte, W.F. (ed.) *Participatory Action Research*, Sage, Newbury Park, Calif.
Argyris, C. and Schön, D. (1996) *Organisational Learning II*, Addison Wesley, New York.
‡Beer, S. (1979) *Heart of the Enterprise*, Wiley, Chichester.
‡Beer, S. (1981) *Brain of the Firm*, Wiley, Chichester.
Bohm, D. (1996) *On Dialogue*, Routledge, London; Nichol, L. (ed.).
Chawla, S. and Renesch, J. (1995) *Learning Organisations*, Productivity Press, Portland, Oreg.
Checkland, P.B. (1981) *Systems Thinking, Systems Practice*, Wiley, Chichester.

Checkland, P.B. and Scholes, J. (1990) *Soft Systems Methodology in Action*, Wiley, Chichester.
Churchman, C. West (1968) *The Systems Approach*, Delacorte Press, New York.
Churchman, C. West (1979) *The Systems Approach and Its Enemies*, Basic Books, New York.
De Geus, A. (1997) *The Living Company*, Harvard Business School Press, Harvard.
Forrester, J.W. (1961) *Industrial Dynamics*, MIT Press, Cambridge, Mass.
Forrester, J.W. (1969) *Principles of Systems*, Wright-Allen Press, Cambridge, Mass.
Fritz, R. (1989) *The Path of Least Resistance*, Fawcett, Columbine.
Garratt, B. (1994) *The Learning Organisation*, Harper Collins, London.
Goodman, M. (1974) *Study Notes in System Dynamics*, Productivity Press, Portland, Oreg.
Johnson-Laird, P.N. (1983) *Mental Models*, Cambridge University Press, Cambridge.
†Kim, D.H. (1993) *Systems Archetypes: Diagnosing Systemic Issues and Designing High Leverage Interventions*, Pegasus Communications, Cambridge, Mass.
Meadows, D.H., Meadows, D. and Randers, J. (1992) *Beyond the Limits*, Chelsea Green Publishing, Post Hills, Vt.
Parker, M. (1990) *Creating Shared Vision*, Dialog International, Oak Park, Ill.
Pedler, M., Burgoyne, J. and Boydell, T. (1991) *The Learning Company*, McGraw-Hill, London.
Richardson, G.P. (1991) *Feedback Thought in Social Science and Systems Theory*, University of Pennsylvania Press, Philadelphia.
Richardson, G.P. and Pugh, A. (1981) *Introduction to System Dynamics Modelling with DYNAMO*, Productivity Press, Portland, Oreg.
†Senge, P. (1990) *The Fifth Discipline: The Art and Practice of the Learning Organisation*, Century, London.
†Senge, P., Kleiner, A., Roberts, C., Ross, R. and Smith, B. (1994) *The Fifth Discipline Fieldbook*, Century, London.
Suarez, R.T. (1998) An inquiry into the historical meaning of *The Fifth Discipline*, *Systemic Practice and Action Research*, 11, 483–502.
†Suzuki, D.T. (1970) Satori. In, Sohl, R. and Carr, A. (eds) *The Gospel According to Zen: Beyond the Death of God*, Mentor, New York.
#*System Dynamics Review*.
Von Bertalanffy, L. (1968) *General System Theory: Foundations, Development, Applications*, Braziller, New York; enlarged edition (1971) Penguin, London.
Wolstenholme, E.F. (1990) *System Enquiry: A System Dynamics Approach*, Wiley, Chichester.

3 Bertalanffy's open systems theory

Ashby, R. (1958) General system theory as a new discipline, *General Systems*, 3, 1–6.
Bogdanov, A. (1996) *Bogdanov's Tektology*, Centre for Systems Studies Press, Hull University; Sadovsky, V.N. and Kelle, V.V. (trans.); Dudley, P. (ed.).
Boulding, K.E. (1956) General system theory: the skeleton of science, *Management Science*, 2, 197–208.
†#*Complexity in Human Systems*.
†#*Emergence*.
Emery, F.E. (ed.) (1981) *Systems Thinking*, (2 volumes) Penguin, Harmondsworth.

Flood, R.L. (1998) Ludwig von Bertalanffy. In, Warner, M. (ed.) *IEBM Handbook of Management Thinking*, International Thomson Business Press, London.

Gray, W. and Rizzo, N. (eds) (1972) *Unity Through Diversity: A Festschrift in Honour of Ludwig von Bertalanffy*, (2 volumes) Gordon and Breach, London and New York.

#*Human Relations.*

†#*International Journal of General Systems.*

Klir, G. (1991) *Facets of Systems Science*, Plenum, New York.

Laszlo, E. (1972) *Introduction to Systems Philosophy*, Gordon and Breach, New York.

†Morgan, G. (1986) *Images of Organization*, Sage, London.

Rapoport, A. (1996) *General System Theory*, Abacus, Tunbridge Wells.

†Rosen, R. (1979) Old trends and new trends in general systems research, *International Journal of General Systems*, 5, 173–181.

†Senge, P. (1990) *The Fifth Discipline: The Art and Practice of the Learning Organisation*, Century, London.

†#*System Dynamics Review.*

†#*Systemic Practice and Action Research.*

†#*Systems Research and Behavioural Science.*

Von Bertalanffy, L. (1933) *Modern Theories of Development*, Oxford University Press, Oxford; Woodger, J.H. (ed.).

Von Bertalanffy, L. (1950) The theory of open systems in physics and biology, *Science*, 11, 23–29.

Von Bertalanffy, L. (1953) *Problems of Life: An Evaluation of Modern Biological Thought*, Wiley, New York; Watts, London.

Von Bertalanffy, L. (1956) General system theory, *General Systems*, 1, 1–10.

Von Bertalanffy, L. (1967) *Robots, Men and Minds: Psychology in the Modern World*, Braziller, New York.

Von Bertalanffy, L. (1968) *Organismic Psychology and Systems Theory*, Clark University Press, Worcester, Mass.

Von Bertalanffy, L. (1968) *General System Theory: Foundations, Development, Applications*, Braziller, New York.

†Von Bertalanffy, L. (1981) *A Systems View of Man*, Westview, Boulding, Calif; La Violette, P.A. (ed.).

4 Beer's organisational cybernetics

†Beer, S. (1959) *Cybernetics and Management*, English Universities, London; Wiley, New York.

†‡Beer, S. (1966) *Decision and Control: The Meaning of Operational Research and Management Cybernetics*, Wiley, Chichester.

†Beer, S. (1968) *Management Science: The Business Use of Operational Research*, Aldus, London.

†‡Beer, S. (1972) *Brain of the Firm*, Allen Lane and Penguin Press, London; Herder and Herder, New York; second edition (1981) Wiley, Chichester and New York.

†‡Beer, S. (1974) *Designing Freedom*, Canadian Broadcasting Company, Toronto; republished (1975) Wiley, Chichester and New York.

‡Beer, S. (1975) *Platform for Change*, Wiley, Chichester and New York.

†‡Beer, S. (1979) *Heart of the Enterprise*, Wiley, Chichester and New York.

†‡Beer, S. (1985) *Diagnosing the System for Organisations*, Wiley, Chichester and New York.

†Beer, S. (1994) *Beyond Dispute: The Invention of Team Syntegrity*, Wiley, Chichester and New York.

Beer, S. (1994) *How Many Grapes Went Into the Wine? Stafford Beer on the Art and Science of Holistic Management*, Wiley, Chichester and New York.

Espejo, R. and Harnden, R. (1989) *The Viable System Model: Interpretations and Applications of Stafford Beer's VSM*, Wiley, Chichester.

Espejo, R. and Schwaninger, M. (1993) *Organisational Fitness: Corporate Effectiveness Through Management Cybernetics*, Campus Verlag, New York.

Feibleman, J.K. (1960) *An Introduction to Peirce's Philosophy Interpreted as a System*, George Allen and Unwin, London.

Flood, R.L. (1998) Stafford Beer. In, Warner, M. (ed.) *IEBM Handbook of Management Thinking*, International Thomson Business Press, London.

Flood, R.L. and Jackson, M.C. (1991) *Creative Problem Solving: Total Systems Intervention*, Wiley, Chichester.

Flood, R.L. and Romm, N.R.A. (1996) *Diversity Management: Triple Loop Learning*, Wiley, Chichester.

Stafford Beer special issue (1990) *Systems Practice*, 3 (3).

5 Ackoff's interactive planning

Ackoff, R.L. (1978) *The Art of Problem Solving*, Wiley, New York.

†Ackoff, R.L. (1981) *Creating the Corporate Future*, Wiley, New York.

Ackoff, R.L. (1986) *Management in Small Doses*, Wiley, New York.

†Ackoff, R.L. (1991) *Ackoff's Fables*, Wiley, New York.

†Ackoff, R.L. (1994) *The Democratic Organisation*, Oxford University Press, New York.

†Ackoff, R.L. (1988–1997) Redesigning the future; regular column in *Systems Practice*.

†Ackoff, R.L. and Rivett, P. (1963) *A Manager's Guide to Operations Research*, Wiley, New York.

†Ackoff, R.L. and Sasieni, M. (1968) *Fundamentals of Operations Research*, Wiley, New York.

Ackoff, R.L. and Emery, F.E. (1972) *On Purposeful Systems*, Tavistock, London.

†Ackoff, R.L., Vergara, E. and Gharajedaghi, J. (1984) *A Guide to Controlling Your Corporation's Future*, Wiley, New York.

Ackoff, R.L., Broholm, P. and Snow, R. (1984) *Revitalizing Western Economies*, Jossey-Bass, San Francisco.

‡Beer, S. (1972) *Brain of the Firm*, Allen Lane and Penguin Press, London; Herder and Herder, New York; second edition (1981) Wiley, Chichester and New York.

Churchman, C. West and Ackoff, R.L. (1950) *Methods of Inquiry*, Educational Publishers Inc., St Louis, Mo.

†Churchman, C. West, Ackoff, R.L. and Arnoff, E.L. (1957) *Introduction to Operations Research*, Wiley, New York.

Flood, R.L. (1998) Russell L. Ackoff. In, Warner, M. *IEBM Handbook of Management Thinking*, International Thomson Press, London.

Flood, R.L. and Jackson, M.C. (1991) *Creative Problem Solving: Total Systems Intervention*, Wiley, Chichester.
Flood, R.L. and Romm, N.R.A. (1996) *Diversity Management: Triple Loop Learning*, Wiley, Chichester.
†Juran, J.M. (1988) *Juran on Planning for Quality*, Free Press, New York.
Keys, P. (ed.) (1995) *Understanding the Process of Operational Research*, Wiley, Chichester.
Lartin-Drake, J.M. and Curran, C.R. (1996) All together now: the circular organisation in a university hospital. Part I – planning and design, *Systems Practice*, 9, 391–402.
Lartin-Drake, J.M., Curran, C.R. and Kruger, N.R. (1996) All together now: the circular organisation in a university hospital. Part II – implementation, *Systems Practice*, 9, 403–420.
†Senge, P. (1990) *The Fifth Discipline: The Art and Practice of the Learning Organisation*, Century, London.
70th Birthday *Festschrift* (1990) *Systems Practice*, 3 (2).

6 Checkland's soft systems approach

†Argyris, C., Putnam, R. and McLain-Smith, D. (1982) *Action Science: Concepts, Methods and Skills for Research and Intervention*, Jossey-Bass, San Francisco.
†Checkland, P.B. (1981) *Systems Thinking, Systems Practice*, Wiley, Chichester.
†Checkland, P.B. (1985) From optimising to learning: a development of systems thinking for the 1990s, *Journal of the Operational Research Society*, 36, 757–767.
†Checkland, P.B. and Scholes, J. (1990) *Soft Systems Methodology in Action*, Wiley, Chichester.
†Checkland, P.B. and Holwell, S. (1998) *Information, Systems and Information Systems*, Wiley, Chichester.
†Jackson, M.C. (1991) *Systems Methodology for the Management Sciences*, Plenum, New York.
Jackson, M.C. (1998) Peter Bernard Checkland. In, Warner, M. (ed.) *IEBM Handbook of Management Thinking*, International Thomson Press, London.
Special issue on action research (1997) *Systems Practice*, 9 (2).

7 Churchman's critical systemic thinking

Ackoff, R.L. (1988) C. West Churchman, *Systems Practice*, 1, 351–356.
Churchman, C. West (1940) *Elements of Logic and Formal Science*, Lippincott, New York.
Churchman, C. West (1948) *Theory of Experimental Inference*, Macmillan, New York.
†Churchman, C. West (1960) *Prediction and Optimal Decision*, Prentice-Hall, Englewood Cliffs, New Jersey.
Churchman, C. West (1968) *The Systems Approach*, Delta, New York.
Churchman, C. West (1968) *Challenge to Reason*, McGraw-Hill, New York.
†Churchman, C. West (1971) *The Design of Inquiring Systems, Basic Concepts of Systems and Organisations*, Basic Books, New York.

†Churchman, C. West (1979) *The Systems Approach and Its Enemies*, Basic Books, New York.
†Churchman, C. West (1982) *Thought and Wisdom*, Intersystems, Seaside, Calif.
†Churchman, C. West (1997) In search of an ethical science: an interview with, C. West Churchman, *Journal of Business Ethics*, 16, 731–744.
Churchman, C. West and Ackoff, R.L. (1950) *Methods of Inquiry*, Educational Publishers Inc., St Louis, Mo.
†Churchman, C. West, Ackoff, R.L. and Arnoff, E.L. (1957) *Introduction to Operations Research*, Wiley, New York.
Flood, R.L. (1998) C. West Churchman. In, Warner, M. (ed.) *IEBM Handbook of Management Thinking*, International Thomson Business Press, London.
Flood, R.L. and Jackson, M.C. (1991) *Critical Systems Thinking: Directed Readings*, Wiley, Chichester.
Keys, P. (ed.) (1995) *Understanding the Process of Operational Research*, Wiley, Chichester.
†#*Management Science*.
Senge, P. (1990) *The Fifth Discipline: The Art and Practice of the Learning Organisation*, Century, London.
Singer, E.A. (1923) *Modern Thinkers and Present Problems*, Henry Holt and Co., New York.
Singer, E.A. (1936) *On the Contented Life*, Henry Holt and Co., New York.
Singer, E.A. (1945) *In Search of a New Way of Life*, Columbia University Press, New York.
†Ulrich, W. (1988) Churchman's 'process of unfolding' – its significance for policy analysis and evaluation, *Systems Practice*, 1, 415–428.
†Ulrich, W. (1994) Can we secure future responsive management through systems thinking and design? *INTERFACES*, 24, 26–37.
Vickers, G. (1970) *Freedom in a Rocking Boat: Changing Values in an Unstable Society*, Basic Books, New York.
75th Birthday *Festschrift* (1989) *Systems Practice*, 1 (4); Ulrich, W. (guest ed.).
80th Birthday *Festschrift* (1994) *INTERFACES*, 24 (1); Koenigsberg, E. and van Gigch, J.P. (guest eds).

8 Senge's *The Fifth Discipline* revisited

Ackoff, R.L. (1981) *Creating the Corporate Future*, Wiley, New York.
Ackoff, R.L. (1994) *The Democratic Organisation*, Oxford University Press, New York.
Argyris, C. and Schön, D. (1985) *Strategy, Change and Defensive Routines*, Ballinger, Cambridge, Mass.
Argyris, C. and Schön, D. (1991) Participatory Action Research and Action Science Compared. In, Whyte, W.F. (ed.) *Participatory Action Research*, Sage, Newbury Park, Calif.
‡Beer, S. (1972) *Brain of the Firm*, Allen Lane and Penguin Press, London; Herder and Herder, New York; second edition (1981) Wiley, Chichester and New York.
‡Beer, S. (1979) *Heart of the Enterprise*, Wiley, Chichester and New York.
‡Beer, S. (1985) *Diagnosing the System for Organisations*, Wiley, Chichester and New York.

Checkland, P.B. (1981) *Systems Thinking, Systems Practice*, Wiley, Chichester.
Checkland, P.B. and Scholes, J. (1990) *Soft Systems Methodology in Action*, Wiley, Chichester.
Churchman, C. West (1968) *The Systems Approach*, Delta, New York.
Churchman, C. West (1979) *The Systems Approach and Its Enemies*, Basic Books, New York.
De Geus, A. (1997) *The Living Company*, Harvard Business School Press, Harvard.
†Marx, K. and Engels, F. (1967) *The Communist Manifesto*, Penguin, London.
†Senge, P. (1990) *The Fifth Discipline: The Art and Practice of the Learning Organisation*, Century, London.
Senge, P., Kleiner, A., Roberts, C., Ross, R. and Smith, B. (1994) *The Fifth Discipline Fieldbook*, Century, London.
Suarez, R.T. (1998) An inquiry into the historical meaning of *The Fifth Discipline*, *Systemic Practice and Action Research*, 11, 483–502.
Von Bertalanffy, L. (1968) *General System Theory: Foundations, Development, Applications*, Braziller, New York.

9 Towards systemic thinking

†Ackoff, R.L. (1974) *Redesigning the Future*, Wiley, New York.
†Berry, T. (1988) *The Dream of the Earth*, Sierra Club, San Francisco.
Bateson, G. (1973) *Steps to an Ecology of Mind*, Paladin, St Albans.
Bohm, D. (1980) *Wholeness and the Implicate Order*, Routledge, London.
Bohm, D. (1994) *Thought as a System*, Routledge, London.
Brown, R.H. (1977) *A Poetic for Sociology: Toward the Logic of Discovery for the Human Sciences*, University of Chicago Press, Chicago.
Capra, F. (1983) *The Turning Point*, Bantam, New York.
Capra, F., Steindl-Rast, D. and Madison, T. (1991) *Belonging to the Universe*, Harper, San Francisco.
Castaneda, C. (1970) *The Teachings of Don Juan: A Yaqui Way of Knowledge*, Penguin, London.
†Checkland, P.B. (1981) *Systems Thinking, Systems Practice*, Wiley, Chichester.
Connerton, P. (1980) *The Tragedy of Enlightenment*, University of Cambridge, Cambridge.
Denzin, N.K. (1991) *Images of Postmodern Society*, Sage, London.
Douglas, M. (1991) *Purity and Danger: An Analysis of the Concepts of Pollution and Taboo*, Routledge, London.
Flood, R.L. and Romm, N.R.A. (1996) *Diversity Management: Triple Loop Learning*, Wiley, Chichester.
Gall, J. (1979) *System-Antics: How Systems Work and Especially How They Fail*, Fontana, London.
Giddens, A. (1991) *Modernity and Self-Identity: Self and Society in the Late Modern Age*, Polity Press, Cambridge.
Gregory, B. (1988) *Inventing Reality: Physics as Language*, Wiley, New York.
Hassard, J. and Parker, M. (eds) (1993) *Postmodernism and Organisations*, Sage, London.
Hesse, M.B. (1966) *Models and Analogies in Science*, University of Notre Dame Press, Notre Dame, Indiana.

Joseph, L.E. (1990) *Gaia: The Growth of an Idea*, Penguin, Harmondsworth.
Koestler, A. and Smythies, J.R. (1969) *Beyond Reductionism*, Hutchinson, London.
Kuhn, T. (1968) *The Structure of Scientific Revolutions*, University of Chicago Press, Chicago; (1970) enlarged second edition.
Lemkow, A. (1990) *The Wholeness Principle*, Quest Books, Wheaton, Ill.
Marx, K. and Engels, F. (1967) *The Communist Manifesto*, Penguin, London.
McKenzie, A.E.E. (1960) *The Major Achievements of Science*, Simon and Schuster, New York.
†Nietzsche, F. (1888) *The Anti-Christ*.
†Popper, K. (1959) *The Logic of Scientific Discovery*, Hutchinson, London.
Porush, D. (1985) *The Soft Machine: Cybernetic Fiction*, Methuen, London.
†Reason, P. (ed.) (1988) *Human Inquiry in Action*, Sage, London.
Reiss, T.J. (1982) *The Discourse of Modernism*, Cornell University Press, Ithaca.
Simons, H.W. and Billig, M. (eds) (1994) *After Postmodernism: Reconstructing Ideology Critique*, Sage, London.
†Sohl, R. and Carr, A. (eds) (1970) *The Gospel According to Zen: Beyond the Death of God*, Mentor, New York.

10 The demise of problems, solutions and normal organisational life

Capra, F. and Flatau, M. (1996) Emergence and Design in Human Organisations: Creative Tension ‘at the Edge of Chaos’. In, *Elegant Solutions: The Power of Systems Thinking*, New Leaders Press, San Francisco.
Cilliers, P. (1998) *Complexity and Postmodernism: Understanding Complex Systems*, Routledge, London.
Coveney, P. and Highfield, R. (1995) *Frontiers of Complexity Theory*, Faber and Faber, London.
Eve, R.A., Horsfall, S. and Lee, M.E. (1997) *Chaos, Complexity and Sociology*, Sage, London.
Kauffman, S.A. (1992) *Origins of Order: Self-Organisation and Selection in Evolution*, Oxford University Press, Oxford.
Kiel, L.D. and Elliot, E. (eds) (1997) *Chaos Theory in the Social Sciences*, University of Michigan Press, Michigan.
Merry, U. (1995) *Coping With Uncertainty: Insights from the New Sciences of Chaos, Self-Organisation and Complexity*, Praeger, Westport, Conn.
Nicolis, G. and Prigogine, I. (1989) *Exploring Complexity*, Freeman, New York.
Pascale, R. (1991) *Managing on the Edge*, Penguin, London.
Prigogine, I. (1980) *From Being to Becoming*, Freeman, San Francisco.
†Prigogine, I. and Stengers, I. (1984) *Order Out of Chaos*, Fontana, London.
Robertson, R. and Combs, A. (eds) (1998) *Chaos Theory in Psychology and the Life Sciences*, Lawrence Erlbaum Associates, Mahwah, NJ; and Hove, UK.
†Stacey, R.D. (1996) *Strategic Management and Organisational Dynamics*, Pitman, London.
Stacey, R.D. (1996) *Complexity and Creativity in Organizations*, Berrett-Koehler, San Francisco.
†Waldrop, M.M. (1992) *Complexity: The Emerging Science at the Edge of Order and Chaos*, Viking, London.

Wheatley, M. (1993) *Leadership and the New Science*, Berret-Koehler, San Francisco.

11 Getting to grips with complexity

†Churchman, C. West (1979) *The Systems Approach and its Enemies*, Basic Books, New York.
†Gouldner, A.W. (1973) *The Coming Crisis of Western Sociology*, Heinemann, London.
†Midgley, G. (1992) The sacred and the profane in critical systems thinking, *Systems Practice*, 5, 5–16.
†Stacey, R.D. (1992) *Managing the Unknowable: Strategic Boundaries Between Order and Chaos in Organisations*, Jossey-Bass, San Francisco.
Ulrich, W. (1983) *Critical Heuristics of Social Planning*, Haupt, Berne.

12 Deepening systemic appreciation

(See 'Further reading' for Chapters 13–17 inclusive.)

13 Window 1: Systems of processes

Born, G. (1994) *Process Management to Quality Improvement*, Wiley Chichester.
Cheryl Currid and Company (1994) *Reengineering Toolkit: 15 Tools and Technologies for Reengineering Your Organisation*, Prima, Rocklin, Calif.
†Crosby, P. (1979) *Quality is Free*, Mentor, London.
Flood, R.L. (1993) *Beyond TQM*, Wiley, Chichester.
†Hammer, M. and Champy, J. (1993) *Reengineering the Corporation: A Manifesto for Business Revolution*, Nicholas Brealey, London.
†Imai, M. (1991) *Kaizen*, McGraw-Hill, Singapore.
†Ishikawa, K. (1976) *Guide to Quality Control*, Asian Productivity Organisation, Tokyo.
Melan, E.H. (1995) *Process Management: A Systems Approach to Total Quality*, Productivity Press, Portland, Oreg.
Obolensky, N. (1994) *Practical Business Re-engineering*, Kogan Page, London.
Ould, M.A. (1995) *Business Processes: Modelling and Analysis For Reengineering and Improvement*, Wiley, Chichester.

14 Window 2: Systems of structure

†Ackoff, R.L. (1994) *The Democratic Organisation*, Oxford University Press, New York.
Banner, D.K. and Gagné, T.E. (1995) *Designing Effective Organisation: Traditional and Transformational Views*, Sage, Thousand Oaks, Calif.
†‡Beer, S. (1972) *Brain of the Firm*, Allen Lane and Penguin Press, London; Herder and Herder, New York; second edition (1981) Wiley, Chichester and New York.
‡Beer, S. (1979) *Heart of the Enterprise*, Wiley, Chichester and New York.
‡Beer, S. (1985) *Diagnosing the System for Organisations*, Wiley, Chichester and New York.
Fairtlough, G. (1989) *Creative Compartments*, Adamantine, London.

Gouldner, A.W. (1954) *Patterns of Industrial Bureaucracy*, Free Press, New York.

Heckscher, C. and Donnellon, A. (eds) (1994) *The Post-Bureaucratic Organisation: New Perspectives on Organizational Change*, Sage, Thousand Oaks, Calif.

Khandwalla, P.N. (1977) *The Design of Organisations*, Harcourt Brace, New York.

Miles, R.E. and Snow, C.C. (1986) Organisations: new concepts for new forms, *California Management Review*, 28.

†Mintzberg, H. (1979) *The Structuring of Organisations*, Prentice-Hall, Englewood Cliffs, NJ.

Semler, R. (1993) *Maverick!*, Arrow, London.

†Von Bertalanffy, L. (1950) The theory of open systems in physics and biology, *Science*, 11, 23–29.

Weber, M. (1947) *The Theory of Social and Economic Organisation*, Free Press, New York.

15 Window 3: Systems of meaning

Ackoff, R.L. (1978) *The Art of Problem Solving*, Wiley, New York.

Ackoff, R.L. (1981) *Creating the Corporate Future*, Wiley, New York.

Allison, G.T. (1971) *Essence of Decision: Explaining the Cuban Missile Crisis*, Little Brown, Boston.

†Argyris, C. and Schön, D. (1990) *Overcoming Organisational Defences*, Allyn & Bacon, Needham Heights, Mass.

Checkland, P.B. (1981) *Systems Thinking, Systems Practice*, Wiley, Chichester.

Checkland, P.B. and Scholes, J. (1990) *Soft Systems Methodology in Action*, Wiley, Chichester.

Fineman, S. (ed.) (1993) *Emotion in Organizations*, Sage, London.

Heron, J. (1992) *Feeling and Personhood: Psychology in Another Key*, Sage, London.

Laing, R.D. (1967) *The Politics of Experience and The Bird of Paradise*, Penguin, London.

Mason, R.O. and Mitroff, I.I. (1981) *Challenging Strategic Planning Assumptions*, Wiley, New York.

Pink Floyd (1994) ‘Keep Talking’. On, *Division Bells*, EMI Music, London.

Vickers, G. (1970) *Freedom in a Rocking Boat: Changing Values in an Unstable Society*, Basic Books, New York.

†Whyte, W.F. (1991) *Participatory Action Research*, Sage, London.

16 Window 4: Systems of knowledge-power

†Alcoff, L. and Potter, E. (eds) (1993) *Feminist Epistemologies*, Routledge, New York and London.

†Bar On, B. (1993) Marginality and Epistemic Privilege. In, Alcoff, L. and Potter, E. (eds) *Feminist Epistemologies*, Routledge, New York and London.

Carr, W. and Kemmis, S. (1986) *Becoming Critical: Education, Knowledge and Action Research*, Deakin University Press, Geelong, Victoria.

Chambers, R. (1997) *Whose Reality Counts?* Intermediate Technology Publications, London.

Clegg, S.R. and Palmer, G. (eds) (1996) *The Politics of Management Knowledge*, Sage, London.

†Code, L. (1993) Taking Subjectivity into Account. In, Alcoff, L. and Potter, E. (eds) *Feminist Epistemologies*, Routledge, New York and London.

Coetzee, J.M. (1982) *Waiting for the Barbarians*, Penguin, New York.

†Fals-Borda, O. and Rahman, M.E. (eds) (1991) *Action and Knowledge: Breaking the Monopoly with Participatory Action Research*, Intermediate Technology Pubs/ Apex Press, New York.

Flood, R.L. (1993) Practising freedom: designing, debating and disemprisoning, *OMEGA*, 21, 7–16.

Freire, P. (1968) *Pedagogy of the Oppressed*, Continuum, New York.

Freire, P. (1996) *Pedagogy of Hope: Reliving Pedagogy of the Oppressed*, Continuum, New York.

†Hölscher, F. and Romm, N.R.A. (1987) Development as a Process of Consciousness. In, Coetzee, J.K. (ed.) *Development is for People*, Macmillan, Johannesburg.

Lather, P. (1991) *Getting Smart: Feminist Research and Pedagogy with/in the Post-modern*, Routledge, London.

Lee, H. (1996) *To Kill a Mockingbird*, Penguin, Harmondsworth.

Lincoln, Y. and Guba, E. (1985) *Naturalistic Enquiry*, Sage, London.

†Marx, K. and Engels, F. (1967) *The Communist Manifesto*, Penguin, London.

Oliver, M. (1990) *The Politics of Disablement*, Macmillan, Basingstoke.

Orwell, G. (1946) *Animal Farm*, Harcourt Brace, Jovanovich, New York.

†Reason, P. (1994) Human Inquiry as Discipline and Practice. In, Reason, P. (ed.) *Participation In Human Inquiry and Action*, Sage, London.

Romm, N.R.A. (1996) Systems Methodologies and Intervention: The Issue of Researcher Responsibility. In, Flood, R.L. and Romm, N.R.A. *Critical Systems Thinking: Current Research and Practice*, Plenum, New York.

Romm, N.R.A. (1998) Interdisciplinary practice as reflexivity, *Systemic Practice and Action Research*, 11, 63–78.

Schratz, M. (1995) *Research as Social Change*, Routledge, London.

†Senge, P. (1990) *The Fifth Discipline: The Art and Practice of the Learning Organisation*, Century, London.

Torbert, W.R. (1991) *The Power of Balance: Transforming Self, Society and Scientific Inquiry*, Sage, London.

Wadsworth, Y. and Epstein, M. (1998) Dialogue between consumers and staff in acute mental health services, *Systemic Practice and Action Research*, 11, 353–380.

Weil, S. (1998) Rhetorics and realities in public service organisations: systemic practice and organisational learning as critically reflexive action research, *Systemic Practice and Action Research*, 11, 37–62.

17 Prismatic thought

De Bono, E. (1990) *Lateral Thinking*, Penguin, London.

Flood, R.L. (1995) *Solving Problem Solving*, Wiley, Chichester.

Fritz, R. (1991) *Creating*, Fawcett, Columbine.

Guenther, H.V. (1989) *From Reductionism to Creativity: RDZOGS-CHEN and the New Sciences of the Mind*, Shambhala, Boston, Mass.

Kim, S.H. (1990) *Essence of Creativity*, Oxford University Press, Oxford.

Koestler, A. (1969) *The Act of Creation*, Hutchinson and Co., London.

†Lakoff, G. and and Johnson, M. (1980) *Metaphors We Live By*, University of Chicago Press, Chicago.

†Morgan, G. (1986) *Images of Organization*, Sage, London.

Ortony, A. (ed.) (1979) *Metaphor and Thought*, University of Cambridge, Cambridge.

Prince, F.A. (1993) *C and the Box: A Paradigm Parable*, Pfeiffer and Co., San Diego.

18 Organisational learning and transformation

†Ackoff, R.L. (1981) *Redesigning the Future*, Wiley, New York.

†Churchman, C. West (1981) *Thought and Wisdom*, Intersystems, Seaside, Calif.

†De Geus, A. (1997) *The Living Company*, Harvard Business School Press, Harvard.

Georgantzas, N.C. and Acar, W. (1995) *Scenario-Driven Planning: Learning to Manage Strategic Uncertainty*, Quorum Books, Westport, Conn.

Heron, J. (1989) *The Facilitators' Handbook*, Kogan Page, London.

†Juran, J.M. (1988) *Juran on Planning for Quality*, Free Press, New York.

†MacIntyre, A. (1981) *After Virtue*, Duckworth, London.

McCalman, J. and Paton, R.A. (1992) *Change Management*, Paul Chapman Publishing, London.

McWhinney, W. (1996) *Creating Paths of Change: Managing Issues and Resolving Problems in Organizations*, Enthusion, Venice, Calif.

Mintzberg, H. (1994) *The Rise and Fall of Strategic Planning*, Prentice-Hall, Hemel Hempstead.

†Morgan, G. (1986) *Images of Organisation*, Sage, Beverley Hills.

Schoemaker, P.J.H. (1993) Multiple scenario development: its conceptual and behavioural foundation, *Strategic Management Journal*, 14, 193–213.

Schwartz, P. (1991) *The Art of the Long View*, Doubleday, New York.

†Senge, P. (1990) *The Fifth Discipline: The Art and Practice of the Learning Organisation*, Century, London.

Stewart, J. (1991) *Managing Change Through Training and Development*, Kogan Page, London.

†Ulrich, W. (1983) *Critical Heuristics of Social Planning*, Haupt, Berne.

Werner, M. (1990) Planning for uncertain futures: building commitment through scenario planning, *Business Horizons*, May/June, 55–58.

Wack, P. (1985) Scenarios: uncharted waters ahead, *Harvard Business Review*, 63, 139–150.

Wack, P. (1985) Scenarios: shooting the rapids, *Harvard Business Review*, 63, 150–161.

19 Systemic evaluation

†‡Beer, S. (1972) *Brain of the Firm*, Allen Lane and Penguin Press, London; Herder and Herder, New York; second edition (1981) Wiley, Chichester and New York.

Bryman, A. (1988) *Quantity and Quality in Social Research*, Unwin Hyman, London.

†Checkland, P.B. and Holwell, S. (1998) Action research: its nature and validity, *Systemic Practice and Action Research*, 11, 9–22.

De Vaus, D.A. (1996) *Surveys in Social Research*, UCL Press, London.

Easterby-Smith, M., Thorpe, R. and Lowe, A. (1991) *Management Research: An Introduction*, Sage, London.

†Flood, R.L. and Carson, E.R. (1988) *Dealing With Complexity: An Introduction to the Theory and Practice of Systems Science*, Plenum, New York; second edition (1992).

Foddy, W.H. (1993) *Constructing Questions for Interviews and Questionnaires: Theory and Practice in Social Research*, Cambridge University Press, Cambridge.

Gill, J. and Johnson, P. (1991) *Research Methods for Managers*, Paul Chapman Publishing, London.

Gummeson, E. (1991) *Qualitative Methods in Management Research*, Sage, London.

20 Instrumental and experiential action

Kolb, D.A. (1984) *Experiential Learning*, Prentice-Hall, Englewood Cliffs, NJ.

Micklethwait, J. and Woolridge, A. (1997) *The Witch Doctors*, Mandarin, London.

Shapiro, E. (1996) *Fad Surfing*, Capstone, Oxford.

21 Local Area Policing (LAP) in York, UK

Flood, R.L. (1993) Quality Management in the Service Sector: North Yorkshire Police. In, *Beyond TQM*, Wiley, Chichester.

Flood, R.L. (1995) *Implementing Local Area Policing in York Division: From Shift to Geographic Policing*, Centre for Systems Studies Press, University of Hull, UK.

Flood, R.L. and Green, P. (1996) TSI in North Yorkshire Police. In, Flood, R.L. and Romm, N.R.A. (eds) *Critical Systems Thinking: Current Research and Practice*, Plenum, New York.

Green, P. (1995) *An Evaluation of Some of the Effects of Local Area Policing (LAP) in North Yorkshire*, Centre for Systems Studies Press, University of Hull, UK.

Green, S. (1995) Managing and Developing a Police Division in a Large Bureaucracy. In, Flood, R.L. *Solving Problem Solving*, Wiley, Chichester.

†Stacey, R.D. (1996) *Strategic Management and Organisational Dynamics*, Pitman, London.

22 Reflections and key insights of systemic thinking

You are invited to reflect on the message of this book and your own practical experiences.

Index

Note: The following items that recur extensively in the text are omitted from the index, 'learning organisation', 'Peter Senge', 'Systemic thinking', and 'The Fifth Discipline'.